CIVIL LIABILITY AND COURTS ACT 2004:

Implications for Personal Injuries Litigation

Civil Liability and Courts Act 2004:

Implications for Personal Injuries Litigation

edited by

Ciarán Craven and William Binchy

First Law

Published in 2005 by
First Law Limited
Merchant's Court,
Merchants Quay,
Dublin 8,
Ireland.
www.firstlaw.ie

Typeset by Gough Typesetting Services, Dublin.

ISBN 1-904480-30-6

A catalogue record for this book
is available from the British Library.

Printed by Johnswood Press

Preface

A civil justice system should strike a fair balance between the rights and duties of the competing interest groups. In the law of torts, the Common Law left it to the judiciary to ensure that this balance was fairly struck and legislative intervention was limited. Since the Civil Liability Act in 1961, the only legislation enacted was specifically targeted at particular problems, for example, the Defamation Act 1961, the Animals Act 1985 and the Occupiers Liability Act 1995. Because of our obligations as members of the EEC (now the EU), the Liability for Defective Products Act 1991 was also introduced.

In earlier times the courts had developed a liability system which was based on "fault" and which obliged the plaintiff to prove his case if he was to succeed. Over the years, the courts, recognising the difficulties which confronted the plaintiff, especially in the industrial accident type of case, intervened in many ways to improve his lot: the original rule in *Donoghue v. Stevenson* was extended to apply to situations far beyond the manufacturer's liability; *res ipsa loquitur* was invented to ease the burden of proof; vicarious liability was widened to catch within its ambit more defendants. These are but a few examples of the judicial response to the rights and entitlements of injured individuals. More recently, the Liability for Defective Products Act 1991 saw the concept of strict liability (greatly modified, it must be said) introduced to improve the lot of those injured by defective products.

Many of these reforms were justified by arguments based on the concept of "enterprise liability" – if an industry created the risk it should bear the cost of the risk. It was in the best position to manage the risk by factoring it into its production cost structure and recovering the expense through price increases. Moreover, with the advent of liability insurance, industry could readily provide in advance for any accidents caused by the industry and spread the cost over all the consumers who used the product. In the case of motor vehicles such liability insurance was made compulsory for users from an early date.

In more recent times in Ireland the public perception has been that the scales have tipped too far in favour of the injured party in this balancing exercise. It was alleged that it was too easy to recover and damages when awarded were too generous. Public authorities became regular targets in "slip and fall" actions and public amenities and entertainments were threatened. Initially, the jury system was blamed: juries were too soft; they made awards that were inconsistent, unpredictable and too high and showed no sympathy for insurance companies. This led to the abolition of the jury trial in personal injury cases. The Supreme Court also responded by imposing a "cap" on general damages, by showing a willingness to substitute its award for that of the trial judge and for penalising plaintiffs who exaggerated their claims and, most recently, by adding a "just and reasonable" requirement to what must be shown before a duty of care is established.

Nevertheless, since subsequent awards made by the judges were not appreciably lower, the demand from employers, politicians, public bodies and the insurance industry for further reform continued until the Personal Injuries Assessment Board was established and the Civil Liability and Courts Act 2004 was passed by the Oireachtas.

These pieces of legislation did not pass into law without a spirited debate between the interested parties and considerable resistance from the legal profession. That political dialogue is history and practising lawyers must now deal quickly with the legislation as passed by the Oireachtas. They are fortunate that in addressing that task they have the present publication as a guide.

Much of the 2004 Act is concerned with pre-trial procedures which are designed to force the parties to make full, early and honest disclosure of their positions and move quickly to an early resolution. The parties are obliged to make offers of settlement and the plaintiff must swear a verifying affidavit, which, if misleading, shall be an offence. There is provision for a mediation conference which it is hoped will encourage settlements. The limitation period is reduced from three years to two. The courts, too, have extended roles in ensuring that the parties comply with the new rules and regulations, in responding to requests for mediation conferences and in appointing persons to give expert evidence. In relation to assessment of damages the courts are obliged to have regard to the *Book of Quantum* published by the Personal Injuries Assessment Board.

It will be some time before one can properly assess whether the legislation achieves these objectives and at what cost. We will have to wait and see.

Professor Binchy and Dr. Craven, as editors, are to be congratulated for examining and analysing these developments and bringing to the early attention of the profession the new requirements imposed on litigants and their advisers and the problems that might arise in the future. The list of contributors commenting on the legislation is impressive and it would be invidious to single out any one for special mention. The practitioner will find most of the immediate questions that arise satisfactorily answered, but (s)he should be warned that some uncertainties remain and will undoubtedly surface in the future. Much will depend on how the Act is applied and interpreted.

Especially welcome is the wider context provided by Professor Steve Hedley of University College Cork and the comparative contribution from Justice Michael Gallagher and John Smith II.

In the meantime, we must all educate ourselves to the new system, and, recognising our respective restricted and limited roles in the compensation process, we must embrace the change.

Bryan M.E. McMahon
Judge of the Circuit Court
July 2005

Table of Contents

Introduction

Ciarán Craven* and William Binchy**

The Civil Liability and Courts Act 2004 represents an important element of the rapidly changing culture of personal injuries litigation in Ireland. Over the past few years, the Oireachtas has transformed the balance of power between plaintiffs and defendants, substantially weakening the entitlements and negotiating positions of plaintiffs. The concern that has been driving the legislature is the desire to reduce insurance costs, to remove unnecessary legal expenses, to thwart fraud and punish exaggeration among plaintiffs and to simplify and speed up litigation. These are clearly excellent goals with which anyone of goodwill would sympathise. What must be questioned is whether these goals are likely to be achieved and at what price.

This book addresses these questions. It consists of a series of papers, many of which derive from presentations at conferences on the legislation organised by the Law School of Trinity College Dublin earlier this year. It seeks to set the legislation in a wider framework as well as focusing on particular areas of interest and concern.

We are very grateful to Professor Steve Hedley, of University College Cork, for allowing us include the text of his Inaugural Lecture, which he delivered to a University audience on January 22, 2004. We are also most grateful to Justice Michael J. Gallagher and John Smith II for their paper on the mediation process in Cook County. Although the context of personal injury litigation in the United States is in many respects radically different from that in Ireland, human nature and motivations do not change and Irish practitioners will benefit greatly from the insights of these authors. The theme of mediation is well developed by Val Corbett of Griffith College Dublin, who places the Irish statutory provisions in a

---

*Barrister-at-Law.
**Regius Professor of Laws, Trinity College Dublin.

broad international context, with special emphasis on Canadian and British approaches.

Paul Quigley, of Trinity College Dublin and New York University School of Law, concentrates on the judicial sequelae to the introduction of the PIAB procedure and suggests an alternative approach. Neville Cox, of Trinity College, examines the new rules relating to collateral benefits and undeclared income. Ray Ryan, also of Trinity College, examines the impact of the Act on the "compensation culture". Our own contributions examine the procedural aspects of the legislation and how particular provisions are likely to affect tort litigation and practice.

We are very grateful to Bart Daly, First Law and to Thérèse Carrick, for their considerable help in bringing the book to publication. We must also thank Gilbert Gough of Gough Typesetting, for his professionalism. Catherine Finnegan of the Law School, Trinity College Dublin, played a crucial role in the development and organisation of the entire project.

Finally we must express our appreciation to the Hon. Judge Bryan McMahon for having agreed to write the Preface to the book. We are greatly encouraged by his participation.

Analysis of legislation before it puts down roots in actual practice is a speculative and uncertain process. [Gray was surely wise to describe legislation as "potential law"] Practitioners, and the wider community, wait with interest and some trepidation, to see whether the Civil Liability and Courts Act 2004 will achieve its worthy goals.

Table of Cases

N

O

P

Table of Legislation

Civil Liability and Courts Act 2004—*contd.*

Civil Liability and Courts Act 2004—*contd.*

STATUTORY INSTRUMENTS

Civil Liability and Courts Act 2004: Procedural Aspects

CIARÁN CRAVEN*

GENERAL

In this chapter the provisions of the Civil Liability and Courts Act 2004, insofar as they relate to the new procedure for the conduct of personal injuries litigation, are examined.

COMMENCEMENT

The following provisions, of relevance to this topic, were commenced on the passing of the Act, *i.e.* on July 21, 2004:

- the definitions section (section 2),
- provisions in relation to the making of orders under the Act (section 3) and,
- provisions in relation to the service of notices (section 4).[1]

Other provisions were commenced by the Civil Liability and Courts Act

---

*Dr Ciarán Craven is a Barrister. He lectures on medical law in the LL.M Degree Programme at Trinity College, Dublin. He is co-author of a textbook on Psychiatry and the Law and the author of several articles on aspects of medical law and tort law.

1 Certain provisions affecting (in particular, ss.54, 4(1) and 30(4) of) the Personal Injuries Assessment Board Act 2003 (ss.31 and 32 respectively) and the courts (funds of suitors – Part 3 Chapter 1 – the issuing of District Court Summonses in criminal matters – s.49 – and the number of judges of the High, Circuit and District Courts – s.56) were also commenced on passing but are no of relevance for present purposes and will not be considered further.

2004 (Commencement) Order (S.I. No.544 of 2004) on September 20, 2004:

- section 1 commencement section,
- section 5 expenses incurred by Minister in the administration of the Act,
- section 6 application of Part 2 (civil liability),
- section 8 letter of claim,
- section 19 evidence,
- section 21 intervention (by the Supreme Court),
- section 22 matters to be taken into account by the court when assessing damages,
- section 25 false evidence, false instructions,
- section 26 fraudulent actions,[2]
- section 29 offences, and
- section 54 exclusion of certain witnesses.[3]

The remaining provisions were commenced on March 31, 2005, *i.e.*:[4]

- section 7 amendment of the Statute of Limitations (Amendment) Act 1991,
- section 9 rules of court,
- section 10 bringing of proceedings,
- section 11 request for further information,
- section 12 defence and counterclaim,
- section 13 pleadings generally,

---

2 William Binchy considers ss.21 and 22 in his discussion, *infra*, p.70.

3 Six other sections, relating to the courts and miscellaneous provisions were also commenced on that date, *i.e.* ss.39, 41, 42, 43, 44 and 55. None are of immediate relevance for present purposes.

4 S.40 (dealing with a relaxation of the *in camera* rule) was also commenced on this date.

- section 14 verifying affidavits,
- section 15 mediation conference,
- section 16 report of chairperson of mediation conference,[5]
- section 17 formal offers,
- section 18 pre-trial hearings,
- section 20 expert evidence,
- section 23 actuarial tables,
- section 24 discount rate,[6]
- section 27 collateral benefits, and
- section 28 income undeclared for tax purposes.[7]

The need to make regulations in relation to certain provisions and to provide for amendments of the Rules of Court was stated to be the reason for the delay in commencing the principal procedural provisions of the Act.[8] On April 1, 2005, orders were made dealing with the nomination of a court-appointed chairperson of a mediation conference[9] and the time for the making of formal offers[10] under the Act.[11] No amendments of the

---

5 Matters arising in relation to mediation, in the context of this Act, are considered in some detail by Val Corbett, *infra*, pp.103 *et seq*. The experience of mediation in Cook County, Illinois is described by Judge Michael Gallagher and John V. Smith II, *infra*, pp.160 *et seq*.

6 William Binchy considers the new statutory regime in respect of limitation periods, formal offers, expert evidence, actuarial tables, and the discount rate, *infra*, pp.44 *et seq*.

7 Neville Cox discusses these two provisions (ss.27 and 28), *infra*, pp.84 *et seq*.

8 The Minister for Justice, Equality and Law Reform, Mr McDowell, in a press release dated September 23, 2004 stated: "In making this [Commencement] Order, I was mindful of the need to ensure that on commencement all the necessary procedures would be in place to ensure the effectiveness of the Act. It was clear to me that in some instances alterations to the Rules of Court were necessary and equally that there is a need to make regulations in regard to certain provisions. For these reasons, I have designate March 31, 2005 as the date on which these sections will come into operation".

9 Civil Liability and Courts Act 2004 (Bodies Prescribed Under Section 15) Order 2005 (Statutory Instrument Number 168 of 2005) The Order prescribes the following bodies for the purposes of section 15(4)(b)(ii)(II) of the Act of 2004: 1. Friary Law, 2. Mediation Forum Ireland, 3. Mediators Institute Ireland, 4. The Bar Council, 5. The Chartered Institute of Arbitrators (Irish Branch) and 6. The Law Society of Ireland.

10 Civil Liability and Courts Act 2004 (Section 17) Order 2005 (S.I. No.169 of 2005)

Rules of Court were commenced at the time. However, Practice Directions, dealing with the Act of 2004, were issued on April 1, 2005 by the Presidents of the District and High Courts to regulate personal injury proceedings commenced after that date "pending the coming into operation of rules of court regulating in detail the procedure and prescribing the forms to be used in such proceedings".[12] A similar Practice Direction was made by the President of the Circuit Court on March 31, 2005. Although the High Court Practice Direction stipulated the form of personal injuries summons to be used in proceedings instituted from March 31, 2005 – and which was in conformity with the Act of 2004[13] – notwithstanding the commencement of the relevant provisions of the Act on that date, and the President's Practice Direction, it was still possible to issue an ordinary Plenary Summons out of the Central Office in a personal injuries action (within the meaning of the Act of 2004), particularly in cases where there was pressure from the Statutes of Limitations.[14] Rules for the purposes of the Act of 2004, made by the Superior Courts Rules Committee, did not come into operation until June 2, 2005.[15]

---

which provides that for the purposes of s.17 the "prescribed date" is the date upon which the personal injuries summons is served on the defendant. It further prescribes the "prescribed period" for the purposes of the section as follows:

"The prescribed period shall:

(a) in the case of the High Court and Circuit Court, commence on the prescribed date and end on the expiration of 14 days after the service of the notice of trial in those proceedings; and

(b) in the case of the District Court, commence on the prescribed date and end on the expiration of 4 days after the delivery of a defence in those proceedings."

11 Other orders were also made, on that day, which are not of immediate relevance. Practitioners might usefully note, however, those in relation to the modification of the *in camera* rule, at least insofar as it applies to matters before professional disciplinary tribunals (Civil Liability and Courts Act 2004 (Bodies Prescribed Under Section 40) Order 2005 (S.I. No.170 of 2005))

12 Practice Direction of the President of the High Court dated April 1, 2005, para.3. Identical provisions appear in the Practice Directions of the Presidents of the Circuit and District Courts published on the same date in the Legal Diary and on the Courts Service website www.courts.ie

13 Civil Liability and Courts Act 2004, ss.10, 13(1)(a) and 14. These are considered in more detail, *infra*, pp.15, 16, 24, 26, 32 *et seq*.

14 The discussion in the text concentrates on the High Court; District Court procedure, and Circuit Court procedure, are set out in the footnotes.

15 Rules of the Superior Courts (Personal Injuries) 2005 (S.I. No.248 of 2005). These are considered in more detail in the description of the new procedure, *infra*, pp.15 *et seq*. Similar rules made by the District Court Rules Committee came into operation

The General Scheme and Scope of the Act

This Act is primarily aimed at procedural changes in personal injuries litigation[16] and applies to a "personal injuries action", *i.e.* an action for the recovery of damages:

- in respect of a wrong for personal injuries, or
- for such injuries and damage to property (but only if both have been caused by the same wrong), or
- a fatal injuries action (under the Civil Liability Act 1961 section 48).

This is very similar to the definition of "civil action", in the Personal Injuries Assessment Board Act 2003 (PIAB Act 2003) which subject to the exclusions set out[17] is "an action intended to be pursued for the purpose of recovering damages, in respect of a wrong, for (a) personal injuries, or (b) both such injuries and damage to property (but only if both have been caused by the same wrong)". This also includes fatal injuries actions.[18]

"Personal injury" for the purpose of the Act of 2004 has the same meaning as in the Civil Liability Act 1961, *i.e.* it includes any disease and any impairment of a person's physical or mental condition. The definitions of plaintiff, defendant, third party and wrong are also those as set out in the Act of 1961, *i.e.* "plaintiff" includes a defendant counter-claiming and a defendant claiming against a co-defendant by notice or otherwise, a "defendant" includes a defendant to a counterclaim, a "third party" includes a fourth party and subsequent party and "wrong" means a tort, breach of contract or breach of trust, whether the act is committed by the person to whom the wrong is attributed or by one for whose acts he is responsible, and whether or not the act is also a crime and whether or not the wrong is intentional.[19]

However, applications under the Garda Compensation Acts and those where the damages being claimed include damages for trespass to the

---

the following day: District Court (Personal Injuries) Rules 2005 (S.I. No.257 of 2005) inserting a new O.39A into those Rules. No such Circuit Court Rules were brought into operation at that time.

[16] Its role in the broader socio-political context is discussed by Ray Ryan, *infra*, p.136.

[17] Personal Injuries Assessment Board Act 2003, s.4(1).

[18] *Ibid.*, s.4(2).

[19] Civil Liability Act 1961, s.2(1).

person or for false imprisonment are excluded from the ambit of the Act of 2004.[20] In this regard it mirrors some of the exclusionary provisions of the PIAB Act – but it does not exclude actions in medical negligence or those intended to be pursued in respect of an alleged breach of Constitutional rights where personal injury is claimed.[21] Nor, indeed, does it appear to exclude an action for personal injuries caused, for instance, by a defamation.

The principal procedural provisions of the Act[22] apply, subject to certain other provisions, to personal injuries actions brought after the date of commencement of those provisions.[23] For most practical purposes, that date is March 31, 2005, although certain sections of the Act apply to proceedings whenever they were brought.[24] Each of the relevant provisions will now be considered in turn.

Actions "Brought after the Date of Commencement"

The first question that arises is when an action is "brought". This assumes particular significance given that many provisions of the Act were commenced on September 20, 2004. Although the amendments of the Statute of Limitations (Amendment) Act 1991,[25] for instance, provided by the Act of 2004 were not commenced until March 31, 2005, the provisions in relation to, for example, the service of a letter of claim were commenced much earlier.[26] The implications of what "brought after the date of commencement" means are, accordingly, considered more fully in the discussion that follows.

---

20 Civil Liability and Courts Act 2004, s.2. The exclusion in respect of the trespassery torts, while set out in the District Court (Personal Injuries) Rules 2005 (S.I. No.257 of 2005), O.39A, r.1, it is not recited in the equivalent provision in RSC, O.1A, r.1.

21 Nor, does it appear to exclude an application for damages pursuant to the European Convention on Human Rights Act 2003 s.3, where such an application is for damages for "injury", which is not defined in that Act.

22 Those in Pt 2 of the Act of 2004, headed "Civil Liability".

23 Civil Liability and Courts Act 2004, s.6.

24 *Ibid.*, s.14(8) (verifying affidavits) and s.26(4) (fraudulent claims).

25 *Ibid.*, s.7.

26 *Ibid.*, s.8.

The Amendment of the Statute of Limitations

Before proceeding to that discussion, however, it is worth noting the reduction of the limitation periods, provided for by the Act, in relation to a range of matters.[27] Thus, the limitation period in section 3(1) of the Statute of Limitations (Amendment) Act 1991 (*i.e.* an action claiming damages in respect of personal injuries caused by negligence, nuisance or breach of duty (whether the duty exists by virtue of a contact or of a provision made by or under a statute or independently of any contract or any such provision)[28] is reduced from three years to two years.[29]

A similar reduction in the limitation period is made in relation to claims pursuant to section 4(1) of the Act of 1991, *i.e.* those maintainable by the estate of an injured person who has died,[30] section 5(1) of that Act, (*i.e.* where the person having the right to bring the action (whether a personal injuries or a fatal injuries action) was under a disability either at the time when the right accrued to him or at the date of his knowledge, the action may be brought at any time before the expiration of 2 years from the date of the cesser of the disability, or the person's death, whichever occurred first)[31] and section 6(1), fatal injuries actions pursuant to section 48 of the Civil Liability Act 1961.[32]

In addition, where the relevant date, *i.e.* the date of accrual of the cause of action or the date of knowledge, whichever occurs later, in respect of an action to which the sections just outlined apply, (sections 3(1), 4(1), 5(1) or 6(1) of the Act of 1991), falls before March 31, 2005,[33] the limitation period prescribed is 2 years from the date of commencement, *i.e.* on or before 30 March 2007 or 3 years from the relevant date, whichever occurs first. In other words, a short stop is applied in relation to those causes of action which have accrued before the commencement date.

---

[27] The broad considerations underlying these amendments are discussed by William Binchy, *infra*, pp.45 *et seq*.

[28] The language here is similar to, but is not the same as, the definition of negligence in the Civil Liability and Courts Act 2004.

[29] Civil Liability and Courts Act 2004, s.7(a).

[30] *Ibid.*, s.7(b).

[31] *Ibid.*, s.7(c).

[32] *Ibid.*, s.7(e).

[33] The commencement date of the Civil Liability and Courts Act 2004 is found in s.7.

How this will operate in practice may result in some curious anomalies. Take, for instance, an injury that occurred on August 1, 2002. Ordinarily the limitation period would expire on July 31, 2005. However, if a claim is made to the PIAB, on July 31, 2004 (because, for example, proceedings were not issued before the date on which application to the PIAB became mandatory) the period beginning on the making of the application and ending six months from the date of issue of an authorisation by the PIAB is disregarded.[34] The PIAB is required to determine a claim within nine months of the date on which the Board receives the respondent's consent to an assessment being made (although if there is more than one respondent, that date may be pushed back further).[35] If the appropriate consent was not obtained until, say, September 1, 2004, the nine-month period runs from that date. However, this time may be extended by a further six months[36] (or further still, with the claimant's consent).[37] Accordingly, an authorisation might not issue for 15 months after September 1, 2004, *i.e.* until November 30, 2005, well after the limitation period would otherwise have expired. But, in these circumstances, where some two years of the limitation period had expired before the application was made to the PIAB, because the time between August 1, 2004 and May 31, 2006[38] is not reckonable for the calculation of time, the limitation period should not expire before 30 May 2007. Because of the short stop, however, in the Act of 2004, that period is abridged and proceedings issued after on or after March 31, 2007 would, therefore, be statute barred.

In effect, therefore, the limitation period may expire in certain cases while a matter is pending before the PIAB. Although this may seem an extreme example, the message is clear: the new limitation regime requires particular attention, at least insofar as the short stop in the Act of 2004 is concerned.

Another issue arises in respect of minors, and those under a disability. The Civil Liability Act 1961 provides that no proceedings shall be maintainable in respect of any cause of action whatsoever which has survived against the estate of a deceased person unless either the proceedings were commenced within the relevant period and were pending

---

[34] Personal Injuries Assessment Board Act 2003, s.50.
[35] *Ibid.*, s.49(2) and (3).
[36] *Ibid.*, s.49(4).
[37] *Ibid.*, s.49(6).
[38] Six months after the issuing of the authorisation in this hypothetical.

at the date of death and proceedings are commenced within the relevant period or within the period of two years after his death, whichever period first expires.[39] Although "relevant period" in that Act means the period of limitation prescribed in the Statutes of Limitation,[40] nevertheless, a short stop applies here too. In *Bank of Ireland v. O'Keeffe*[41] Barron J considered that the relevant period also included "not only the basic period of limitation laid down by the Statute but also the extension of such basic period by reason of such matters as acknowledgements in writing, mistake etc." However, in *Moynihan v. Greensmyth*[42] a minor who was injured in a road traffic accident instituted proceedings against the defendant who had been killed in that accident within three years of the date on which the accident occurred, even though the Statute did not ordinarily expire until three years after she would have attained her majority, which was some years hence. Statute bar having been pleaded, the plaintiff unsuccessfully challenged the constitutional validity of the section. The Supreme Court held that there was no unjust attack on the alleged property rights of the infant plaintiff because the State had to strike a balance between those alleged rights and the rights of other persons interested in the early completion of the administration of the deceased's estate. The claim was, accordingly, statute barred not having been instituted within two years of the defendant's death.[43]

The question, therefore, arises in relation to the short stop provided in the Act of 2004 as to whether or not the "relevant date" in that Act is likely to have the meaning ascribed to it by Barron J in *O'Keeffe* or one that is considerably more restrictive. Whatever about the policy arguments that might justify a short stop that would act to bar claims that were otherwise commenced within the limitation period (as ordinarily understood) where estates have to be administered, the same policy considerations can hardly be considered to apply in ordinary personal injuries litigation. In addition, applying a restrictive interpretation would produce a significant anomaly: a minor, or a person under a disability, in respect

---

[39] Civil Liability Act 1961, s.9(2).

[40] *Ibid.*, s.9(1).

[41] Unreported, High Court, December 3, 1986.

[42] [1977] I.R. 55.

[43] See, in particular, Kerr, A *The Civil Liability Acts 1961 and 1964* (Round Hall Press, Dublin, 1993), pp.23–25. Another example of this section in operation is found in *Yardley (a minor) v. Boyd* [2004] I.E.H.C. 385 (December 14, 2004) (Herbert J.).

of whose action the relevant date fell before March 31, 2005, would be statute barred two years after that date, notwithstanding ongoing minority or disability whereas those whose relevant dates fell after March 31, 2005 would not be. The shorter limitation period of two years (after the cesser of minority or disability) would, of course, apply after that date.

Having said that, the placing of the amendments to the Statute of Limitations (Amendment) Act 1991 in Part 2 of the Act, under the heading "Civil Liability" raises a drafting anomaly. Section 6 of the Act of 2004, which describes the application of that Part states:

> "Subject to *sections 14(8), 25(4), 26(4), 27(3) and 28(2)*, a provision of this Part applies only to personal injuries actions brought after the date of the commencement of that provision."

Therefore, the amendments of the Statute of Limitations (Amendment) Act 1991 should, also, only apply to such actions brought after March 31, 2005. That, however, would produce a definitional circularity that is irreconcilable and is manifestly inconsistent with the provisions, in particular, in relation to the short stop, already described.

The "Letter of Claim"[44]

The Act provides that where a plaintiff in a personal injuries action fails, without reasonable cause, to serve a notice in writing on the alleged wrongdoer, before the expiration of 2 months from the date of the cause of action, or as soon as practicable thereafter, stating the nature of the wrong alleged to have been committed, the court hearing the action may draw such inferences from the failure as appear proper and, where the interests of justice so require, make no order as to the plaintiff's costs or deduct that amount as it considers appropriate from those costs that would otherwise have been payable.[45] The date of the cause of action means the date of accrual of the cause of action or the date of knowledge, whichever occurs later.[46] Although this provision is cast in terms of the

[44] William Binchy considers other aspects of this requirement, *infra*, pp.48 *et seq.*
[45] Civil Liability and Courts Act 2004, s.8(1).
[46] *Ibid.*, s.8(2).

language of the Statute of Limitations (Amendment) Act 1991, the Statute does not apply in relation to a letter of claim, such that the minority or disability of a plaintiff is not expressly taken into consideration.

A letter of claim must be addressed to the person concerned by name and may be served on or given to him or her by delivering, or by leaving it at, or sending it by registered post to, the address at which (s)he ordinarily resides or, in a case in which an address for service has been furnished, at that address.[47] or by sending it by prepaid registered letter to that address. That said, the provision, superficially at least, seems relatively anodyne, apart from the obviously truncated period within which a letter of claim has to be served. However, it self-evidently applies to any personal injuries action "brought" after September 20, 2004, the date of the commencement of this section. "Brought", in this context, can only realistically mean "initiated" or commenced by the issuing (within the relevant rules) of the appropriate civil proceedings.[48] It can hardly, for instance, mean service of, for example, a Plenary Summons or a Civil Bill. Given the three year limitation period for actions claiming damages for personal injuries which exists in respect of causes of action that accrued prior to March 31, 2005 – and also the twelve month period within which, after issuing, a Plenary Summons may be served – it will manifestly not be possible to comply with this provision of the Act of 2004 in many cases that have already been initiated. Will the fact that such a transitional consequence has occurred be sufficient to constitute a "reasonable cause" within the meaning of the Act? Self-evidently it should: but given the

---

[47] *Ibid.*, s.4(1) and Rules of the Superior Courts (Personal Injuries) 2005 (S.I. No.248 of 2005) para.10 amending RSC, O.121, by inserting a new r.9. Insofar as a company within the meaning of the Companies Acts 1963 to 2003 is concerned, it is deemed to be ordinarily resident at its registered office; every other body corporate and unincorporated body is deemed to be ordinarily resident at its principal office or place of business (*ibid.*, s.4(2)).

[48] A Plenary Summons, Ordinary Civil Bill or Civil Summons (before March 31, 2005), or, as appropriate, a Personal Injuries Summons (on foot of a Practice Direction, between March 31, 2005 and June 2, 2005 (in the High Court) or June 3, 2005 (in the District Court)) or, at least insofar as High Court and District Court proceedings are concerned between those dates, the usual civil proceedings issued out of those courts, or a Personal Injuries Summons (within the meaning of the Rules) issued on or after June 2, 2005 in the High Court or on or after June 3, 2005 in the District Court. Amended Circuit Court Rules are awaited and, accordingly, the Practice Direction of the President of the Circuit Court dated March 31, 2005 and the unamended Rules apply. *Supra*, pp.3 and 6.

relatively draconian nature of the possible sanction that might be imposed for default, it would have been preferable to have had an express transitional provision in this regard.

Be that as it may, looking beyond such temporary matters, other issues arise for consideration. Thus, for instance, a question arises as to the necessity for the provision in the first instance. Is it the case that there is (or was) such manifest abuse of the litigation process that defendants were forced unnecessarily into litigation that could have been avoided by the delivery of a letter of claim? Where a claim is notified very late after the event complained of, it may well be that relevant witnesses will no longer be available or the locus may have changed.[49] However, practitioners working in this area well know that it is exceptionally rare for a defendant to do other than ignore any such letter or, in response, to nominate a solicitor to accept service of subsequent proceedings on receipt of a letter of claim. Where an O'Byrne letter (or, more correctly, a letter pursuant to the provisions of the Courts of Justice Act 1936, section 78) is delivered, the response invariably does not amount to an admission, or apportionment, of liability by the proposed defendants. There may, of course, be circumstances where the sending of a letter of claim might result in a wrongly named defendant being identified early and, thus, avoiding the unnecessary issue and service of proceedings on such a person. But, even in such a situation, if a person is wrongly identified and proceedings are discontinued after service, for instance, after the entry of an Appearance, the costs provisions in, in particular, RSC Order 99, rule 5, should be sufficient to deal with the matter. Deducting such amount from the plaintiff's costs that were attributable to the failure to deliver a letter of claim before the issuing of proceedings should not be beyond the ordinary powers of the courts when dealing with the matter of costs. What inferences might otherwise be properly drawn by a failure to serve a letter of claim is difficult to fathom.

Secondly, the question arises as to what constitutes a proper letter of claim. The statutory provision goes no further than to provide that it

---

[49] In relation to what has been termed "pre-commencement" delay (as distinct from "post-commencement" delay, see *MacH v. M*, unreported, High Court, Peart J., March 3, 2004. Insofar as prejudice caused by the death of a party or an otherwise important witness is concerned, see *Anglo-Irish Beef Processors Ltd & anor v. Montgomery*, unreported, Supreme Court, July 31, 2002 and *McCarthy v. South Infirmary-Victoria Hospital Ltd* [2004] I.E.H.C. 429 (Abbott J.).

must state "the nature of the wrong alleged to have been committed". Many letters of claim, at present, set out the factual circumstances surrounding the occurrence of the injuries sustained by the plaintiff, as well as identifying the legal nature of the wrong alleged to have been committed. There is nothing in the Act of 2004 to suggest that it requires anything further. However, given some of the other provisions in relation to pleadings,[50] prudence would seem to dictate that the nature of the wrong alleged to have been committed be stated precisely and not in the terms of an omnibus "negligence and breach of duty and/or breach of statutory duty and/or breach of contract and/or nuisance" format. Given the very short period involved, this may be difficult. That said, perhaps anomalously, the court is not required to have regard to inconsistencies between the letter of claim and the subsequent pleadings (as may sometimes occur). The only focus of the court, in this area, is on the failure to serve such a letter.

Thirdly, the time within which a letter of claim must be served is very short – two months, or "as soon as practicable thereafter".[51] What was or was not practicable is, of course, a matter of fact to be determined after the event and given the myriad of circumstances that might conspire to delay in the service of a letter of claim, e.g. illness, minority, disability, treatment, failure to seek legal advice and so on, a natural anxiety might arise to effect service within the time prescribed. The court, while concerned with the failure to deliver a letter of claim, without reasonable cause, must be considered to have regard not alone to the reasonableness of such excuse as might be offered but also as to whether or not the letter was served as soon as was practicable thereafter.[52] The onus placed on plaintiffs and their legal advisers is, in the circumstances, formidable as it is not difficult to foresee actions arising against lawyers for breach of contract or retainer, and in negligence, where a court makes a determination as to costs adverse to a plaintiff because of a failure at the letter of claim stage

---

[50] *Infra*, p.32.

[51] The legislative policy of seeking to speed up litigation is reflected in judicial pronouncements: see, in particular, *Gilroy v. Flynn* [2004] I.E.S.C. 98 (December 3, 2004) *per* Hardiman J. referring to *McMullen v. Ireland* E.C.H.R. 422/97/98 (July 29, 2004) and the European Convention on Human Rights Act 2003.

[52] In delay cases, a distinction has been drawn between an "explanation" and an "excuse". See, in particular, *Byrne v. Minister for Defence & ors*, unreported, High Court, Peart J., April 26, 2005.

However, an issue also arises in respect of those cases which require a consent from the PIAB before proceedings can be initiated. Such cases constitute the bulk of personal injuries cases, the most obvious and immediate exception being in respect of medical negligence actions: in most such cases, compliance with the statutory time limit is likely to prove difficult, given the nature of the injuries and difficulty in proof of the wrongs involved. A plain reading of the Act of 2004 clearly requires a letter of claim to be sent to a proposed defendant even before any requirement arises to submit the matter, in the first instance, to the PIAB. Thus, it creates a general obligation – with a discretion on the part of the court to waive, effectively, the requirements of the Act – without any express exception in relation to the PIAB. To assert that, accordingly, it will result in a plethora of unnecessary procedural difficulties, in relation to formulating letters of claim – even in those cases where the PIAB assessment is ultimately accepted by the parties – does not quite state the full extent of the curiosity of this anomaly.

In addition, because of the discretionary – and, thus, uncertain - nature of the circumstances in which non-compliance with the statutory provisions might not give rise to a penalty on the plaintiff, it could effectively be considered to require plaintiffs who are sick and ill and recovering from injuries inflicted by a defendant to instruct lawyers as soon as possible. Were it to be considered to have this effect, surely it is contrary to public policy in that it runs the risk of initiating, at least to a preliminary extent, a litigation process in relation to injuries that might otherwise be considered to involve unstateable cases. The appropriateness of inquiries that might ordinarily be regarded as necessary, before initiating proceedings, for instance, in medical negligence actions, is not considered.[53] There is no good reason why such circumstances, *i.e.* the making of appropriate inquiries, could not constitute "reasonable cause" for a failure to serve a letter of claim promptly. That the provisions are

---

[53] The initiation and prosecution of cases involving professional negligence without adequate supporting evidence, in advance, has been characterised as irresponsible and an abuse of process. See, in particular, *Reidy v. National Maternity Hospital*, unreported, High Court, Barr J., July 31, 1997 endorsed by in *Connolly v. Casey & Murphy (t/a Casey & Murphy) & Fitzgibbon*, unreported High Court, Kelly J., June 12, 1998 and approved in *Cooke v. Cronin & Neary*, unreported, Supreme Court, July 14, 1999 (Denham, Keane and Lynch JJ.).

cast in the terms that they are, however, militates against practitioners seeking to justify any delay or failure, after the event, absent express provision for exceptions.[54]

The Bringing of Proceedings: The Personal Injuries Summons

General

The Act of 2004 requires that proceedings in respect of a personal injuries action are to be commenced – irrespective of the level of the court involved – by way of a personal injuries summons.[55] Such a summons must specify:

- the plaintiff's name, address, occupation and PPN,
- the defendant's name, address and occupation (if known),
- the injuries alleged to have been occasioned by the defendant's wrong,
- full particulars of all items of special damage being claimed,
- full particulars of the acts of the defendant constituting the wrong and the circumstances relating to the commission of the wrong, and
- full particulars of each instance of negligence by the defendant.[56]

A failure to comply with these provisions may result in the courts' staying the plaintiff's action until the (s)he complies with such conditions as the court may specify or, indeed, if the court considers that the interests of justice so require, the dismissing of the plaintiff's action. Any failure must also be taken into account when the court is deciding whether to make an order for the payment of the plaintiff's costs in the action, or the

---

[54] Although not directly on point, as to the initiation of professional negligence proceedings without the necessary evidence, when a hard statutory time limit is about to expire, see *Cunningham v. Neary & Ors* [2004] I.E.S.C. 43 (July 20, 2004) *per* McGuinness J.

[55] Civil Liability and Courts Act 2004, s.10(1). See, also, Rules of the Superior Courts (Personal Injuries) 2005 (S.I. No.248 of 2005) and, in the case of District court Proceedings, District Court (Personal Injuries) Rules 2005 (S.I. No.257 of 2005) inserting a new O.39A into those Rules and Practice Direction of the President of the Circuit Court dated March 31, 2005.

[56] *Ibid.*, s.10(2).

amount of those costs.[57] In addition, the court is entitled to draw such inferences as appear proper from a failure to comply with the statutory requirements.[58]

In practical terms, it might not be considered that these provisions herald a wholly new procedure, insofar as personal injuries litigation is concerned. Certainly, the requirement of a single summons similar in form irrespective of the court in which the action is to be heard simplifies matters somewhat. However, given that the case must be fully pleaded in the High Court on the issuing of the summons, unlike the situation that pertained up to the commencement of the relevant rules of court,[59] it is obvious that the practical difficulties will be protean, particularly in complex matters as often arise in cases involving professional negligence which take some considerable time to investigate. Such difficulties need not be over-stated and will be obvious.

Insofar as High Court proceedings[60] are concerned, the rules require that a personal injuries action be instituted by an originating summons, for the commencement of plenary proceedings with pleadings and hearing on oral evidence.[61] It is further provided that, unless otherwise expressly provided for, the provisions of the rules that apply to a plenary summons, with appropriate modifications, also apply to a personal injuries summons.[62] In other words, the rules in relation to service[63] and renewal[64]

---

[57] *Ibid.*, s.10(3).
[58] *Ibid.*, s.10(4).
[59] *Supra*, p.15.
[60] Relevant variations in the procedure in the other courts are set out in the footnotes throughout the discussion
[61] RSC O.1A, r.3. The form of the summons, called a personal injuries summons, is specified in Appendix CC (see, also District Court Rules O.39A, r.3(1) in the form No. 39A 1, Schedule C; Circuit Court Practice Direction para. 4).
[62] *Ibid.*, r.4. (See, also, Circuit Court Practice Direction para. 9 and District Court Rules O.39A, r.3(2), in relation to a civil summons.)
[63] RSC O.9 to 11B. That the rules provide for a period of twelve months (or such further period for which the summons may be renewed in accordance with O.8) within which a personal injuries summons must be served hardly seems consonant with the shortened times otherwise provided for in the Act of 2004, specifically, the two month period for service of a letter of claim and the two year limitation period for personal injuries actions. In addition, any advantage, in respect of being able to issue a summons in order to stop the limitation clock, and delay its service because, for example, investigations for the purpose of drafting a statement of claim were ongoing, simply does not accrue under the new procedure.
[64] RSC O.8.

of a High Court summons also apply.[65] Certain provisions of the rules, however, do not apply in personal injuries actions.[66] Although a statement of claim is not required,[67] the provisions of the rules that apply to a statement of claim, save where otherwise expressly provided for, where appropriate and with appropriate modifications, also apply to a personal injuries summons.

The personal injuries summons required by the Rules of the Superior Courts must be headed "Personal Injuries Summons" and is in the form of a Plenary Summons.[68] However, the indorsement of claim is other than general.[69] It must set out the reliefs claimed for personal injuries suffered by the plaintiff,[70] and set out in numbered paragraphs, full and detailed particulars of:

(i) the nature of the claim and of each allegation, assertion or plea comprising that claim;

(ii) the injuries to the plaintiff alleged to have been occasioned by the wrong of the defendant;

(iii) the acts of the defendant constituting the said wrong and the circumstances relating to the commission of the said wrong, and

(iv) each instance of negligence by the defendant.

In addition, the indorsement must also contain a schedule of full particulars

---

65 The capacity in which a person sues also remains a matter for indorsement on the summons (RSC O.4, r.9). However, as the whole of the claim is also required to be set out, any difficulties that might otherwise have been encountered by the application of this rule are now obviated.

66 RSC O.19, rr.1 and 3 (delivery of a statement of claim, defence, set-off or counterclaim and pleading generally) and O.21, r.6 (non-requirement of a denial or defence as to damages claimed). In the event of a conflict between the rules in relation to personal injuries and any other provision of the Rules of the Superior Courts, the provision of the personal injuries rules, in respect of personal injuries actions, prevails. See, O.1A, r.2. An equivalent provision is found in District Court Rules O.39A, r.2(2).

67 RSC O.1A r.7(1).

68 In the District Court, it is headed "Personal Injuries Summons Civil Liability and Courts Act 2004, Section 10".

69 RSC O.4 r.2 as inserted by the Rules of the Superior Courts (Personal Injuries) 2005, para.5.

70 The capacity in which the plaintiff sues must be specified here. See, RSC O.4, r.9.

of all items of special damage in respect of which the plaintiff is making a claim.[71]

The rules suggest a format in which the indorsement might be presented as follows:[72]

1. description of the parties;
2. the nature of the claim;
3. the acts of the defendant alleged to constitute a wrong, each instance of negligence by the defendant, all other relevant circumstances in relation to the commission of the said wrong and any other assertion or plea concerning same;
4. the injuries to the plaintiff alleged to have been occasioned by the wrong of the defendant, and
5. the reliefs sought.[73]

A schedule, setting out particulars of items of special damage, is also suggested. Insofar as particulars of a general allegation are concerned, these should be set out in the indorsement under the paragraph containing such an allegation and headed "Particulars" of whatever that allegation is, e.g. negligence, breach of duty etc. If these are lengthy, in the alternative, they may be scheduled to the indorsement or set out on additional sheets appended to the personal injuries summons at the time of issue and service.

In addition to the usual signature required on a Plenary Summons in relation to its issuing and the usual indorsement of service, a personal injuries summons must also contain the plaintiff's personal details, as follows:

---

[71] In the District Court, the requirements are identical, District Court Rules O.39A, r.5.

[72] RSC O. 1A r.3. The form of the Summons in the District Court is broadly similar to that in the High Court (see, District Court Rules O.39A, rr.4 and 5 and O.39A 1 Sch.C). In the Circuit Court, see, Practice Direction, Form 1. The Civil Liability and Courts Act 2004, s.13(2) requires that the pleadings in a personal injuries action be in such form as are prescribed by rules of court.

[73] Where indorsements are required for the purpose of serving out of the jurisdiction pursuant to Council Regulation 44/2001, these should be inserted here. In the District Court, the details of the basis upon which jurisdiction is claimed must also be given. See, Form. No.39A 1 Sch.C.

1. the address at which the plaintiff ordinarily resides, and the address for service, if different;
2. the plaintiff's occupation;
3. the plaintiff's date of birth in day, month and year format, and
4. the plaintiff's Personal Public Service Number.[74]

Where the action is being instituted for the benefit of the dependants of a deceased person, the summons must specify the date of birth and the Personal Public Service Number of the deceased person, and the name, address and date of birth of each dependant.[75]

Having set out the requirements under the Act of 2004 and the rules, a number of observations are apposite. Firstly, there is the requirement that the plaintiff's Personal Public Service Number (or PPN) be included on the personal injuries summons. A PPN – as originally envisaged – was allocated to each citizen to provide a single, unique identifier for a member of the public's dealings with the public service.[76] Although its attraction in terms of being able to identify a plaintiff who might use one of several names or other identifiers is obvious, it does not appear that, as originally envisaged, a PPN could properly be used for non-public service access purposes. The PIAB is a specified body within the meaning of the social welfare legislation.[77] The Act of 2004 requires the disclosure of a person's PPN in circumstances where it would otherwise be unlawful and it expands considerably the circumstances in which a person can be

[74] If the plaintiff has not been issued with a Personal Public Service Number, this must be stated. RSC O.1A, r.5(3) (and District Court Rules O.39A, r.4(ii)). For a further discussion of this issue, see *supra*, p.15.

[75] RSC O.1A, r.5(1) and (2). The provision in relation to statutory dependants is wholly consistent with the requirements in actions pursuant to the Civil Liability Act 1961, s.48 as heretofore.

[76] Social Welfare (Consolidation) Act 1993, s.223 as inserted by the Social Welfare Act 1998, s.14, as amended by the Social Welfare (Miscellaneous Provisions) Act 2000, s.32 as extended by the Social Welfare (Miscellaneous Provisions) Act 2002, s.12 as extended by the Social Welfare (Miscellaneous Provisions) Act 2003, s.10 as amended by the Personal Injuries Assessment Board Act 2003, s.84 and as extended by the Social Welfare (Miscellaneous Provisions) Act 2004, s.11 and as extended by the Social Welfare and Pensions Act 2005, s.15. In the amendments and extensions, the range of specified bodies has been considerably expanded.

[77] Personal Injuries Assessment Board Act 2003, s.84.

required to disclose it. It raises obvious data protection issues,[78] which are beyond the scope of the current discussion. It merits noting however, that insofar as the PIAB is permitted to furnish information to a central database,[79] which is subject to the data protection legislative regime,[80] and that the Courts Service is under a duty to establish and maintain a register of personal injuries actions,[81] to be made available to "such persons as establish to the satisfaction of the Courts Service a sufficient interest in seeking access to it",[82] in neither instance is there provision for the storage or registration of a person's PPN. This begs the question, in the circumstances: for what purpose is its disclosure required? Matters in relation to social welfare payments and revenue affairs can otherwise be adequately dealt with, at least in the High Court.[83]

Secondly, it should be noted that "negligence", here, has an extended meaning and includes "nuisance and breach of duty (whether the duty exists by virtue of a contact, a provision of a statute, an instrument under

---

78 Data Protection Act 1988 as amended by the Data Protection (Amendment) Act 2003.

79 Personal Injuries Assessment Board Act 2003, s.86(3) which provides:

"The Board may supply the following, and no other particulars, for the purpose of their being entered in a central database and, by means of that database, being disclosed to other persons who have access to that database, namely—

(*a*) the name and address of a claimant who has made an application under *section 11*,

(*b*) the date on which the accident or incident, the subject of that application, is alleged in that application to have occurred,

(*c*) the name and address of the person or each of the persons who the claimant alleges in the application is or are liable to him or her in respect of the relevant claim concerned, and

(*d*) the name of the insurance company or undertaking, if any, which has entered into a policy of insurance with the person or any of the persons referred to in *paragraph (c)* and which policy provides an indemnity in respect of the claimant's proposed proceedings."

80 *Supra*, n.78 and 79 and *infra*, n.82.

81 Civil Liability and Courts Act 2004, s.30. The register must contain the name and address of the solicitor for each party to a personal injuries action, the name and occupation of each party and the address at which (s)he ordinarily resides as specified in the pleadings. This section has not, as yet, been commenced.

82 This must, surely, include persons who make applications under the Data Protection Act 1988 as amended by the Data Protection (Amendment) Act 2003, and under the Freedom of Information Act 1997, s.7, especially in relation to matters dealt with in s.28 of that Act (access to personal information).

83 See, in particular, the Courts and Court Officers Act 1995, s.45(1)(a)(iv) and (v) and RSC O.39, r.46(2) (Rules of the Superior Courts (No.6) (Disclosure of Reports and Statements) 1998 (S.I. No.391 of 1998).

a statute, or otherwise)."[84] Nuisance is frequently pleaded inappropriately in personal injuries actions and its inclusion – as part of the definition of negligence[85] – it might be speculated, will simply perpetuate the pleading of a head of claim that is often of little or no relevance whatsoever. What the costs implications will be of alleging and pleading a particular legal wrong that the evidence – or the summons itself – does not sustain is uncertain. What is clear, however, as already noted, is that personal injury allegedly caused by a breach of a constitutional right comes within the ambit of the Act.

Thirdly, it might be noted that the personal injuries summons also provides for the pleading of evidence, and not just a summary of the facts which, if established, forms the basis of the legal wrongs alleged.[86] This arises both from the language of the Act itself and the rules of court. The difficulties here are self-evident should an action proceed to trial and the evidence that is given – whether in chief or under cross-examination – materially differs from what is set out in the personal injuries summons.[87] Although the statutory provisions seem to admit of interlocutory applications similar to those that are now brought (in particular in relation to a request for what the Act terms "further information")[88] it is by no means clear – from the use of the word "full" in relation to particulars of special damage and particulars of the acts and circumstances of the commission of an alleged wrong and the particulars of negligence (in the Act and the rules) – that such particulars might be updated after the issuing of the personal injuries summons.

What of a situation, however, where the injuries are unfolding, or

---

[84] Civil Liability and Courts Act 2004, s.2.

[85] It is not included, for instance, in the definition of negligence in the Civil Liability Act 1961, s.2(1). However, the Statute of Limitations (Amendment) Act 1991, s.3(1) as amended by the Civil Liability and Courts Act 2004, s.7(a) applies a two year limitation period to personal injuries caused by nuisance.

[86] This view is supported by the exclusions, from the rules dealing with personal injuries summonses (RSC O.1A) of O.19, r.3, in relation to pleading generally: *supra*, n.00 and the insertion of a new r.5(1) in O.19 by the rules of the Superior Courts (Personal Injuries) 2005 (S.I. No.248 of 2005) para.8.

[87] This is a matter of importance, too, in relation to the swearing of verifying affidavits, pursuant to the Civil Liability and Courts Act 2004, s.14, *infra*, p.33, and fraudulent and exaggerated claims, s.26, *infra*, p.39. This last matter is considered further by William Binchy in his chapter, *infra*, p.74.

[88] Civil Liability and Courts Act 2004, s.11.

investigations are continuing and, accordingly, updated particulars of personal injuries are required? The adjective "full" is not applied to personal injuries in the Act (although it is, in the rules)[89] and it is obviously desirable that it should be possible to deliver such particulars, when known, in order that the matters in issue might be identified. The better view must be that the particulars of the injuries suffered that must be pleaded are those alleged to have been occasioned by the wrong of the defendant, *at the time of the issuing of the summons*.

However, it is difficult to reconcile such a construction with the use of the word "full" in the statutory provisions in respect of pleadings generally.[90] A restrictive interpretation would, at least in the context of special damages, be manifestly inconsistent with the disclosure rules currently in force insofar as personal injuries actions in the High Court are concerned.[91] Although the power to make rules of court pursuant to the Act of 2004[92] is limited to rules that "do not derogate from, and are not inconsistent with, any provision" of the Act,[93] it merits noting that the rules that apply in the High Court ostensibly deal with this matter in a pragmatic way. They provide that where a plaintiff alleges that he was unable, at the time at which a personal injuries summons was issued, to include in it any of the information required to be specified, (s)he must include in the personal injuries summons a statement of the reasons why it is claimed that any such information could not be provided at the time of issue. The plaintiff must then, at the time the personal injuries summons is served or "as soon as may be thereafter (whether by amendment or otherwise)" provide such of the information required as was not included originally."[94] It remains to be seen whether this provision of the rules sustains challenge.

---

89 *Supra*, pp.17 *et seq*.
90 *Infra*., p.32.
91 RSC, O.39, r.46(2) (Rules of the Superior Courts (No.6) (Disclosure of Reports and Statements) 1998 (S.I. No.391 of 1998).
92 Civil Liability and Courts Act 2004, s.9.
93 *Ibid*., s.9(4)(a).
94 RSC, O.1A, r.6

Default of Pleading: The Personal Injuries Summons[95]

One of the principal obligations on the court in relation to the management of personal injuries actions, is to ensure that parties comply with rules of court so that the "trial of personal injuries actions within a reasonable period of their having been commenced is secured."[96] To this end, the Act also provides that where the time within which a certain step is to be taken is prescribed, that period must not be extended unless the parties to the action agree to its being extended or the court considers that in all of the circumstances, the extension of time is necessary or expedient to enable the action to be properly prosecuted or defended and the interests of justice require the extension of time in question.[97] The rules applicable in the High Court expressly provide for the enlargement of time in this regard.[98] For the purpose of ensuring compliance with the rules, the court is empowered to make such orders as to the payment of costs as it considers appropriate.[99] This, obviously, is not limited to those rules in relation to specified time limits.

Under the Act of 2004, the jurisdiction of the court to stay or to dismiss proceedings is expressly extended to non-compliance with the requirements for a personal injuries summons. The court may, in such circumstances, direct that the action not proceed any further until the plaintiff complies with such conditions as the court may specify or, where it considers that the interests of justice so require, dismiss the plaintiff's action. Any application, for a stay or a dismissal of the plaintiff's action on such a ground, must be by way of motion on notice, grounded on an affidavit.[100] However, the order sought will not be made unless the defendant has first written to the plaintiff seeking compliance, a period

---

95 Default issues arising in personal injuries proceedings in the District and Circuit Courts are considered in the footnotes in the relevant discussion of the High Court procedure.

96 Civil Liability and Courts Act 2004, s.9(1).

97 *Ibid.*, s.9(2).

98 Rules of the Superior Courts (Personal Injuries) 2005 (S.I. No.248 of 2005), para.11 inserting a new rule 7 into RSC, O.122. It is, however, stated to be "subject to any relevant provision of statute" such as, for instance, the Civil Liability and Courts Act 2004, s.9(2).

99 Civil Liability and Courts Act 2004, s.9(3).

100 RSC, O.1A, r.11(1)(i). See, also, District Court Rules, O.39A, r.8(1)(i): the form of the notice of application in the District Court is set out in Form 39A.5 Sch.C.

of 28 days[101] for compliance with the defendant's request had been allowed and the plaintiff has failed, refused or neglected to comply with the request.[102] Furthermore, no application for judgment or other relief in default of pleading will be granted in a personal injuries action unless the moving party has satisfied the court that he has verified his previous pleadings in that action on oath.[103] However, if the default is in relation to a personal injuries summons, the defendant may not have delivered a defence and, therefore, there will be no "previous pleadings". It also remains to be seen how these provisions will harmonise, in practice, with the rules in relation to updating the personal injuries summons, if it has issued without all the statutory requirements having been complied with.[104]

In addition, the court must take any failure to comply with the statutory requirements into account when deciding whether to make an order as to the payment of the costs of the action concerned or the amount of those costs.[105] However, as already set out, the rules applicable in the High Court admit of non-compliance with the statutory requirement and its subsequently being remedied.[106] The court hearing the action is also entitled to draw such inferences from the failure to comply with the provisions of the personal injuries summons as appear proper.[107] Accordingly, non-compliance with a requirement is relevant at both the interlocutory and hearing stages. This might reasonably be considered a power considerably wider than the courts currently expressly enjoy. Whereas the provisions in relation to costs seem unexceptional, it is unclear what inferences might be drawn from a failure to comply with a procedural provision, other than that the plaintiff, or his legal advisers, are dilatory in the prosecution of the action.

Appearance

As in other actions, an appearance must be entered to the personal injuries

---

[101] In the District Court, the period is 14 days; District Court Rules, O.39A, r.8(1).
[102] RSC O.1A, r.11(1).
[103] *Ibid.*, r.11(2). No such provision, in this regard, appears in the District Court Rules.
[104] *Ibid.*, r.6, *supra*, n.94.
[105] Civil Liability and Courts Act 2004, s.10(3).
[106] *Supra*, pp.16 *et seq.*
[107] Civil Liability and Courts Act 2004, s.10(4).

summons within eight days of service[108] and the ordinary rules of court apply, in this regard.[109] In default of appearance by any defendant, the plaintiff may apply to the court by motion for judgment in the action in default of appearance upon filing in the Central Office an affidavit of service of the personal injuries summons and an affidavit verifying[110] the contents of the summons.[111] Similar provisions apply where there is default of appearance to a personal injuries summons served on a defendant outside the jurisdiction.[112]

Request for Further Information

Standard particulars that are often raised in personal injuries actions relate to any previous injuries sustained by a plaintiff and to social welfare and income matters. The Act of 2004 deals with such requests expressly and requires the provision by a plaintiff to a defendant, on the defendant's request, with:

- particulars of any personal injuries action brought by the plaintiff in which a court made an award of damages or which was withdrawn or settled,
- particulars of any injuries sustained or treatment administered to the plaintiff that would have a bearing on the personal injuries to which the action relates,

---

[108] RSC, O.12. No express provision is made in the Rules of the Superior Courts (Personal Injuries) 2005 (S.I. No.248 of 2005) in relation to the time for an appearance to a personal injuries summons. RSC, O.1A, r.4 must, accordingly, apply. In the District Court, no Appearance is required and a defendant who intends to defend the proceedings must deliver to the plaintiff, or his solicitor, and to the District Court Clerk a defence within 28 days after the service of the personal injuries summons; District Court Rules, O.39A, r.6. In the Circuit Court, see Practice Direction para. 9, applying the normal rules for Circuit court proceedings.

[109] See, RSC, O.1A, r.8 and Form No.5 in Appendix A Pt II. The Act of 2004 is silent on this procedural point.

[110] *Infra.*, p.33.

[111] RSC, O.13, r.6A as inserted by the Rules of the Superior Courts (Personal Injuries) 2005 (S.I. No.248 of 2005), para.6.

[112] RSC, O.13A, r.3 as inserted by the Rules of the Superior Courts (Personal Injuries) 2005 (S.I. No.248 of 2005), para.7.

- the name of any persons from whom the plaintiff received such medical treatment,[113] and
- documents (of such a class as may be prescribed from time to time by the Minister) from the Revenue Commissioners or the Minister for Social and Family Affairs relating to any earnings or other income in respect of which the plaintiff is making a claim.[114]

This information, in the Act, is referred to as "further information". A failure to comply with such a request attracts the same range of sanctions as apply to a failure to comply with the statutory provisions in relation to a personal injuries summons, *i.e.* the action may be stayed or dismissed and the failure must be taken into account by the court, at the hearing of the action,[115] in deciding whether to make any order as to the payment of the costs of the action or the amount of those costs.[116] In addition, may draw such inferences, at the hearing of the action, as appear proper from a failure to provide information in relation to previous actions, injuries or the identity of those from whom treatment was received.[117]

An application to stay or dismiss the plaintiff's action on the grounds of a failure to provide further information as requested, must be made by motion on notice grounded on an affidavit sworn by the defendant.[118] As in the case of default in relation to a personal injuries summons, the order sought will not be made unless the defendant has first written to the plaintiff seeking compliance, a period of 28 days[119] for compliance with the defendant's request had been allowed and the plaintiff has failed, refused or neglected to comply with the request.[120] Furthermore, no

---

[113] Civil Liability and Courts Act 2004, s.11(1).

[114] *Ibid.*, s.11(2). The Revenue Commissioners and the Minister for Social and Family Affairs are required to furnish the plaintiff with the relevant documents, on his request, *ibid.*, s.11(5).

[115] This is not as express in the provisions relating to default in relation to the personal injuries summons. See, Civil Liability and Courts Act 2004, s.10(3)(b).

[116] Civil Liability and Courts Act 2004, s.11(3).

[117] *Ibid.*, s.11(4); this does not apply, curiously, in relation to a failure to provide revenue and social welfare information or to a failure to seek that information.

[118] RSC, O.1A, r.11(1)(ii). (Insofar as the District Court is concerned, District Court Rules O.39A, r.8(1)(ii): the form of the notice of application in the District Court is set out in Form 39A.5 Sch.C.)

[119] The period in the District Court is 14 days; District Court Rules, O.39A, r.8(1).

[120] RSC, O.1A, r.11(1).

application for judgment or other relief in default of pleading will be granted in a personal injuries action unless the moving party has satisfied the court that he has verified his previous pleadings in that action on oath.[121] Unlike in the case of default in relation to a personal injuries summons, however, a defence may have been delivered, by the time the request for further information is made and, accordingly, it will be necessary, in those circumstances to have the contents of the defence verified on affidavit.

The mischief sought to be addressed by this statutory provision is self-evident and reflects a prevailing concern on the part of the insurance sector that serial litigators have been successful in numerous, separate personal injuries actions. That said, insofar as particulars of injuries sustained or treatment administered to a plaintiff that would have a bearing on the injuries to which a particular action relates are concerned, a question arises as to how disclosure of such particulars is to be assessed. In other words, is the plaintiff's, or his legal adviser's, subjective view sufficient or will the objective assessment of a medical practitioner be required? Insofar as discovery is concerned, the relevance of a particular document is determined by the party making the discovery. Should a similar rule be applied here too? If an independent objective approach is to be required, more extensive medical reports than are currently provided will unarguably be required.

This, then, leads to consideration of the requirement to furnish the identities of persons from whom the plaintiff received treatment previously. Although the word "treatment" is used alone in relation to the requirement to furnish particulars, insofar as the identity of the person who provided the treatment is concerned, the adjectives " such medical" are added (although there is no previous mention of the word "medical" in the relevant section). Whereas it can hardly be considered likely that "medical", in this context, is to be construed overly narrowly, such as to exclude dental, surgical or psychiatric treatment, (especially given the definition of personal injury – which is the same as that in the Civil Liability Act 1961), the question does arise as to whether or not persons providing non-medical treatment, either of the orthodox or "alternative" variety, also require to be identified, e.g. physiotherapists, psychologists,

---

121 *Ibid.*, r.11(2). An identical provision does not arise in the District Court Rules.

acupuncturists *et al*. It must be the case, however, that the provision is directed at the widest possible disclosure of information.[122] That the drafting does not reflect that intention is regrettable.

Defence and Counterclaim

Defence

A defence to a personal injuries action, unlike a defence in other proceedings must specify:

- the allegations specified or the matters pleaded in the summons of which the defendant (i) does not require proof and (ii) those of which (s)he requires proof,
- the grounds on which the defendant claims that (s)he is not liable for any injuries suffered by the plaintiff, and
- the grounds of any contributory negligence alleged.[123]

In the High Court, the rules require that the defence be delivered (by each defendant) within eight weeks of the service of the personal injuries summons.[124] Insofar as the form of the defence is concerned,[125] in addition to the matters set out, it must also contain full and detailed particulars of each denial or traverse, and of each allegation, assertion or plea, comprising the defendant's defence[126] and, where appropriate, a counter-schedule setting out the defence to items of special damage claimed by the plaintiff. Particulars of a general denial, traverse, allegation, assertion

[122] In this context, see C. Craven, "Personal Injuries Assessment Board Act 2003: Medico-Legal Aspects" in Quigley and Binchy (eds.), *The Personal Injuries Assessment Board: Implications for Legal Practice* (First Law, 2004), p.47 *et seq*., and *McGrory v. ESB* [2003] 3 I.R. 407.

[123] Civil Liability and Courts Act 2004, s.12(1).

[124] RSC, O.1A, r.8. (In the District Court, there being no Appearance, the defence must be delivered within 28 days of service of the District Court Personal Injuries Summons; District Court Rules O.39A, r.6). The Circuit Court Practice Direction is silent on the point and, therefore, the usual rules in relation to default of defence must apply; see para.9. The Act of 2004 is silent in relation to this time limit.

[125] As to the form of pleadings, *supra*, pp.15 *et seq*. and *infra*, pp.32 *et seq*.

[126] Civil Liability and Courts Act 2004, s.13, *infra*, p.32, "Pleadings Generally".

or plea may be set out in the defence under the paragraph containing them and headed "Particulars" of whatever it is, e.g. contributory negligence. If they are lengthy, they may, in the alternative, be scheduled to the defence or set out on additional sheets appended to the defence at the time of service.[127] Insofar as a plea of contributory negligence is concerned, it must be the case that specifying that a failure to mitigate one's own loss, a provision of the Civil Liability Act 1961 or acts alleged to amount to negligence on the part of plaintiff will be sufficient for such purposes, as they are now. There is nothing in the Act of 2004 to suggest that anything other than that which procedure now requires is necessary.

Although there is provision in the rules that apply to personal injuries proceedings in the High Court for the updating or amendment of a personal injuries summons in circumstances where, at the time of issuing, the plaintiff was unable to include some of the information required to be specified in it,[128] there is no analogous provision in relation to a defence.[129] Accordingly, the usual rules in relation to the amendment of pleadings must apply.[130]

In addition to the usually applicable rules in relation to default in pleading,[131] a defendant's failure to comply with the statutory requirements attracts the same range of sanctions as apply to a plaintiff's failure to comply with the provisions in relation to a personal injuries summons, *i.e.* the action may be stayed or judgment given in favour of the plaintiff and the failure must be taken into account by the court when deciding whether to make any order as to the payment of the costs of the action or the amount of those costs.[132] In addition, the court hearing the action may draw such inferences as appear proper from a defendant's

---

[127] Form No.2 in Appendix CC to the Rules of the Superior Courts. (In the District Court, the form is Form 39A.2 Sch.C; in the Circuit Court, the Practice Direction specifies Form 2 – both are broadly similar). See, also *infra*, p.32, "Pleadings Generally".

[128] RSC, O.1A, r.6, *supra*, n.94 and 104.

[129] In this regard, see the discussion in relation to pleadings generally, which impact on the contents of a defence more than on a personal injuries summons or counterclaim, *infra*, p.32. However, the fact that an interlocutory application might be made seeking an order for the delivery of further and better particulars (RSC O.1A, r.11(1)(iv)), *infra*, p.37 may avail a defendant in this regard.

[130] RSC, O.28, subject to O.1A, r.2.

[131] RSC, O.27, subject to O.1A, r.2.

[132] Civil Liability and Courts Act 2004, s.12(3); the reference to the taking into account

failure to comply with the provisions,[133] although what such inferences might be are unclear.

As in the case of default in relation to a personal injuries summons[134] or a request for further information,[135] an application to stay the action or for judgment against the defendant on the grounds of a failure to comply with the statutory provisions in relation to a defence or counterclaim, must be made by motion on notice grounded on an affidavit sworn by the plaintiff.[136] As in the other cases of default, the order sought will not be made unless the plaintiff has first written to the defendant seeking compliance, a period of 28 days[137] for compliance with the plaintiff's request had been allowed and the defendant has failed, refused or neglected to comply with the request.[138] As in the other cases, too, no application for judgment or other relief in default of pleading will be granted in a personal injuries action unless the moving party has satisfied the court that he has verified his previous pleadings in that action on oath.[139] Accordingly, it will be necessary, in those circumstances to have the contents of the personal injuries summons verified on affidavit.[140]

Counterclaim

A counterclaim, for its part, must specify the matters required of a plaintiff in a personal injuries summons, other than, of course, the name and address of the plaintiff, which are already set out in the personal injuries summons.[141] Where any defendant makes a counterclaim, that must be appended to the defence[142] and its form[143] is, for all practical purposes, identical to that of a personal injuries summons.[144]

By virtue of the definition of plaintiff in the Act (*i.e.* it includes a

---

of "such failure *or refusal*" (*emphasis* added) in paragraph (b) of the subsection is odd as the section does not refer to any refusal whatsoever.

133 *Ibid.*, s.12(4).

134 *Supra*, p.23.

135 *Supra*, p.25.

136 RSC, O.11, r.11(1)(iii). (See, also, District Court Rules, O.39A, r.8(1)(iv): the form of the notice of application in the District Court is set out in Form 39A.5 Sch.C.)

137 The period in the District Court is 14 days; District Court Rules, O.39A, r.8(1).

138 RSC, O. A, r.11(1).

139 *Ibid.*, r.11(2). (See, also, District Court Rules O.39A, r.8(3))

140 This is expressly provided for in District Court Rules, O.39A, r.8(3).

141 Civil Liability and Courts Act 2004, s.12(2); *supra*, p.15.

142 RSC O.1A, r.8, and, accordingly, delivered at the same time. (In the District Court,

defendant counter-claiming)[145] the provisions in relation to default by a plaintiff, whether in relation to a personal injuries summons[146] or on foot of a request for further information,[147] apply here too.[148] The comments already set out in respect of the personal injuries summons apply generally.[149]

Reply and Defence to Counterclaim

Reply

Although the Act of 2004 does not expressly refer to any pleading after a defence or counterclaim, the rules applicable in the High Court provide that a plaintiff who wishes to join issue with a defendant's defence may deliver a reply within six weeks of the delivery of the defence.[150] A reply, if it contains any assertion or allegation of fact, must be verified on oath.[151]

Defence to counterclaim

A plaintiff is required to deliver a defence to any counterclaim within eight weeks of the delivery of the counterclaim and it must comply with the requirements of the Act of 2004 applicable to a defence.[152]

---

see District Court Rules O.39A, r.6, in the Circuit Court, see Practice Direction para.5).

143 *Supra*, pp.15 *et seq.*

144 Form No. 3 in Appendix CC to the Rules of the Superior Courts, Form 39A .3 Schedule C in the District Court.

145 *Supra*, n.30.

146 *Supra*, p.23.

147 *Supra*, p.25.

148 The provisions of the Civil Liability Act 2004, s.12(3) and (4), which are in similar terms, also apply, perhaps in an otiose manner.

149 *Supra*, pp.15 *et seq.*

150 RSC, O.1A, r.9.

151 *Ibid.*, rr.9 and 10.

152 *Ibid.*, r.9. The form is in Form No.2 Appendix CC, in other words, the same as a defence, with such modifications as may be necessary. (See, also, the equivalent provision in the Circuit Court Practice Direction para.5, where no time limit is specified).

Pleadings Generally

Notwithstanding the specific provisions in relation to the contents of a personal injuries summons, defence and counterclaim, the Act of 2004 goes on to impose general requirements in respect of pleadings.[153] In this context, "pleading" in relation to a personal injuries action, means not alone a personal injuries summons, a defence or a defence and counterclaim, but it also includes any other document (other than an affidavit or a report prepared by a person who is not a party to the action) that, under rules of court is required to be, or may be, served (within such period as is prescribed by the rules) by one party to the action on another.[154] Although service of a letter of claim,[155] or of a notice of an offer of terms of settlement,[156] is not required by rules of court but, rather, by the Act of 2004 itself, the rules applicable in High Court proceedings, somewhat anomalously, make provision for both.[157] That said, the rules make no provision for the making of requests, or the delivery of responses to requests, for "further information".[158] Disclosure schedules seem to be caught by the definition, as is a reply and a defence to a counterclaim. Having regard to what is required by the Act in relation to "pleadings" it is not entirely clear what else may be included.[159]

The Act requires that where a pleading is served by a plaintiff, it must contain full and detailed particulars of the claim of which the action consists and of each allegation, assertion or plea comprising that claim.[160]

---

[153] Civil Liability and Courts Act 2004, s.13 and RSC, O.19, r.5(1) as inserted by the rules of the Superior Courts (Personal Injuries) 2005 (Statutory Instrument Number 248 of 2005) para. 8.

[154] *Ibid.*, s.2. The same definition is adopted in RSC, O.1A, r.1 and District Court Rules, O.39A, r.1.

[155] *Supra*, p.10.

[156] Civil Liability and Courts Act 2004, s.17.

[157] *Supra*, n.00. See, also, RSC, O.1A, r.13. There is no equivalent provision in the District Court Rules; the Circuit Court Practice Direction merely refers to the statutory requirement.

[158] Having regard to the language of s.14 of the Act of 2004 and RSC, O.1A, r.10 (verifying affidavits), *infra*, p.33, such a request or response could not be regarded as a "pleading".

[159] In this context, however, given the provisions of s.14(8)(b) of the Act in relation to the requirement to swear a verifying affidavit in a case which was brought before March 31, 2005, it must extend, given the terms of the definition, to the pleadings in such cases too, including the Statement of Claim, *infra*, p.33.

[160] Civil Liability and Courts Act 2004, s.13(1)(a).

This, in fact, adds nothing to the requirements already in the Act in relation to a personal injuries summons, other than to require that, in addition, full particulars of the injuries alleged must also be there set out.[161] It does, however, as in the context of a defence, amplify what is required of a defence to a counterclaim and define the requirements of a reply. Furthermore, it might be observed that it is difficult to envisage how such particulars might be necessary or set out in other than a personal injuries summons or a reply (or a counterclaim).

Where a pleading is served by a defendant or a third party, the Act of 2004 requires that it contains full and detailed particulars of each denial or traverse, and of each allegation, assertion or plea comprising the defence.[162] Unlike in the case of a personal injuries summons, this provision does add to the drafting requirements of a defence (including a third party defence) and this is reflected in the provisions of the rules in relation to a defence.[163] However, one can only speculate as to how full and detailed particulars of a denial or traverse are to be drafted.

If the new provisions in relation to pleadings do no more than define the matters actually in issue between the parties to a personal injuries action they should be unproblematic. Although that is the function of pleadings, as understood, narrowing the matters in issue often does not occur until close to trial. The thrust of the new regime, accordingly, is that of expeditious – and, presumably, less costly – litigation.

Verifying Affidavits

Where any pleading in a personal injuries action containing assertions or allegations (probably confined to a personal injuries summons, reply and defence to a counterclaim for the reasons already set out)[164] is served or a defendant or a defendant is provided with further information[165] an affidavit verifying those assertions or allegations or the further information must be sworn by the plaintiff or, in the case of an infant or a person of

---

161 As RSC, O.1A requires see *supra*, pp.15 *et seq.*
162 Civil Liability and Courts Act 2004, s.13(1)(b).
163 *Supra*, pp.28 *et seq.*
164 *Supra*, p.31.
165 *Supra*, p.25.

unsound mind, by the next friend or committee.[166] Similarly, where a defendant or a third party serves on another party to the action any pleading containing assertions or allegations, a verifying affidavit is also required.[167] Where the affidavit is sworn by a next friend or committee, the affidavit is required to state that (s)he honestly believes the assertions, allegations or further information to be true in respect of those matters of which (s)he does not have personal knowledge.[168] Given that such a requirement exists in every affidavit, this statutory provision might be considered otiose. That no such provision exists in relation to verifying affidavits sworn by plaintiffs, defendants or third parties – where personal knowledge of the meaning of certain allegations of, for instance, negligence or breach of duty, may not exist – impliedly demonstrates the non-necessity for such a requirement to be express.

Verifying affidavits are, generally, required to be lodged in court[169] (by filing in the Central Office)[170] not later than 21 days after service of the pleading concerned, or such longer period as the court may direct or the parties may agree.[171] The rules[172] provide that a verifying affidavit, if not separate to the pleading or other document, may be endorsed on it.[173] A copy of the verifying affidavit must be delivered to the party to whom the pleading or other document is to be delivered. Where endorsed on the pleading or document, the copy of the affidavit must be delivered within the time prescribed for the delivery of the pleading or document in question (e.g. 28 days after service of the summons in the case of the defence in the High Court). Otherwise, the default 21-day (or agreed)

---

[166] Civil Liability and Courts Act 2004, s.14(1).

[167] *Ibid.*, s.14(2).

[168] *Ibid.*, s.14(3).

[169] Including the Master's Court and the County Registrar's list: *ibid.*, s.14(6).

[170] RSC, O.1A, r.10(3). In the case of the District Court, this is by lodging the original affidavit duly stamped with the District Court Clerk: District Court Rules, O.39A, r.7(4). In the Circuit Court, filing in the Circuit Court Office "in the usual way" is prescribed: Practice Direction para.7.

[171] Civil Liability and Courts Act 2004, s.14(4)(a). How this is consistent with the foreshortening of other time limits is not easy to discern, in this particular area.

[172] In this regard, the provisions of RSC O.1A, r.10 are virtually identical to District Court Rules, O.39A, r.7. In the Circuit Court, see Practice Direction para.6.

[173] RSC, O.1A, r.10(1). The form is set out in Form No.4, Appendix CC. (See, also, District Court Rules, O.39A, r.7(1) and Form 39A.4 Schedule C and Circuit Court Practice Direction, para.6, Form 3).

period applies.[174] In this regard, it should be noted that where the copy of the verifying affidavit is delivered subsequent to the pleading or document in question, the time prescribed in the rules for the delivery of any pleading or other document in reply only runs from the date of the delivery of that copy affidavit.[175] Thus, for example, the time within which the defence must be delivered only begins to run from the date on which the copy of the affidavit verifying the personal injuries summons is delivered, if it is not endorsed on the summons itself and it is delivered subsequent to the service of the summons.

The rules[176] also provide that the affidavit is to contain an averment to the effect that the deponent is aware that it is an offence to make a statement in the affidavit that is false or misleading in any material respect and that the deponent knows to be false or misleading.[177] What is material, of course, is a matter for the court to decide.[178] The penalty prescribed for such an offence is very significant: it is punishable, on conviction on indictment, by a fine not exceeding €100,000 and/or a term of imprisonment not exceeding 10 years.[179] However, the offence is triable in the District Court where the court is of the opinion that it is a minor offence and fit to be tried summarily, the accused elects a summary trial and the DPP consents to such a disposition. In those circumstances, on summary conviction, the punishment prescribed is a fine not exceeding €3,000 and/or imprisonment not exceeding 12 months.[180] In terms of the scale of punishment, what is prescribed for many non-fatal offences against the person is a useful comparator.

Thus, in practical terms, a pleading should not be delivered without a verifying affidavit having been sworn, which affidavit will then fix the evidence to be adduced by the swearing party at trial. This will, in essence,

---

174 *Ibid.*, r.10(2). (See, District Court Rules, O.39A, r.7(2)).

175 *Ibid.*, r.10(4). (See, District Court Rules, O.39A, r.7(3). In the case of the District Court Rules, the reference, in this regard, is to the affidavit, not the copy affidavit).

176 RSC Form No.4 Appendix CC, District Court Rules, Form 39A.4 Schedule C, Circuit Court Practice Direction Form 3.

177 This reflects the requirement of the Civil Liability and Courts Act 2004, s.14(7). The offence is created by s.14(5).

178 See the discussion by William Binchy in relation to this issue generally, *infra*, pp.44 *et seq*.

179 Civil Liability and Courts Act 2004, s.29(1). It should be noted that these penal provisions were commenced on September 20, 2004.

180 *Ibid.*, s.29(2) and (3).

require each party to litigation to read and examine any pleading drafted by the legal advisers and to satisfy him- or herself that it is correct in all material respects. A high standard of precision, not always obvious in current pleadings, e.g. in relation to dates, places, circumstances of accident, will, accordingly, be required. The time for doing this may also be circumscribed.

In respect of actions brought after the date of commencement of this provision of the Act, *i.e.* March 31, 2005, any difficulty, in this regard may be principally administrative in nature. However, it should be noted that the Act also provides that in personal injuries actions brought before the commencement of the provisions in relation to verifying affidavits, a party to the action may require another party to swear a verifying affidavit, not later than 21 days before the date fixed for the trial of the action.[181] Whether this means the date specified in the Notice of Trial – which is a masterful fiction – or the actual date on which the case is listed for hearing is unclear although to make any sense of the provision it must be considered to mean the latter. Thus, this provision ostensibly applies to all personal injuries actions currently pending, although the harmonising of the definition of pleading within the meaning of the Act and pleading generally may not entirely straightforward.[182] Filing of the verifying affidavit in the Central Office must take place not later than 7 days before the date fixed for the trial, in such circumstances.[183] The other provisions in the rules in relation to the swearing and delivery of verifying affidavits[184] are not immediately applicable.[185]

Interlocutory Applications

As with other proceedings in the High Court, the rules, in relation to personal injuries actions also provide for the making of certain

[181] *Ibid.*, s.14(8)(b).
[182] *Supra*, p.32.
[183] Civil Liability and Courts Act 2004, s.14(4)(b).
[184] *Supra*, p.33.
[185] However, see Circuit Court Practice Direction, para.6, which requires that the same form of verifying affidavit be used in proceedings brought before March 31, 2005 in the circumstances referred to in s.14(8) of the Act of 2004.

interlocutory applications.[186] In addition to those already set out (in relation to applications to stay or dismiss the action by reason of the plaintiff's failure to comply with the requirements of a personal injuries summons,[187] or with a request to provide further information,[188] or for a stay of the action and judgment against a defendant by reason of the defendant's failure to comply with the provisions in relation to a defence or counterclaim)[189] applications may also be made for an order for the delivery of further and better particulars of any pleading[190] and in relation to having evidence in the action given by affidavit.[191]

An application for an order for the delivery of further and better particulars must be made by motion on notice grounded on an affidavit sworn by the party seeking the particulars.[192] As in applications for orders in default of statutory compliance, the order sought will not be made unless the moving party has first written to the relevant opposing party

---

[186] Insofar as the District Court is concerned, District Court Rules, O.39A, r.8(1) also provides for the making of the following applications in a personal injuries action: (i) under s.9(2) of the Act (in the absence of agreement between or among the parties) for the extension of the period provided, within which any document may be served or thing may be done, (ii) by a party for a direction under s.15 of the Act that a mediation conference be held, (iii) to order the delivery by the opposing party of further and better particulars of any pleading delivered, (iv) by a party wishing to have evidence in the action given by affidavit, under s.19 of the Act and (v) by a party wishing to have an approved person appointed to carry out any investigation and to give any evidence in the action in relation to any matter, under s.20 of the Act. How this last application arises, however, on a plain reading of s.20 is unclear. Both the form of the notice to be given and the order to be made are specified (District Court Rules, Form 39A.5 and Form 39A.6 Sch.C respectively). The rules in relation to notice and the giving of a 14 day warning letter apply as with interlocutory applications for relief in default of pleading, e.g. *supra*, p.23. In the Circuit Court, an application for any interlocutory order "referred to in Pt 2 of the Act" (*i.e.* in default of statutory compliance, application for a mediation conference) may be made by motion on notice in the ordinary way: Practice Direction, para.8.

[187] *Supra*, p.15.

[188] *Supra*, p.25.

[189] *Supra*, pp.28 *et seq.*

[190] RSC O. 1A, r.11(1)(iv). If the rules in relation to pleadings are complied with, it is not clear how many such applications might arise. However, see pp.23 *et seq. supra*. There appears to be more than a minimal overlap with other applications in relation to non-compliance with the statutory formalities in relation to drafting, *supra*, p.24. That the Act of 2004 contemplates such steps, eminently practical though they may be, is uncertain.

[191] *Ibid.*, r.11(1)(v). See, the Civil Liability and Courts Act 2004, s.19.

[192] *Ibid.*, r.11(1).

seeking compliance with the request for the particulars, a period of 28 days for compliance with the request has been allowed and the other party has failed, refused or neglected to comply with the request.[193] As in the other cases, too, no application for the relief sought will be granted in a personal injuries action unless the moving party has satisfied the court that he has verified his previous pleadings in that action on oath.[194]

Affidavit Evidence

Although the rules applicable in High Court proceedings require that a personal injuries action shall be instituted by an "originating summons, for the commencement of plenary proceedings with pleadings *and hearing on oral evidence*"[195] (*emphasis* added) the Act of 2004 further provides that in such an action, evidence as to any matter shall, where the court so directs, be given by affidavit.[196] This may arise, for example, in relation to formal evidence of a non-contentious nature, e.g. the proving of photographs, x-rays etc. Such evidence, and evidence in the nature of reports, however, may, of course, always be agreed by the parties, in any event However, any direction by the court in a personal injuries action in relation to affidavit evidence does not operate to deny any party the right to cross-examine a witness who has given such evidence.[197]

Whereas personal injuries actions, by their nature, generally require plenary hearing, this provision can hardly be considered to represent a particular departure from current, standard practice. Application can always be made to cross-examine a deponent on his or her affidavit.

Exclusion of Certain Witnesses

The Act of 2004 provides that the court, in a personal injuries action may, upon the application of a party to that action, direct that a person,

---

[193] *Ibid.*
[194] RSC, O.1A, r.11(2).
[195] *Ibid.*, r.3.
[196] Civil Liability and Court Act 2004, s.19(1). See, also, RSC, O.1A, r.11(1)(v) and District Court Rules, O.39A, r.8(1)(vii).
[197] *Ibid.*, s.19(2).

other than another party or an expert witness,[198] who it is intended will be called to give evidence at the trial, shall not attend that trial until called to give evidence. In addition, where a court gives such a direction, it may give all such other directions as it considers necessary or expedient to secure that a such a witness does not communicate with other witnesses who it is intended will be called to give evidence at the trial or receive information such as might influence him or her when giving evidence.[199] Although this is a new provision in our civil procedure, the mischief sought to be addressed is obvious. The underlying assumption that experts might not also be subject to a "cushion" effect is, however, questionable.

Offence in Relation to False Evidence, False Instructions and Fraudulent Actions

False evidence

Not alone is it an offence to swear a verifying affidavit that is misleading and is known to be so,[200] a person who gives or adduces, or dishonestly causes to be given or adduced, evidence in a personal injuries action that is false or misleading in any material respect, knowing it to be false or misleading, is also guilty of an offence.[201] Such an offence is punishable in the same manner as an offence in relation to a verifying affidavit.[202]

False instructions

Similarly, a person who gives, or dishonestly causes to be given, an instruction or information,[203] in relation to a personal injuries action, to a solicitor, or a person acting on behalf of a solicitor, or an expert[204] that

---

198 An expert witness, in this context, means a person it is intended will be called as a witness to give expert evidence at trial of that action: *ibid.*, s.54(3)
199 *Ibid.*, s.54.
200 *Supra*, p.35.
201 Civil Liability and Courts Act 2004, s.25(1).
202 *Supra*, p35.
203 See, in this regard, *Philip v. Ryan* [2004] I.E.S.C. 105 (December 17, 2004).
204 An expert is a person who has a special skill or expertise and who has been engaged by one of the parties to give expert evidence in the action or, for the purposes of or in contemplation of a personal injuries action, has been requested to carry out an

is false or misleading in any material respect, knowing it to be so is guilty of an offence. This too, is punishable in the same manner as the other offences in the Act.[205]

For the purposes of these provisions, an act is done dishonestly if the person does it with the intention of misleading the court.[206] In this regard, it should be noted that these provisions apply not alone to personal injuries actions brought on or after their commencement (which was September 20, 2004) but also to actions "pending" on that date.[207] "Pending", in this context, must refer to actions which have already been initiated but which have not yet been determined. In effect, therefore, the provisions apply to all proceedings currently extant, and are not solely applicable to those initiated after that date.

What merits noting in this context, is the use of the adjective "any" in relation to "material respect". The offence is committed, therefore, assuming proof of the other elements, once the court has been misled in relation to *any* matter of significance. That, of course, will involve an assessment of materiality.

Fraudulent actions

Where a plaintiff gives or adduces, or dishonestly causes to be given or adduced, evidence that is false or misleading, in any material respect, knowing it to be so, not alone does that constitute an offence but the court is required to dismiss the action unless, for reasons that the court is required to state in its decision, the dismissal of the action would result in injustice being done.[208] Dishonestly, for the purposes of this provision, has the same meaning as set out above in relation to false evidence.[209]

Similarly, if the court is satisfied that a person has sworn an affidavit that is false or misleading in any material respect, knowing it was false

---

examination or investigation in relation to any matter for which such special skill or expertise is necessary: Civil Liability and Courts Act 2004, s.25(5).

205 *Ibid.*, s.25(2).

206 *Ibid.*, s.25(3).

207 *Ibid.*, s.25(4).

208 Civil Liability and Courts Act 2004, s.26(1). See the discussion by William Binchy, *infra*, p.74 *et seq*.

209 *Ibid.*, s.26(3).

or misleading when swearing the affidavit, a similar sanction attaches.[210] Cognate provisions, however, do not apply to defendants.

These provisions also apply not alone to personal injuries actions brought on or after their commencement (September 20, 2004) but also to actions "pending" on that date.[211] "Pending", in this context, has the same meaning as that already discussed in the context of false evidence and false instructions.[212]

Other Matters

General

Issues in relation to court-appointed experts, intervention in the Supreme Court, actuarial tables and discount rates, collateral benefits and mediation are considered more fully by other contributors. Insofar as formal offers are concerned, although this is discussed in some detail by William Binchy,[213] it merits noting that the rules of court contribute nothing by way of clarification to the issues he identifies. They merely require that copies of the plaintiff's notice of an offer of terms of settlement[214] and of the defendant's notice[215] must be lodged in court by being filed (together with an affidavit as to their service on the opposing party) in the Central Office as soon as may be after the expiry of the prescribed period.[216]

Pre-trial hearings

In relation to pre-trial hearings, the Act of 2004 provides that, in a personal injuries action, the court, if it considers it appropriate, is to direct that a hearing be held before the trial for the purposes of determining what

---

[210] *Ibid.*, s.26(2).
[211] *Ibid.*, s.26(4).
[212] *Supra*, p.39.
[213] *Infra*, pp.54 *et seq.*
[214] Civil Liability and Courts Act 2004, s.17(1).
[215] *Ibid.*, s.17(2).
[216] *Ibid.*, s.17(3). See, RSC, O.1A, r.13 (the form of the notice is in Form No.5 in Appendix CC) which is in terms, virtually identical to District Court Rules, O.39A, r.10 (Form 39A.7 Sch.C applies. See, also, Circuit Court Practice Direction, para.7 Form 4). In relation to the "relevant date" and the "prescribed period" *supra*, p.7.

matters are in dispute.[217] All parties to the action are entitled to be heard[218] at a hearing held pursuant to any such direction, which hearing is to be presided over by, in an action brought in the High Court,[219] a High Court judge, the Master or a Deputy Master of the High Court or a nominated[220] officer as directed by the President of the High Court.[221]

The person presiding over a pre-trial hearing may give such directions and make such orders as may be necessary for the purposes of determining what matters relating to the action are in dispute.[222] However, any direction given or order made at such a hearing where the person presiding is other than a judge may be appealed to the court by the party affected.[223] How these provisions will operate in practice and how they will harmonise with those in relation to mediation remains to be seen.[224]

What might be said by way of summary, to this chapter, is that the principal procedural provisions of the Act of 2004 clearly indicate a new regime in which time limits and drafting precision assume particular importance, and in which the parties to personal injuries litigation play more central roles than, perhaps, heretofore. The rules of court, however, in many instances, do not appear, at first blush, to be wholly consistent with what the Act seems, expressly, to require. That said, the anomalies and difficulties identified are more than idle curiosities. Given the enormous range of actions affected – from the perspective of both the

---

[217] *Ibid.*, s.18(1). The pleadings regime, it might have been considered, should have been largely sufficient for that purpose. This power is in addition to the power of the court to give directions in relation to any matter in a personal injuries action, *ibid.*, s.18(4). Note that District Court Rules, O. 39A r.11 contemplates that an application for such a hearing be made by one of the parties. This does not immediately arise on a plain reading of s.18 of the Act of 2004.

[218] *Ibid.*, s.18(2).

[219] Where the action is brought in the Circuit Court, the hearing is presided over by a Circuit Court judge, the appropriate county registrar or a member of the staff of the Circuit court Office in the county in which the action was brought, as the President of the circuit Court may direct, Civil Liability and Courts Act 2004, s.18(3)(b). In the case of an action brought in the District Court, a District Judge will preside, *ibid.*, s.18(3)(c).

[220] Nominated under the Courts (Supplemental Provisions) Act 1961, Sch.8, para.6(1).

[221] Civil Liability and Courts Act 2004, s.18(3)(a).

[222] RSC, O.1A, r.14(1).

[223] *Ibid.* r.14(2).

[224] In this regard, see District Court Rules, O.39A, r.11.

courts and the public – such anomalies and difficulties can hardly be considered merely unfortunate.

The Impact of the New Act on Tort Law

WILLIAM BINCHY*

We are witnessing a radical transformation in the culture of personal injuries legislation. The Oireachtas has enacted two pieces of legislation – the Personal Injuries Assessment Board Act 2003[1] and the Civil Liability and Courts Act 2004 – which are designed to bring down the cost of insurance, root out false claims, smooth the path of litigation, encourage settlement and generally make the lot of defendants happier than before. This is a major project, carrying the risk of injustice to vulnerable victims of wrongs. Time will tell whether the two Acts succeed in their goals, and at what price.

The theme of this chapter is the 2004 Act. It does several things, most of which are directed towards restricting the latitude afforded under the law previously to plaintiffs in personal injuries litigation. It reduces the limitations period from three to two years. It requires plaintiffs to issue a letter of claim, within two months as a general rule, notifying the alleged wrongdoer of the alleged wrong. It transforms the process of initiating litigation, and of pleadings generally, by requiring greater specificity, earlier than under the previous dispensation. It requires the plaintiff to swear a verifying affidavit and creates criminal sanctions for knowingly false or misleading statements therein as well as for the giving or adducing of evidence known to be false or misleading.

The Act also includes new machinery for a mediation conference, designed to encourage settlement, and for the making of formal offers. It

---

*Regius Professor of Laws, Trinity College Dublin.

1 For analysis, see P. Quigley & W. Binchy eds., *The Personal Injuries Assessment Board Act 2003: Implications for Legal Practice* (First Law, Dublin, 2004) and David Nolan, "The Personal Injuries Assessment Board Act 2003: A Critical Analysis", 9 *Bar Review* 7 (2004).

empowers the court to appoint an independent expert and changes several aspects of the law relating to damages, most notably by requiring the court to have regard to the Book of Quantum published by the PIAB. As a further discouragement to fraudulent claimants it establishes a register of personal injuries actions, which will reveal the number of times plaintiffs have previously participated in litigation.

These are the main features of the legislation. Other contributors will be addressing in detail particular aspects of the Act. This chapter will seek to concentrate on those provisions that are likely to impact on the substance of tort litigation, directly or indirectly.

Limitation of Actions

Personal injury litigation, prior to the enactment of the 2004 Act, had to be initiated within three years of the date of accrual of the right of action or the "date of knowledge" (whichever occurred later), as a result of the passage of the Statute of Limitations (Amendment) Act 1991, which introduced the "discoverability" principle for personal injury litigation.[2] In essence, the clock does not start to tick under the 1991 Act until one could reasonably be aware that one has been injured, that the injury is significant and that it is attributable to the defendant's conduct.[3]

Section 7 of the 2004 Act reduces the relevant period from three years to two years, from both the date of accrual of the cause of action and the "date of knowledge".[4]

---

2 See McMahon & Binchy, *Law of Torts* (3rd ed., Butterworths, Dublin, 2000), para.46.21ff.

3 It is not necessary that one should reasonably be aware that this conduct was tortious: it is enough that the factual causal connection between the factual occurrence of that conduct and the injury should have been reasonably discoverable. This has occasioned considerable difficulty for the courts in regard to medical interventions which have no justification but which appear reasonably to the patient to have had a therapeutic purpose and outcome. Cf. *Gough v. Neary* [2003] I.E.S.C. 39; [2003] 3 I.R. 92, *Cunningham v. Neary* [2004] I.E.S.C. 43 (Supreme Court, July 20, 2004).

4 As to the transitional cases, para.(d) of s.7 inserts the following section (s.5A) into the 1991 Act:

> "(1) Where the relevant date in respect of a cause of action falls before the commencement of s.7 of the Civil Liability and Courts Act 2004, an action (being an action to which sections 3(1), 4(1), 5(1) or 6(1) of this Act applies) in respect of that cause of action shall not be brought after the expiration of—

The limitation provision in the Bill as initiated[5] provided for only a 1-year limitation period. This was roundly condemned by Senators and the Minister, at the close of the Second Reading in the Seanad, indicated[6] that he would reflect on the matter. By Committee Stage, the Minister had capitulated. Responding to an amendment proposed by Senator Terry, Mr. McDowell explained his change of mind on the basis that the States Claims Agency had communicated with him its belief that one year was too short a period for medical negligence claims:

> "Although this Bill has gone through a drafting and scrutiny process in the Attorney General's office, it strikes me, when I think about the effect on medical negligence cases, there could be a question mark over its proportionality in constitutional terms, for example, where somebody in the rehabilitation hospital in Dun Laoghaire has one year in which to decide on these weighty matters … ,
>
> The Law Society has also made the point to me that cases of medical negligence are complex and require time to establish the facts. I know from my experience as a barrister that even an enthusiastic solicitor seeking to marshall all the facts and get all the relevant reports will be hard pressed to get much of the material lined up so that the barristers can advise the client, if it is a case that requires advice, on who the appropriate defendant should be and on whether it was the anaesthetist, the surgeon or the hospital who was responsible for the medical catastrophe. Also, obtaining medical reports here frequently requires going outside the country and the laying out of considerable amounts of money.
>
> I pay tribute to members of the legal profession who carry much

---

(a) 2 years from the said commencement, or

(b) 3 years from the relevant date, whichever occurs first.

(2) In this section 'relevant date' means the date of accrual of the cause of action or the date of knowledge of the person concerned as respects that cause of action whichever occurs later."

The effect of this provision is that if a plaintiff had a claim which, for example, had knocked up six months on the limitations clock by the time s.7 is commenced, there will only be a further eighteen months remaining on the limitations clock. Ciarán Craven, *supra*, pp.1 *et seq*., identifies other difficulties in regard to this transitional provision, especially in the context of applications to PIAB.

5 Then numbered s.6.

6 Seanad Debates, March 11, 2004, col.1833.

> of the slack in terms of undertaking to pay fees for consultants in cases where there is a considerable risk to themselves that nothing will come of it. Often one must arrange for one's client to be examined by somebody outside the country, arrange trips abroad and join a queue if the client requires examination by a busy specialist in the United Kingdom or wherever. One cannot just click one's fingers and get an instant report from such a person, even in an ideal world."[7]

The Minister proved impervious, however, to the suggestion – forcibly made by several Senators and Deputies – that medical negligence claims might need a longer limitation period than two years and might be deserving of a special period. In favour of a special, longer period, several arguments were canvassed: the difficulty of getting expert witnesses, the trust that many patients repose in their doctors which may cause them to hesitate before initiating a claim against them, as well as the fact that, under the Personal Injuries Assessment Board Act 2003, the Statute of Limitations is suspended for a personal injury claim while it is being assessed by the PIAB, whereas medical negligence claims fall outside the scope of the 2003 Act and thus lose this period of grace. Moreover, forcing lawyers to initiate claims before the case has been properly prepared compromises the plaintiff, the defendant and the administration of justice.

The Minister's arguments against an extension for medical negligence claims are not fully convincing:

> "I reflected carefully on this and it is not as easy as members might think. Frequently a single incident has several consequences. For example, where a person is knocked down and breaks a limb, he or she is brought to hospital and treated, either correctly or not. It may happen some months after the injuries have settled that he or she should have been warned that the bone had settled in the wrong position, that there should have been an X-ray follow-up and, had he or she been property advised, a new treatment to mitigate the effects of the accident should have been given. There is a series of single incidents that lead to a multiplicity of claims.

---

[7] Seanad Debates, June 3, 2004, col.1573.

I am concerned that, if the two year limit were to be imposed but it would be extended to three years where an additional claim for medical negligence would he made, a claimant would be tempted to allege that he was badly treated. In turn, he would launch a joint action against the original motorist and the doctor, claiming that between them his injuries resulted in a limp. Mixed claims would be difficult to disentangle.

Defensive medicine is also damaging to the national interest. Claiming that the boat must be put out for victims of medical negligence because they are a special category ignores that we want doctors to treat people in an effective and efficient way. It is not a public policy aim to encourage medical negligence claims and put them into a wholly different category from ordinary negligence claims. It is never pleasant to be on the receiving end of a professional negligence claim. A doctor, in working out what went wrong, will have to recreate the situation from the patient's treatment notes to determine if care was adequate. On public policy grounds, I am not as sympathetic as most Deputies are to free range for medical negligence plaintiffs. I tend to believe that the pendulum may have swung too far in favour of liability. If one has a case in medical negligence, then bearing in mind the new law and the new time period which starts at the point of knowledge, which is quite generous in its own way, two years should be sufficient for people with claims against doctors to have those claims articulated, put in writing and commenced."[8]

This defence of the two-year period for medical negligence claims does not address the concerns that were advanced in favour of a longer period. The instance cited by the Minister of a claim against both a motorist and a doctor is clearly an exceptional one.

Letter of Claim

Section 8 contains a new requirement, that plaintiffs in personal injury

---

[8] Dáil Select Committee on Justice, Equality, Defence and Women's Rights, July 6, 2004, col.1215.

litigation serve notice on the alleged wrongdoer, stating the nature of the wrong alleged to have been committed. It provides as follows:

> "(1) Where a plaintiff in a personal injuries action fails, without reasonable cause, to serve a notice in writing, before the expiration of 2 months from the date of the cause of action, or as soon as practicable thereafter, on the wrongdoer or alleged wrongdoer stating the nature of the wrong alleged to have been committed by him or her, the court hearing the action may—
> (a) draw such inferences from the failure as appear proper, and
> (b) where the interests of justice so require—
> (i) make no order as to the payment of costs to the plaintiff, or
> (ii) deduct such amount from the costs that would, but for this section, be payable to the plaintiff as it considers appropriate.
> (2) In this section "date of the cause of action" means—
> (a) the date of accrual of the cause of action, or
> (b) the date of knowledge, as respects the cause of action concerned, of the person against whom the wrong was committed or alleged to have been committed,
> whichever occurs later."

The Minister was confident that the section would not involve oppression on the plaintiffs. He observed that:

> "anybody who knows the general disposition of the court knows that section will not be interpreted in a draconian or unreasonable way. It will only be invoked where the interests of justice require that something be done in regard to the costs because the plaintiff, without reasonable cause, failed to put the defendant on notice that a case was being taken. It is not simply that there was a failure without reasonable cause. It is also that the interests of justice require that the defendant be assisted by the penalisation as to cost issues.
>
> In practice, it will not have a dramatic effect on genuine cases or people who did not get their act together. I do not think the courts would so interpret it. There is every reason to believe the courts will interpret it in a reasonable way. They will say that if a solicitor

> had a clear indication of the crash or an industrial accident, he or she should have written a letter to the other side stating, for example, that a person dropped a hammer on his foot at work last week and was not wearing protective boots. There is no reason that they should not be alerted within two months of being made aware of it. That is not draconian."[9]

One can see the merit of encouraging solicitors not to sit on claims: it is unfair to defendants that they should learn of a claim perhaps a month short of the expiry of the limitation period, when they have little or no recollection of the day of the alleged accident. Of course the courts have the power to dismiss litigation taken within the limitation period on the basis of inordinate and inexcusable delay, but this will help only a small number of defendants facing such difficulties.

Nevertheless, two months is a very short period. In a matter of less than nine weeks, many victims of a tort will simply be recovering from their injuries; they will not yet have consulted a lawyer. Other victims may not yet be aware that they have a right of action against the wrongdoer. The "discoverability" principle introduced by the Statute of Limitations (Amendment) Act 1991 and incorporated into section 8 of the 2004 Act will often not avail them as they will be perfectly aware that they have received a significant injury as a result of the wrongdoer's conduct but may lack the legal sophistication to be aware that they have a right to sue the wrongdoer.[10]

It will be hard to know how section 8 will harmonise with the policy of the Personal Injuries Assessment Board Act 2003. Section 8 requires very early intervention by victims of tortious wrongdoing. Prudence would dictate that this intervention be made only after legal advice has been obtained: a badly framed statement of the nature of the alleged wrong could damage the prospects of success in litigation. Yet the 2003 Act is designed to encourage victims (mistakenly, I would suggest) *not* to see the need for lawyers to vindicate their claim. One must wonder whether the need to serve a notice under section 8 is yet widely known in the community – especially the community of employees, pedestrians and

---

[9] Seanad Debates, June 3, 2004, col.1588.

[10] Cf. *Guerin v. Guerin* [1992] 2 I.R. 287, analysed by Byrne & Binchy, *Annual Review of Irish Law 1992* (Round Hall Press, Dublin), pp.436–437.

adventurous young boys[11] who comprise a sizeable proportion of personal injury claimants. The best advice that can be given to the victims of a tort is that they should *immediately* contact a lawyer. How this is going to reduce the incidence of litigation is not easy to discern.[12]

Mediation Conferences[13]

It is now appropriate to examine the effect of sections 15 and 16 of the Act which provide for the holding of a mediation conference, with a chairperson, under the direction of the court.

Section 15 empowers the court, on the request of any party, at any time before trial, if it considers that the holding of a meeting would assist in reaching a settlement, to direct the parties "to meet and discuss and attempt to settle the action".[14] The parties are obliged to "comply with that direction."[15] This meeting, referred to as a "mediation conference," is to take place "at a time and place agreed by the parties"[16] or, where they do not agree, at a time and place specified by the court.[17]

The mediation conference has a chairperson appointed by agreement

---

[11] The litigation tends to involve boys rather than girls. I am aware of no case in which the contributory negligence of a girl has been addressed by the court, save *Rooney v. Connolly* [1986] I.R. 56; [1987] I.L.R.M. 758, where the activity, far from involving an adventurous escape, was the lighting of a candle in a church. Since s.8 sets out a 2-month limit without express reference to the Statute of Limitations, the clock does not stop for disability based on minority. This should not prejudice the interests of children, however, since the provisos regarding "reasonable cause", practicability and the "interests of justice" give the court a wide discretion. This, and related issues, are taken up in more detail by Ciaran Craven, above, pp.1 *et seq*.

[12] Niall O'Neill, Claims Manager, Corporate Broking Coyle Hamilton, *Civil Liability & Courts Bill 2003* (Coyle Hamilton 03 Cover Notes, December 2003) (http://newsweaver.ie/coylehamilton/e_article000204884.cfm) has observed, regarding the two months' notification requirement, that:

> "[w]hile this proposal gives defendants the opportunity to investigate claims much earlier, it may actually bring about an increase in claims, as injured persons, who have not yet made up their mind about claims, will be forced to do so much earlier, in order to avoid the penalty on costs."

[13] Val Corbett considers this issue in detail at pp.103 *et seq*.

[14] S.15(1).

[15] S.15(2).

[16] S.15(3).

[17] *Id.*

of all the parties[18] or, in default of agreement, by the court.[19] In the latter (but not the former) case, the chairperson must be a practising barrister or solicitor of five years' standing or a person nominated by a body prescribed by order of the Minister.[20] These bodies, prescribed by S.I No.168 of 2005, are Friary Law, Mediation Forum—Ireland, Mediators' Institute of Ireland, the Bar Council of Ireland, the Chartered Institute of Arbitrators Irish Branch and the Law Society.

The notes of the chairperson and all communications during the mediation conference and any records or other evidence of the conference are confidential and may not be used in evidence in any proceedings, civil or criminal.[21] The costs incurred in the holding of the mediation conference are to be paid "by such party to the personal injuries action concerned as the court hearing the action shall direct."[22]

The chairperson submits a report to the court. If the mediation conference did not take place, the report must state the reasons as to why it did not.[23] Where it did take place, the report must state whether or not a settlement has been reached and, if so, its terms; the agreement must be signed by the parties.[24] Each party is given a copy of this report.[25] At the conclusion of the action the court hears submissions from the parties. If satisfied that "a party to the action failed to comply with a direction under section 15(1)",[26] the court may direct that party to pay all or some of the costs of the action incurred after the giving of the direction under section 15(1).[27]

This section provokes a number of comments. First, it is to be noted that the initiative for the holding of a mediation conference rests with any of the parties to the litigation: the court cannot direct that such a conference take place of its own motion. Even where a party makes a request for a mediation conference, the court will make a direction for it

---

[18] S.15(4)(a).
[19] S.15(4)(b)(i).
[20] S.15(4)(b)(ii).
[21] S.15(5).
[22] S.15(6).
[23] S.16(1)(a).
[24] S.16(1)(b).
[25] S.16(2).
[26] S.16(3)(b). The direction under s.15(1) is to the parties "to meet to discuss and attempt to settle" the action.
[27] S.16(3).

to be held only if it considers that this would assist in reaching a settlement in the action. Whether the court must have specific grounds for that view or can make a direction, acting on the *a priori* principle that settlement should always be attempted, is not clear. The language of section 15(1)(b) suggests that the former interpretation is preferable.

Next, the section envisages that only one mediation conference will take place: it refers to "a time" rather than "a time or times". This hardly means that a conference, once initiated, could not be adjourned by the chairperson, with the consent of the parties, with the intention of concluding it at some later stage; but if, at the end of a conference, there is no agreement that the conference be reconvened, that would appear to be that. It may even be the case that commonsense must yield to the actual language of section 15 and that a consensual adjournment is not permitted under the section – that what is provided for is one shot at a settlement rather than a settlement process.

The next issue concerns the parties' obligations under section 15. What are they actually required to do? The crucial provision is section 15(1), under which the court directs that the parties "meet to discuss and attempt to settle the action." Failure to comply with this direction renders a party liable to an order relating to costs. Clearly a point blank refusal, or a wilful omission, to meet the other party at all will constitute such a failure; but what is the position where a party turns up but indicates no desire whatsoever to settle the case? Do the words "attempt to settle the action" import some genuine substantive attempt? There must be serious difficulties with such an interpretation. Let us take a case where a defendant sincerely believes that the claim is fraudulent. The only terms on which he or she will "settle" the action may be that the plaintiff withdraws the claim. Clearly there can be no obligation on the defendant to offer a penny.[28] If a defendant takes the stance of complete opposition to the claim, is the chairperson to involve himself or herself in an assessment of whether that stance is *bona fide* or reasonable? How could the chairperson come to any sound conclusion on the basis of one meeting? Section 15 does not require the chairperson to brief himself or herself on the merits of the claim: that would be an adjudicatory function well beyond what the mediation (or settlement) process envisages. Moreover the terms

[28] Cf. s.17(2) of the Act.

of the report prescribed by section 16 give no support for this interpretation of the chairperson's role.

One must conclude, therefore, that the strong likelihood is that the sanction for failure to comply with a direction under section 15(1) will, in practice, be limited to cases where the party simply does not participate in the conference rather than adopts what, in the view of the chairperson, is an entirely unreasonable stance.

Section 15 is lacking in any detail of the chairperson's role, other than to chair a process the purpose of which is to seek to reach a settlement of the action. Whether the chairperson is strongly interventionist or entirely passive seems to be a matter for him or her to determine.

It is worth noting that anyone can be a chairperson if the parties agree: no qualifications are required. It is only where the court makes the appointment, in default of such agreement, that the qualifications mentioned in section 15(4)(b)(ii) are relevant.

Formal Offers

A new procedure, requiring the parties to make formal offers of terms of settlement to each other, is prescribed by sections 17. It is important because it is backed by a sanction: the court, when addressing the costs issue, must have regard to the terms of the respective formal offers and the reasonableness of the conduct of the parties in making them. The section provides as follows:

> "(1) The plaintiff in a personal injuries action shall, after the prescribed date, serve a notice in writing of an offer of terms of settlement on the defendant.
>
> (2) The defendant in a personal injuries action shall, after the prescribed date, serve a notice in writing on the plaintiff—
>
> (a) of an offer of terms of settlement, or
>
> (b) stating that he or she is not prepared to pay any sum of money to the plaintiff in settlement of the action.
>
> (3) A copy of a formal offer shall, after the expiration of the prescribed period be lodged in court by, or on behalf of, the plaintiff or defendant, as the case may be.
>
> (4) The terms of a formal offer shall not be communicated to the

judge in the trial of a personal injuries action until after he or she has delivered judgment in the action.

(5) The court shall, when considering the making of an order as to the payment of the costs in a personal injuries action have regard to—

(a) the terms of a formal offer, and

(b) the reasonableness of the conduct of the parties in making their formal offers.

(6) This section is in addition to and not in substitution for any rule of court providing for the payment into court of a sum of money in satisfaction of a cause of action or the making of an offer of tender of payment to the other party or parties to an action.

(7) In this section—

"formal offer" means an offer under subsection (1) or (2)(a), or a statement under subsection (2)(b);

"prescribed date" means such date before the date of the commencement of the trial of the personal injuries action concerned as is prescribed by order of the Minister;

"prescribed period" means such period commencing on the prescribed date as is prescribed by order of the Minister."

The Minister, when discussing the Bill at Select Committee stage in the Dáil (when the provision referred to "final" rather than "formal" offers) was uncharacteristically uncertain about how the section was meant to operate in practice, as the following extract indicates:

> **"Mr. J. O'Keeffe:** I wish to raise some concerns about section 16 generally. Normally in dealing with a claim, one expects the defendant or the defendant's insurers to make an offer. If they do not, in many cases they should. Here, however, we are also requiring the plaintiff to serve notice in writing of an offer of terms of settlement. Has this been thought through? Is it fair to the plaintiff? Normally, the plaintiff makes a claim. It is then up to the defendant to declare that the plaintiff does not have a claim, to tell him or her to go to the Devil, to defend or otherwise state the claim is worth a certain amount. The initiative is taken by the defendant and the plaintiff may or may not make a counter offer once negotiations start. I wonder if the Minister has thought through what will happen

> and when this procedure will be initiated. As he well knows, haggling often occurs in the Round Hall of the Four Courts. …
>
> **Mr. McDowell:** The plaintiff will make the first offer because he or she must do so after the prescribed date, whereas the defendant—
>
> **Mr. J. O'Keeffe:** That would be contrary to normal practice.
>
> **Mr. McDowell:** Sorry, I should not say it will be in that order.
>
> **Mr. J. O'Keeffe:** I am sure the Minister appreciates that normal practice is that the plaintiff makes his or her case and, if necessary, issues proceedings. It is then a matter for the insurance company to come up with an offer. Here we seem to be inverting the procedure.…
>
> [I]t should be a matter for the defence to make its offer in response to the claim first.
>
> **Mr. McDowell:** There is nothing to stop the defence from doing so. The rules on lodgement still apply.
>
> **Mr. J. O'Keeffe:** I accept that.
>
> **Mr. McDowell:** The defence can make its offer at any stage."[29]

The question of who offers first is, as Deputy O'Keeffe pointed out, of considerable importance. Yet section 17, in its final form, has not clarified the matter. This is unfortunate. Whereas, of course, one might have considered that the ministerial order might have required the parties to make their offers without prior sight of their opponents' offers, this is not, in fact, the case.

Even that strategy would not make matters easy for a plaintiff. While clearly a plaintiff who asks for "a million euro for a broken finger and not a halfpenny less"[30] will be acting totally unreasonably and perhaps deserving of some sanction on costs,[31] the position becomes more troublesome where the plaintiff places a very high value on his or her claim. Why should the plaintiff not do so? Is the underlying thrust of

---

[29] Dáil Select Committee, July 6, 2004, cols 1243–1245.

[30] The Minister's example, *id.*, cols 124.

[31] One must question whether such a sanction, even in cases where plaintiffs take such an unreasonable stance, is necessary or even appropriate. The lodgment procedure seems sufficient to protect the interests of defendants in these cases. Moreover, no sane defendant will heed such wild negotiating techniques.

section 17 that the plaintiff should be intimidated by the fear of a costs sanction into formally offering less than he or she estimates the claim at its best? Is section 17 really about forcing plaintiffs to compromise on the fullest worth of the claim?

Note that the defendant is under similar, but not identical, pressures. The defendant may be contesting liability. If the defendant reasonably believes that there is a 60% chance of successfully defending a claim worth €100,000, and offers €40,000 and goes down, is the court to investigate, not merely the quantum issue, but the propriety of the defendant's assessment of the strength or weaknesses of the claim? A judge who has just found in favour of a plaintiff on the issue of liability is hardly likely to sympathise with a defendant's assessment that the claim is unmeritorious.

An incidental conundrum may also be mentioned. If a defendant is already liable to pay the plaintiff's costs, because, for example, the defendant was negligent and the court awards high damages, how can the court use a costs sanction further against the defendant for breach of section 17?

Expert Evidence

Section 20 enables the court to appoint an expert witness, in addition to any other expert witness called by the parties. The section provides as follows:

> "(1) In a personal injuries action, the court may appoint such approved persons as it considers appropriate to carry out investigations into, and give expert evidence in relation to, such matters as the court directs.
>
> (2) A party in a personal injuries action shall cooperate with a person appointed under this section and shall, in particular, provide the person with—
>
> (a) (i) any report or other document prepared by the party, or
>
> (ii) any report or other document prepared on behalf of the party concerned, for the purposes of or in contemplation of the personal injuries action,
>
> and

(b) any document or information used or referred to for the purpose of preparing the report.

(3) The costs incurred in the appointment of, and carrying out of an investigation by, a person appointed under this section shall be paid by such party to the personal injuries action concerned as the court hearing the action shall direct.

(4) A party in a personal injuries action shall be entitled to cross-examine a person appointed under this section in relation to any matter that he or she was appointed to investigate and give expert evidence on.

(5) The President of the High Court in consultation with the President of the Circuit Court and the President of the District Court shall approve such persons as he or she considers appropriate for the purposes of this section, and a person so approved is in this section referred to as an 'approved person'."

The Minister sought to justify this innovation as follows:

> "In many personal injuries actions, conflicting evidence from experts must be decided by the court. Section 19 allows a court to appoint approved persons to investigate and give expert evidence on any issue the court may direct. The section also provides that any party to a personal injuries action shall co-operate with an approved person. An "approved person" is a person approved by the President of the High Court, in consultation with the Presidents of the Circuit and District Courts, for the purposes of the section. The intention behind this provision is that an expert, independent of any expert witness retained by the parties, could be appointed to assist the court. To take a medical example, a court might decide to appoint its own medical assessor, who will testify and be liable to cross examination, but will give an objective view to the court having listened to the medical experts on either side."[32]

Although it is true that the parties may cross-examine the court-appointed expert and may call expert witnesses themselves, one may wonder about

---

[32] Seanad Debates, March 11, col.1808.

the justification for this change. Let us consider some of the difficulties it involves.

First, it appears to call into question the truthfulness and objectivity of expert witnesses called by the parties. The court-appointed witness is presented by the Minister as giving an "objective view": the implication is that the court is not otherwise in receipt of such evidence. Undoubtedly some expert witnesses may tend towards partisanship[33] and it would be sensible to acknowledge this fact clearly; but such a weakness is not limited to expert witnesses; judges are well used to responding to it when it presents itself; moreover, it is the function of cross-examination to expose it to the gaze of the court.

Second, there is a danger that a court-appointed witness might be regarded by the court as offering more reliable evidence than the parties' experts. That will clearly not necessarily be the case where these experts give objective evidence.

Third, the use of a court- appointed expert witness may have an effect detrimental to plaintiffs who are seeking to advance a theory that contradicts orthodox practice. In the case of medicine, for example, the test for professional negligence set out in *Dunne v. National Maternity Hospital*[34] imposes liability where a particular customary practice is one with inherent defects that ought to be obvious to anyone giving the matter consideration. This involves a challenge to the accepted wisdom of the profession. A person chosen by the court from a panel of experts may tend towards the centre of conventional thought within the profession. This means that, in such a case, the plaintiff may have the handicap of having to pitch his or her expert witness, arguing in favour of a new approach, against two expert witnesses. Conversely, a defendant doctor who has conscientiously deviated from customary practice may well find that his or her expert has to do battle with two expert witnesses.

---

[33] Cf. Hilary Delany & Declan McGrath, *Civil Procedure in the Superior Courts* (Thompson Round Hall, Dublin, 2001), para.19.035, Harrison, "Reconceptualizing the Expert Witness: Social Costs, Current Controls and Proposed Responses", 18 Yale J. on Regulation 253 (2001) and Perrin, "Expert Witness Testimony: Back to the Future", 29 U. Richmond L. Rev. 1389 (1995). For consideration of the court's power to appoint its own expert in various federal and state codes in the United States of America, see Cecil & Willging, "Accepting *Daubert's* Invitation: Defining a Role for Court-Appointed Experts in Assessing Scientific Validity", 43 Emory L.J. 995 (1994).

[34] [1989] I.R. 91.

Next one may ask: What will be the position where a scientific controversy is at the heart of the litigation? There are two difficulties with the role of the court-appointed expert here. First, the selection by the court of a particular expert may have an influence on the outcome of the case. Take a practical example: a plaintiff claims that her condition of multiple sclerosis is attributable to an accident caused by the defendant's negligence. The crucial scientific issue in the case is whether multiple sclerosis can be caused by trauma. If the panel of experts contains experts taking opposing views of this issue, what is the court to do? Is it to apprise itself of the respective views of the experts before making a selection of one of them or should it simply take potluck? What is it to do where it is aware of the view of some of the experts on the panel but not of others?

A second difficulty arises where an expert is chosen from the panel and gives evidence (let us say) that multiple sclerosis cannot be caused by traumatic injury. The court is theoretically free to reject that view and to favour the evidence given by the plaintiff's expert witness. To do so, however, would be to stigmatise the quality of the evidence of the expert witness on a straightforward scientific issue and, indirectly, the wisdom of the President of the High Court in having put that witness on the panel. A new pressure has been placed on judges which is unfair to them and even more unfair to litigants.

At a philosophical level, there are problems with compromising the values underlying the adversarial system. These may seem remote from daily practice but that is not in fact the case. No enterprise can thrive if based on inconsistent values as to what it should seek to achieve.

At the core of the adversarial system, surely, is the notion that the parties to be litigation have the function of defining the issues, adducing evidence and challenging each other's case through cross-examination and the adducing of opposing evidence. The trial judge has the function of adjudicating on the issues on the evidence presented to the court. It is not the judge's function, generally speaking, to assume the mantle of Hercule Poirot, prescribing the scope of the evidence that should be adduced and engaging in an enquiry into the true situation.[35] The

---

[35] Cf. *Air Canada v. Secretary of State for Trade* [1983] 2 A.C. 394 at 438 (HL, *per* Lord Wilberforce):

> "The task of the court is to do, and be seen to be doing, justice between the parties… There is no higher or independent duty to ascertain some independent

inquisitorial process, favoured in continental European legal systems, serves that goal. The judge takes control and the parties play a secondary, subservient role.[36]

This is not to suggest that the adversarial system is an inadequate vehicle for the emergence of the truth. On the contrary, with the central role it gives to cross-examination – in Wigmore's famous description, "beyond doubt the greatest legal enquiry ever invented for the discovery of the truth"[37] – the adversarial system can claim to advance the interests of truth, generally, in a rigorous manner. Whatever force there may be in the concerns that expert witnesses can overimpress juries, the suggestion that a seasoned High Court judge would call for the blandishments of expert witnesses chosen by parties is not convincing.

Now it may be possible to argue that we should replace the adversarial system by the inquisitorial system. This would be a truly radical change for our legal culture and should be contemplated only after a most thorough comparative analysis of the competing systems and an assessment of the probable outcome from the standpoint of justice. No such enquiry has even been proposed, let alone begun, in Ireland. Yet this Act introduces into the very heart of the adversarial system an essentially inquisitorial element, based on the thinnest of rationales, with no clear guidance to the court as to how to accommodate and nurture the cuckoo that has been placed in the nest.[38]

One should keep a sense of proportion: the change may turn out not to be seismic, in view of the facts that the trial judge retains a discretion

---

truth. It often happens, from the imperfection of evidence, or the withholding of it, sometimes by the party in whose favour it would tell if presented, that an adjudication has to be made which is not, and is known not to be, the whole truth of the matter: yet, if the decision has been in accordance with the available evidence and the law, justice will have been fairly done."

36 See Schroeder, "Problems Faced by the Imperial Expert Witness in Court: The Continental View", 34 Temple L.Q. 378 (1961).

37 Wigmore, *Treatise on the Anglo-American System of Evidence in Trials at Common Law* (3rd ed., 1940), vol. 5, para.1367.

38 If there are serious, empirically supported, concerns about the inability of the adversarial system to cope with partisanship among expert witnesses, one could first contemplate possible changes within the adversarial model rather than rushing to create an inquisitional/adversarial hybrid. These changes could include the imposition of a duty of care in negligence of expert witnesses and the reduction of absolute privilege to qualified privilege in defamation: see further Alford, "The Basic Witness in Louisiana Tort Law: Existing Mechanisms of Control and Proposals for Change", 61 La L. Rev. 181 (2000).

as to whether to appoint an expert witness and the parties retain the right of cross-examination. As against this, it would be wise to keep in mind that the PIAB procedure is deeply inquisitorial; the PIAB computation of assessment of damages has been linked to the courts by section 22 of the 2004 Act; there may be here an inexorable underlying shift away from the adversarial process of compensation for personal injury in Ireland.

The Act does not explain the scope of the court-appointed expert witness' power to carry out investigations into "such matters as the court directs."[39] How extensive can these investigations be? Is the expert to take on the role of investigator of the truth of the plaintiff's assertions or of the evidence of other witnesses? Does the duty of co-operation[40] resting on parties to the action (but not, expressly at all events, on witnesses other than the parties) include the obligation to answer fully and truthfully all questions that the expert chooses to ask? The effect of section 20(2) is to weaken substantially the protection awarded to parties by legal professional privilege, since reports which would have been shielded from the scrutiny of the court without the consent of the party concerned are now to come within its range of vision, through the agency of the court-appointed expert.

Neither does the Act clarify the status of the expert evidence given by the expert witness to the court after he or she has carried out these investigations. The easy answer would be that this expert evidence should be treated in the same way as the evidence given by experts chosen by the parties; but it is of a somewhat different character, being based on a power of investigation backed by compulsion.[41] Time will tell whether the court-appointed expert will be treated as essentially an expert witness or will become a judicial surrogate, ferreting out information on behalf of the court on the basis of an inquisitional rather than adversarial philosophy.

---

[39] S.20(1).
[40] S.20(2).
[41] S.20 expresses no specific sanction for breach of the obligation to cooperate prescribed in s.20(2). It would seem, at a minimum, that such a breach would constitute civil contempt; it could well be criminal contempt and perhaps constitute the offence of interfering with the administration of justice.

DAMAGES' AWARDS

Turning now to consider some of the changes in relation to damages awards which the Act makes, it should be noted this theme is in much greater detail elsewhere.[42]

1. Actuarial Tables

Section 23 provides as follows:

> "(1) The Minister may, by regulations, prescribe actuarial tables for the purpose of their being referred to by the courts when assessing damages in personal injuries actions in respect of future financial loss.
>
> (2) A court in a personal injuries action shall, in assessing damages in respect of future financial loss, refer to such actuarial tables (if any) as are prescribed under subsection (1).
>
> (3) In this section "actuarial tables" means actuarial tables prepared by a person designated for that purpose by a body prescribed by regulations made by the Minister."

The Minister explained the purpose of the provision as follows:

> "This is a new innovation, but it is not unprecedented internationally, whereby the Minister can prescribe actuarial tables by regulations for the purpose of their being referred to by the courts when assessing damages in respect of future financial loss.
>
> If one loses an income stream for the rest of one's life, at the moment in Ireland if it is a serious case an actuary comes to court and gives evidence by reference to actuarial tables as to what the appropriate multiplier for a capital sum should be. I am not in the slightest anti the actuarial profession whose members are skilled and wonderful people, but it is a waste of their time to have them hanging around courts to give fundamentally statistical advice by way of evidence when, as in certain other common law countries comparable to ours, it is possible to do so by a standard form table which can be varied from time to time to reflect realities. Somebody

---

42 See Neville Cox, *infra*, pp.84 *et seq.*

> once asked 'What is the definition of an extrovert actuary?' to which the reply was 'An extrovert actuary is one who looks at your shoes when he is talking to you'."[43]

2. Discount rate

Section 24 gives the Minister power to prescribe the discount rate for determining the current value of future financial loss for the purposes of assessing damages. The section provides as follows:

> "(1) The Minister may, by regulations, prescribe the discount rate that shall apply for the purposes of the assessment of damages in respect of future financial loss.
>
> (2) Regulations under subsection (1) may prescribe different rates in respect of different classes of financial loss or different periods of time.
>
> (3) The court may apply a discount rate other than the rate prescribed under subsection (1) if it considers that the application of the rate prescribed would result in injustice being done.
>
> (4) In this section "discount rate" means, in relation to the assessment of damages by a court, the rate commonly referred to by that name that is applied by the court for the purpose of determining the current value of any future financial loss."

A few points may be noted. First, the court has power, under section 24(3), to depart from the Ministerial preference, but only where not to do so "would result in injustice being done". That is a fairly stiff test. The thrust of section 24 is to give to the Minister the power to shape the quantum of damages' awards, with greater impact in relation to the serious cases. If a court considered that the Minister's prescription was insufficiently generous to plaintiffs in general, it might be brave enough to depart from it on the basis that not to do would "result in injustice being done". This phrase may, however, suggest a more individuated enquiry as to the circumstances to the specific case rather than some a priori disagreement between the courts and the executive as to the appropriate quantum of damages. In short, I suspect that courts are likely

[43] Seanad Debates, June 3, 2004, col.1607.

to taken the ministerial prescription as the default rate, to be departed from only where the specific circumstances of the case so ordain.

It should be noted, secondly, that although the section is not expressly limited to personal injuries actions, section 6 would seem to limit it in this way, since it provides that (subject to certain identified sections other than section 24) a provision of Part 2 – of which section 24 is one – "applies only to personal injuries actions brought after the date of the commencement of that provision."

It may be of interest to look briefly at how matters had been operating up to the passage of the 2004 Act. In *McEneaney v. Monaghan County Council*,[44] O'Sullivan J. gave an important judgment on how the discount rate should be calculated for the purposes of actuarial evidence. In determining a plaintiff's future loss, account must be taken of the estimated duration of that loss and the relevant interest rate used to translate the expected loss into a capital sum equivalent. The real rate of interest – that is, the nominal rate less the rate of inflation – has traditionally been taken by actuaries calculating these sums in Ireland at 46. This was considered to be an appropriate value for the return which a prudent person might expect after inflation on a relatively risk-free portfolio in the early 1980s.

In *McEneaney*, where the plaintiff had a life expectancy of 39 years, O'Sullivan J. described as "compelling" Lord Lloyd of Berwick's reasoning in *Wells v. Wells*,[45] to the following effect:

> "The ordinary investor may be presumed to have enough to live on. He can meet his day-to-day requirements. If the equity market suffers a catastrophic fall, as it did in 1972, he has no immediate need to sell. He can abide his time, and wait until the equity market eventually recovers.
>
> The plaintiffs are not in the same happy position. They are not ordinary investors in the sense that they can wait for long term recovery, remembering that it was not until 1989 that equity prices regained their old pre-1972 level in real terms. For they need the income, and a portion of their capital, every year to meet their current cost of care. A plaintiff who invested the whole of his award in

---

[44] Unreported, High Court, July 26, 2001.
[45] [1998] 3 All E.R. 481.

equities in 1972 would have found that their real value had fallen by 41% in 1973 and by a further 62% in 1974. The real value of the income on his equities had also fallen.

So it does not follow that a prudent investment for the ordinary investor is a prudent investment for the plaintiffs. Equities may well prove the best long-term investment. But their volatility over the short term creates a serious risk. This risk was well understood by the experts. Indeed [one of them] conceded that if you are investing so as to meet a plaintiff's needs over a period of five years, or even ten years, it would be foolish to invest in equities. But that concession, properly made as it was on the evidence, is fatal to the defendant 's case. For, as [another expert] pointed out in reply, every long period starts with a short period. If there is a substantial fall in equities in the first five or ten years, during which the plaintiff will have had to call on part of his capital to meet his needs, and will have had to realise that part of his capital in a depressed market, the depleted fund may never recover.

While therefore I agree with the Court of Appeal that, in calculating the lump sum, courts are entitled to assume that the plaintiff will behave prudently, I do not agree that what is prudent for the ordinary investor is necessarily prudent for the plaintiff. Indeed the opposite may be the case. What the prudent plaintiff needs is an investment 'which will bring him the income he requires without the risks inherent in the equity market'; which brings us back to the ILGS."

Later in his speech, when giving reasons for his conclusion that the judges' calculations had been correctly based on the assumption that the plaintiff would invest his damages in the ILGS, he stated:

"Although this will result in a heavier burden on these defendants, and, if the principle is applied across the board, on the insurance industry in general, I can see nothing unjust. It is true that insurance premiums may have been fixed on the basis of the 4 to 5 % discount rate indicated in *Cookson v. Knowles*[46] and the earlier authorities. But this was only because there was then no better way allowing

[46] [1979] 1 A.C. 556.

for future inflation. The objective was always the same. No doubt insurance premiums will have to increase in order to take account of the new lower rate of discount. Whether this is something which the country can afford is not a subject on which your Lordships were addressed. So we are not in a position to form any view as to the wider consequences.

For a plaintiff who is not in a position to take risks, and who wishes to protect himself against inflation in the short term of up to ten years, it is clearly prudent to invest in ILGS. It cannot therefore be assumed that he will invest in equities and gilts. Still less is it his duty to invest in equities and gilts in order to mitigate his loss. …

Logically the same applies to a plaintiff investing for the long term. In any event it is desirable to have a single rate applying across the board, in order to facilitate settlements and to save the expense of expert evidence at the trial. …

How the plaintiff, or the majority of plaintiffs, in fact invest their money is irrelevant …".

In *McEneaney*, O'Sullivan J., adopting this analysis noted that, on the evidence there was no equivalent in Ireland of the ILGS. Accordingly he had to approach the assessment of the sum required to produce the appropriate annuity for the plaintiff over the following 39 years on the basis that it would yield "a reasonably secure and reliable stream of annual funding (comprising income and capital)" and, to that end, that the investment of the award should be "as risk free as reasonably possible in the absence of an equivalent of the ILGS in the UK."

One economist had given evidence to the effect that the actuarial discount rate should be 2%. Another had suggested a figure of 2.5% accepting a prudent element of equities investment. O'Sullivan J. considered that the appropriate rate for general calculation purposes should be 2.5%.

There had been uncontroverted evidence that the annual average rate of increase of medical and other costs was nearly 6%–3% in excess of the general annual average rate of increase over the period since *Cooke v. Walsh*[47] had been decided. The expert evidence was to the effect that this

[47] [1984] I.L.R.M. 208.

was likely to continue to be the case. Accordingly, O'Sullivan J. proceeded on the basis of actuarial figures calculated on this premise.

3. The Book of Quantum

The legislation contains an important provision relating to the *Book of Quantum* created under the Personal Injuries Assessment Board Act 2003.

The PIAB published its *Book of Quantum* in June 2004. It is a curious document. Whilst it lists ranges of awards for injuries to the head, arm, neck, back, trunk, legs, feet and toes, psychiatric injuries or post-traumatic stress disorder are not mentioned. The manner in which the range of awards is presented is also worthy of comment. A skull fracture with no loss of consciousness, for example, resulting in serious and permanent conditions generates a range of award between €61,000 and €96,700. This specificity for relatively high awards is replicated in some other award ranges in the *Book of Quantum*. No lawyer advising a client or seeking to negotiate a settlement would work on a figure with this degree of fussy detail: so why does the *Book of Quantum* do so? One answer may be that it represents the exact mathematical average of the awards and settlements that founded the basis of the comparisons contained in the Book. Yet no such specificity is contained in the very highest ranges relating to the most serious injuries. The effect on a legally unsophisticated claimant might well be to induce a belief that the computation process has some objective scientific basis which must be respected. The claimant may say to himself or herself: I don't understand how they do it but there must be some basis, which I cannot understand, governing this process.

This hierarchical relationship between the Board and the claimant may cause him or her to acquiesce in the process but it fails to capture the essence of the claimant's position from the standpoint of justice. The claimant is the putative victim of a legal wrong who is seeking vindication of his or her legal entitlements. He or she is not a supplicant for a handout from a State agency nor a suspected malingerer whose credibility is to be subjected to the inquisitorial scrutiny of State officials. Reading through the *Book of Quantum*, the experience is not dissimilar to perusing a document from the social welfare authorities where a culture of hostility towards the supplicant and suspicion of his or her *bona fides* was the dominant traditional culture.

The highest award in the *Book of Quantum* is €3000,000 for

quadriplegia or paraplegia. This reflects the cap placed on awards of this general character in *Sinnott v. Quinnsworth Ltd.*[48] As to whether the other amounts are generous, time will tell. The fact that a range of awards is provided naturally makes it hard to anticipate future practice. One might have thought it prudent for the PIAB, in the early years at least, to make awards that could not easily be criticised as being less than the tariff applied in the courts.

Testing this hypothesis against a decision of the Supreme Court in 2004, it could not be said to have been confirmed.

The *Book of Quantum* prescribes €62,800 to €85,900 for "serious and permanent" back conditions. In *Breen v. Fagan and the Motor Insurers Bureau of Ireland*,[49] the Supreme Court upheld an award of €80,000 general damages to a young woman for injuries to her neck and back. The trial judge accepted the plaintiff's "very strong evidence" of the pain she suffered, and in particular the continuing pain in her back, which affected her very considerably in the morning. McGuinness J., in her judgment in the Supreme Court, noted that the trial judge had gone on to say that pain was subjective and on the medical evidence in her case did not appear to be as bad as other similar cases which he had heard that day. As against this, he accepted the evidence of the plaintiff's surgeon that the plaintiff had suffered degenerative changes to her lumbar region which were shown objectively on MRI. The surgeon had also given evidence of likely further degeneration over time.

The Supreme Court, upholding the award, considered that, whilst it "might be thought to be on the high side on the face of the evidence," it fell within the range in respect of which the Supreme Court ought not to intervene.

The injury in this case could not possibly be regarded as being at the upper end of "serious and permanent" back injury, yet the amount awarded, and upheld on appeal, was the maximum prescribed by the *Book of Quantum*.

The *Book of Quantum* contains no figures for psychiatric or psychological injury, in spite of the fact that this kind of injury is a feature of many cases, sometimes as a freestanding claim but more usually as an

---

48 [1984] I.L.R.M. 523.

49 Unreported, Supreme Court, May 14, 2004.

exacerbating element to physical injuries. Post traumatic stress disorder is a head of damages in very many claims.[50]

In *Ledwith v. Bus Atha Cliath/Dublin Bus*,[51] the Supreme Court, albeit with some reluctance, upheld an award of €90,000 general damages to a bus conductor who had been assaulted by drunken men carrying bottles. He had received only a laceration of his lip but he also sustained a post-traumatic stress disorder. If victims of torts were to peruse the *Book of Quantum*, unaided by professional legal advice, they would have no effective notice that a trivial physical injury might generate an entitlement to very substantial damages if accompanied by such a psychiatric or psychological condition.

While the *Book of Quantum* makes a brief reference to the entitlement to be awarded compensation for loss of earnings or other financial loss, it lays no great stress upon it. A victim, without professional legal advice, cannot be expected to appreciate that the amounts mentioned in great detail in the book of quantum, often with a specificity in respect of high amounts that makes one ponder deeply upon the underlying motivation, in many cases represent only a small fraction of the total amount to which victims are entitled.

Turning to the way in which the Personal Injuries Assessment Board Act 2003 has been integrated with the Civil Liability and Courts Act 2004, section 22 of the 2004 Act provides as follows:

> "(1) The court shall, in assessing damages in a personal injuries action, have regard to the Book of Quantum.
>
> (2) Subsection (1) shall not operate to prohibit a court from having regard to matters other than the Book of Quantum when assessing damages in a personal injuries action.
>
> (3) In this section 'Book of Quantum' means the Book of Quantum required to be prepared and published by the Personal Injuries Assessment Board under the Act of 2003."

The Minister explained his understanding of the provision as follows:

> "There is a precedent in that there was a guideline for the Army

[50] See, however, s.17 of the PIAB Act 2003, s.17(1)(ii)(II).
[51] Unreported, Supreme Court, June 24, 2003.

deafness claims. It is not mandatory, a court is free to disregard it if it wishes but it asks courts to have regard to the Book of Quantum.

If one is a judge in a Circuit Court in Tipperary town, with counsel from both sides addressing a case, and one is trying to decide how much a broken leg or hand is worth, it is useful at least to have a document which addresses that issue. It may be that the judge in his or her independent judicial function regards it as low or high in the circumstances of the particular case but it is in the interests of uniformity in the administration of justice that there should be some general document available to which the Judiciary can have regard, even if it is not strictly legally bound. Subsection (2) makes it clear this is not an exhaustive procedure or that the court cannot have regard to matters not covered by the Book of Quantum. It is a serious advance in an effort to bring consistency in uniformity to the question of damages. ...

I want to make it clear to judges that they are expected to have regard to the contents of this Book of Quantum, that it is their legal duty to have regard to it and to consult it. I do not want a price list that is invariable in every case which counsel could consult and say a case is worth a given amount and that is it. Injuries vary from case to case, for example, a broken ankle can be very serious or less so.

It is beyond the wit of man and woman to devise an exact scale of damages in these matters. ...

This is a major new step. It would be unlawful for a court to decide damages without having regard to the Book of Quantum, but it would not be unlawful to deviate from it. The High Court, on appeal from the Circuit Court, would be in a position to ask why was there a departure from the Book of Quantum and if there were grounds to justify it. It is an effort to bring consistency but not uniformity into the application of the law."[52]

It is worth recalling, in the context of the army deafness litigation, that the Government enacted the Civil Liability (Assessment of Hearing Injury) Act 1998, section 4 of which provides as follows:

"(1) In all proceedings claiming damages for personal injury arising

---

[52] Seanad Debates, June 3, 2004, cols 1602–1603.

> from hearing loss, the courts shall, in determining the extent of the injuries suffered, have regard to Chapter 7 (Irish Hearing Disability Assessment System) of the Report and, in particular, to the matters set out in paragraph 1 (Summary) and Table 4 (Disability Percentage Age Correction Factor) to paragraph 7 (Age Related Hearing Loss Correction) of that Chapter, and the said paragraph 1 and Table 4 are, for convenience of reference, set out in Part I and Part II, respectively, of the Schedule to this Act.
>
> (2) In all proceedings claiming damages for personal injury arising from tinnitus, the courts shall, in determining the extent of the injuries suffered, have regard to the classification method contained in paragraph 9 (Tinnitus) of Chapter 7 (Irish Hearing Disability Assessment System) of the Report."

Commenting on this provision, in *Hanley v. Minister for Defence*,[53] Keane J. observed:

> "The policy underlying the Act is obvious. Although it is not confined in its terms to the many cases brought against the present defendants, it was, of course, the legislative response to what may fairly be described as a 'litigation crisis' confronting the State. The objective was clearly to ensure that, while those who had suffered hearing loss as a result of negligence were fairly compensated, the amount of that compensation should, so far as possible, be assessed by courts in a manner which reflects the basic principle that like cases should be treated alike. It was also no doubt envisaged that such an approach would facilitate the early compromise of claims of this nature with a consequent significant reduction in the huge burden of legal costs involved.
>
> While it is the duty of the courts to give effect to the legislative policy enshrined in the Act, every case which comes before them for assessment must be considered in the light of its particular facts. The Act indeed implicitly acknowledges that this should be the appropriate approach by doing no more than requiring the court to 'have regard' to the relevant sections of the Green Book."

[53] [1999] 4 I.R. 393.

Keane J. approved of what Lavan J. had said in *Green v. Minister for Defence*:[54]

> "The requirement to 'have regard to' the Green Book does not … impose a duty upon the Court to adhere strictly to its terms. Therefore, while the court must consider the approach adopted in the Green Book, it reserves the right to consider alternative approaches. The Court may then determine which is the most appropriate solution in each individual case. In the absence of a more appropriate alternative solution … established to the satisfaction of the Court, the statutory formula should be applied. The circumstances in which the statutory formula is not applied may in fact transpire to be as limited as the defendants' submissions suggest. However, this will be a matter for the determination of the Court in the circumstances of each individual case."

It seems clear that section 22 of the 2004 Act would not be declared unconstitutional on the basis of interference by the Oireachtas in the exercise of the judicial power. It is nothing like the offending provision in *Maher v. Attorney General*[55] which purported to give to a certificate regarding the alcohol in a blood specimen the status of conclusive evidence, Section 22 merely requires the court to "have regard" to certain evidence, while leaving the court perfectly free to have regard to other evidence. A purist court might complain about being *required* to have regard to evidence to which it otherwise might attach absolutely no weight; it seems far more likely that a court would consider this obligation as going no further than to take account of the *Book of Quantum, for what it is worth evidentially,* which may be very little or not at all in some cases. Thus, for example, in a case involving post-traumatic stress disorder, which is not covered by the *Book of Quantum*, the trial judge would merely state in his or her judgment that he or she had "had regard" to the *Book of Quantum* and found that it had thrown no light on the issue requiring resolution.

Having said this, it should also be said that section 22 represents a coded message from the Oireachtas to the courts that the former would

---

[54] [1998] 4 I.R. 464.

[55] [1973] I.R. 140. See further G. Hogan & G. Whyte (eds), *Kelly: The Irish Constitution* (4th ed., Lexis Nexis, Dublin, 2003), paras 6.1.120ff.

greatly prefer if the latter went a considerable distance towards adopting the ranges of awards prescribed by the *Book of Quantum*. This appears to be what Herbert J. did in *Meagher v. Shamrock Public Houses Ltd t/a The Ambassador Hotel*.[56] Indeed, in the decision of the Supreme Court in *Nolan v. Murphy*,[57] reference was made to the *Book of Quantum* without any sign of hesitation or of a desire to create clear blue water between it and the courts.

Fraud or Exaggeration

Before considering section 26 of the 2004 Act, a brief look at the previous caselaw is merited. In *Vesey v. Bus Éireann*,[58] and *Shelly-Morris v. Bus Átha Cliath/Dublin Bus*,[59] the Supreme Court took a strong stance against exaggerated claims. Hardiman J., in *Vesey* raised the question, *obiter*, whether exaggeration might in some cases amount to an abuse of the judicial process.

In *Shelly-Morris,* he cited with approval what Lord Denning had said in *Goldsmith v. Sperrings*:[60]

> "In a civilised society, legal process is the machinery for keeping order and doing justice. It can be used properly or it can be abused. It is used properly when it is invoked by the vindication of men's rights of the enforcement of just claims. It is abused when it is diverted from its true course as to serve extortion or oppression: or to exert pressure so as to achieve an improper end. When it is so abused it is a tort, a wrong known to the law. The judges can and will intervene to stop it. They will stay the legal process if they can before any harm is done. If they cannot stop it in time, and harm is done, they will give damages against the wrong doer".

Commenting on this passage and another cited in *Shelly-Morris*, Hardiman J. observed that he had:

---

[56] High Court, February 16, 2005.
[57] Supreme Court, March 18, 2005.
[58] [2001] 4 I.R. 192.
[59] [2003] 1 I.R. 232; [2003] 2 I.L.R.M. 12.
[60] [1977] All E.R. 566.

> "no doubt that these principles are equally applicable in this jurisdiction. It must not be thought that a falsehood in respect of one aspect of the claim will, at worst, lead to that particular part of the claim being reduced or disallowed. The Courts have a power and a duty to protect their own processes, being made the vehicle of unjustified recovery. In a proper case this will be done by staying or striking out the plaintiff's proceedings."

In *O'Connor v. Bus Átha Cliath/Dublin Bus*,[61] the issue was revisited but not resolved. In *O'Connor* video evidence of the plaintiff's activities had been hard to reconcile with his evidence as to the extent of his injury. O'Donovan J. had concluded on the evidence that although the plaintiff had grossly exaggerated the symptoms, he had not told deliberate lies and believed everything that he had said. O'Donovan J. thought that he was 'basically an honest person". An attempt on appeal to challenge these findings was unsuccessful. The Court – Denham, Murray and Hardiman JJ. – proceeded on the basis that what Hardiman J. had said earlier was *obiter*. Perhaps not surprisingly, Hardiman J. persisted in his view, whilst conceding that for the purposes of the instant case it was again *obiter*. Murray J., making the same concession about his own, opposing view, in the instant case, observed that abuse of process:

> "is a term which is applied to stay or dismiss proceedings before trial to prevent an action proceeding any further and has not been applied at the conclusion of a trial, apart from the exceptional case where an alleged abuse of process is the cause of action itself. A party which suffers harm caused by the abuse of process may have a cause of action against the other party for damages for that harm.[62] That arises where harm is proved to have been done by a tortious wrongdoer, the person who has abused the process of the court, and he or she is liable to pay damages measured by reference to the harm done to the injured party. That is quite different from denying

---

[61] [2003] I.E.S.C. 66 (December 18, 2003); [2003] 4 I.R. 459.

[62] Citing *Speed Seal Products Ltd v. Paddington and Anor* [1986] 1 All E.R. 91, which Murray J. noted, referred to the American *Second Restatement of the Law of Tort* (1977) to that effect, and the observations of Denning M.R. in *Goldsmith v. Sperrings Ltd* [1977] 2 All E.R. 566 at 574 in an application to stay proceedings before trial.

damages to a plaintiff without reference to any, if any, harm or loss sustained by a defendant (thus relieving the latter of his or her legal liability) in a case where part of the plaintiff's claim is rejected because of deliberate exaggeration while part is found to have been proved. In the present case there has been no claim (or counterclaim) for such harm or loss.

So far as I am aware there has been no case in this jurisdiction, England or the United States where proceedings have been stayed or dismissed for an abuse of the process of the court or imposing on another party where the abuse is alleged to comprise of deliberate exaggerations or falsehoods by the plaintiff in the course of his or her evidence at a trial where the plaintiff has otherwise been held to have established that at least part of his or her claim was valid and entitled to some award of damages.

In such circumstances it is the judgment of the court which has governed the issues and the plaintiff loses any claim based on such evidence. Of course where there is cogent or tangible evidence of fraud the court may in circumstances where it considers it proper to do so direct that the relevant papers in the case be referred to the Director of Public Prosecutions. A plaintiff may also be penalised in costs since the court enjoys a wide discretion having regard to wanton and substantial waste of the court's time.

I hesitate for present purposes to consider whether the term 'abuse of process' should be qualified as a term of art since 'abuse' is capable of such a wide meaning and may take many forms. In an appropriate case it may fall to be decided whether it is inherent in the jurisdiction of the court to treat false evidence at a trial as coming within the meaning of that term (and in one sense, a single falsehood could fall within the notion of abuse). If that were to be so it would also be necessary to decide the form of order which could be made by a court and the criteria for its application and whether the question of an abuse of process would fall to be tried as a discrete issue in each case where it was raised. Any right of a party to sue for damage suffered as a result of an abuse of process would also have to be taken into account. These are just some of the issues which it seems to me would have to be addressed should the court, in an appropriate case, have to decide whether the term abuse of process is capable of being applied to cases of such a nature."

Section 26 of the 2004 Act *requires* the court to dismiss a personal injuries action where the plaintiff gives or adduces, or dishonestly causes to be given or adduced evidence that is false or misleading, in any material respect, and that he or she knows to be false or misleading, *unless*, for reasons that the court must state in its decision, the dismissal would result in injustice being done. An act is done "dishonestly" by a person if he or she does it with the intention of misleading the court.

The introduction of section 26 appears to be a clear attempt by the Oireachtas to weaken the position of plaintiffs whose claim is tainted by untruthfulness in some respect. Its proviso probably preserves the common law position, so far as it can be gleaned from *Vesey, Shelly-Morris* and *O'Connor*. It leaves for another day resolution of the exact circumstances in which an exaggerating plaintiff should be denied any remedy. Clearly section 26 would not apply to someone such as the plaintiff in the *O'Connor* case, who was not dishonest, having no intent to mislead the court.

The Minister was apparently content with the principle that untruthfulness should be met by an outright dismissal. He stated:

> "People must understand that if they take personal injuries actions, they will lose out if they come other than with clean hands as genuine claimants. If they come with dishonest intent either to exaggerate or tell lies about their case, they will get nothing.
>
> I, for example, a plaintiff states that as a result of fracturing his or her leg he or she can no longer play golf and subsequently a video is shown to the court of the person playing golf, the person will not only get the extra damages he or she would have got as a result of not being able to play golf but will also lose the full damages and the case will be thrown out of court emphatically."[63]

It remains to be seen whether the courts will take a more nuanced view. What is not clear is whether the court is free to take, and articulate, a position, *a priori*, that a general rule denying compensation to a plaintiff who is untruthful in any material respect is one that would result in injustice being done. In other words, does the "out clause" given by the section on the issue of justice permit the court to articulate a value that is

---

[63] Dáil Debates, June 30, 2004, col.765.

inconsistent with the value adopted by the section? Of course the issue is unlikely to surface because the court is always free to conclude, in *the particular circumstances*, that to deny compensation to the particular plaintiff would result in injustice being done. It would be encouraging to see the courts accepting the *renvoi* given to them by the section and asserting their own understanding of how justice is best served, as a matter of general principle.

Mulkern v. Flesk,[64] is the first decision in which section 26 of the Act is analysed. The plaintiff had been involved in a traffic accident. Liability was not contested. The defendant obtained through discovery the records of a job application made by the plaintiff subsequent to the accident in which she had not mentioned the accident and asserted that she was in good health and specifically that she had never suffered from back injury. When the inconsistency between her claim and what she had stated in these documents was put to her in correspondence by the defendants' solicitor, she acknowledged the disparity but explained it was on the basis that she had been working as a shop assistant, that her back pain was so intense that she needed to avoid constantly standing and that the new job offered this possibility.

Kelly J. declined to dismiss the claim. Having heard the plaintiff's evidence as well as the evidence of doctors who had treated her, he concluded:

> "Before the court could apply the provisions of section 26(1) of the Act it would have to be satisfied as a matter of probability that the evidence given by the plaintiff was false or misleading in a material respect and that the plaintiff knew her evidence to be false and misleading.
>
> I do not accept that the plaintiff gave false or misleading evidence. It is not to her credit that she told untruths to her prospective employer. I am satisfied that she very much wanted and indeed needed to obtain employment with Boston Scientific. That may explain why she was untruthful in her dealings with that employer although it does not excuse such behaviour. But I do not accept that she gave false or misleading evidence to the court. …

[64] Unreported, High Court, February 25, 2005.

> I am of opinion that once the plaintiff realised that the defendants had found her out in her untruths she decided to make a clean breast of it and admit to the court her wrongdoing in that regard. That wrongdoing was admitted at the outset. It was admitted in pre-trial correspondence, by her counsel in opening the case and in her own evidence in chief. She may well have given false and misleading information to her employer but I do not believe that she did so on oath before the court and consequently I am satisfied that the provisions of the section do not apply."

One has to wonder whether the interests of justice are truly being served by section 26. *Mulkern v. Flesk* captures the dilemma that many people who are not well off may confront. They may be driven by economic necessity to suppress certain facts in order to avoid financial disaster. If in this case the documents had not be discovered but instead a surprise witness from the new employer had given evidence, there is a real prospect that the claim would be dismissed. Would that really have been a fair result?

Invited Submissions to the Supreme Court

Section 21 of the Act is a very curious innovation. It provides as follows:

> "(1) The Supreme Court may, upon an appeal to it in a personal injuries action, invite such persons as it considers appropriate to make submissions to the court—
> (a) in relation to any matter concerning either liability or damages that it considers to be of exceptional public importance, and
> (b) if the action belongs to a class of causes of action in which the same or a similar matter arises.
> (2) The Supreme Court may perform functions under subsection (1), either—
> (a) upon receiving a request in that behalf from a party to the personal injuries action concerned, or from a person who is not such a party, or
> (b) where no such request is made.
> (3) Where a person declines an invitation to make submissions

under this section he or she shall inform the court in writing stating his or her reason for so declining."

What is this section seeking to achieve? First, it is clear that the Supreme Court's power of invitation can be activated either on the request of a party to the personal injuries action[65] or of anyone else or by the court itself, without any request to it. Secondly, it appears that the Supreme Court is free, but not obliged, to adhere to such a request by inviting "such persons as it considers appropriate" to make submissions to it. The section gives no guidance as to the qualifications or other qualities that might render persons "appropriate" to the task, nor does it throw light on their number or on whether they need represent both sides of the issue that requires determination on appeal. It would appear that they need not.

As to the kind of case in which the power may be exercised, it must be one involving "any matter concerning either liability or damages" that the Supreme Court considers to be of exceptional public importance and the action "belongs to a class of causes of action in which the same or a similar matter arises." The word "liability" is highly elastic. It obviously includes issues relating to the duty[66] or standard[67] of care. Less obviously, it may extend to issues relating to contributory negligence,[68] voluntary assumption of risk[69] or the *ex turpi causa* defence,[70] all of which, in part or in whole, arguably relate to the *non-ascription* of liability. A matter concerning "damages" clearly includes such issues as the categories for assessment of damages.[71] Arguably it includes issues relating to remoteness of damage,[72] which is concerned with the limits of liability. It may well be that the notion of liability could be regarded by the Court as being sufficiently broad to encompass any case raising the question whether a defendant should be found liable to compensate the plaintiff *in the particular circumstances of that case*.

---

65 The section is drafted in a way that does not expressly require that this party actually be participating in the appeal; perhaps this can be inferred.

66 Cf. McMahon & Binchy, *op. cit.*, Chap.6.

67 Cf. *id.* Chap.7.

68 Cf. *id.* paras 20.02–20.60.

69 Cf. *id.* paras 20.61–20.92.

70 Cf. *id.* paras 20.93–20.108.

71 Cf. *id.* Chap. 44.

72 This was the Minister's interpretation of the provision: Seanad Debates, March 4, 2004, col.1809. See further McMahon & Binchy, *op. cit.*, Chap.3.

The provisos are twofold. The first is that the Court must consider that the matter is one of "exceptional public importance". This concept is familiar in the context of limitations on the entitlement to appeal against certain judgments, generally in a public law context. The second is that the action must "belon[g] to a class of causes of action in which the same or a similar matter arises." What exactly does a "class of causes of action" comprise? Must there be a series of related claims before the courts? If so, what degree of connectedness must there be as regards defendant or defendants or as regards plaintiffs? If the concept of class does not carry with it a connotation of several actual claims but rather an abstract category of claims that could be taken, what are the parameters to this concept? It is easy to regard the tort of negligence as being capable of being broken into categories of duty: one recalls Lord Macmillan's observation that "[t]he categories of negligence are never closed". But how sharply should the notion of class of causes of actions be defined in this context?

One suspects that the court will not attempt to lay down any clear guidelines on this question but will instead proceed more by way of broad intuition that a particular claim has the potential for significant downstream effects on the incidence of litigation. For example, in *Barclay v. An Post*,[73] McGuinness J. rejected a claim by a postal worker that An Post (and its predecessor, the Department of Posts and Telegraphs) had been negligent in exposing him and other workers to the risk of back pain from having to bend to deliver mail to letterboxes placed at the bottom of front doors in private residences. The plaintiff's argument was that the defendant either ought to have secured from the Department of the Environment a bye-law locating letterboxes higher up on doors or ought not to have required its workers to deliver letters to doors with dangerously low letterboxes. McGuinness J. held on the evidence that the defendant, an employer, had just about done enough to discharge its duty of care to its postal workers.[74] Had she come to the opposite conclusion, An Post would no doubt have faced, potentially, thousands of claims. Yet there was nothing novel about the relevant legal principles in this litigation.

---

[73] [1998] 2 I.L.R.M. 385.

[74] Though McGuinness J. did impose liability on the defendant for having exposed the plaintiff to the risk of recurrence of his back injury by giving him (albeit at his option) work involving low letter boxes after he had already been injured by work of this kind.

The issue was one merely of applying traditional, well established principles to the facts and making a value-judgment as to whether the defendant had complied with the standard of care required of employers generally. No extension of the frontiers of liability or of the duty of care was in issue: all that was involved was the prospect that a defendant could be exposed to claims from a great many plaintiffs. The same, incidentally, could be said of the Army deafness litigation, though the subjective character of the injury in that context was an exacerbating factor so far as estimating the potential range of claims was concerned.

Why should the prospect of the imposition of widespread liability on an admittedly negligent defendant whose negligence is well established by traditional principles be a reason for the Supreme Court to invite submissions from outsiders? It may be unpleasant for defendants to have to face a large bill but it is hard to articulate a principled reason for the Supreme Court to go to their aid by inviting submissions from people or groups who are not involved in the litigation, the intended effect of which will be to make it more likely for the court to find in favour of the defendant. Yet this is what the framers of the section appear intent on encouraging.

The Minister stated:

> "Section 20 is an important provision dealing with intervention in personal injuries actions. It provides that where an appeal is taken to the Supreme Court, the court may, where it considers that any matter in the case is of exceptional public importance and the action is one of a class of claims in which the same or similar matters arise, invite appropriate persons to make submissions to it. Such an intervention may come about at the initiative of the court, at the request of any party or of any person who is not a party. An issue may arise in a series of cases which is of exceptional public importance and goes beyond the interests of the parties before the court.
>
> This could, for example occur within the ambit of nervous shock. If, for example, when walking down a street I witness a collision between two people causing fatal injury to one of them and I suffer shock and injury on account of what I have witnessed, the ambit of that right to claim damages has serious implications. Recently, for example, we had a case where somebody working in a hospital

> accident and emergency unit or a morgue claimed damages after suffering nervous shock arising from a traffic accident.
>
> This gives rise to the question of reasonable foreseeability and proximity. This is not just a matter of a good or bad barrister spending an afternoon in court arguing the toss between a plaintiff or a defendant and coming to a conclusion on this issue. The Attorney General or others may want to tell the Supreme Court that such a High Court decision extends the concept of reasonable foreseeability or proximity too far and will have general repercussions if it becomes a general application."[75]

What seems to be envisaged here is that, where there is a prospect that one defendant, or a range of defendants, may face wide-ranging liability, the Supreme Court should seek to ensure that the strongest arguments against that prospect are advanced. This does not seem a very even-handed approach. If we take the case of the wrongful sustained exposure by an employer of its employees to the risk of injury, would it be fairer for the court to side with the negligent employer or the injured employees? The best answer perhaps is that it should not be in the business of siding with either party; the next best answer, it is suggested that the court should strive to advance the vindication of the rights of the injured victims of a serious tort than protect the interests of the wrongdoer.

It may well be the case that the Minister's apparent interpretation of the section is mistaken and that the Supreme Court will exercise its jurisdiction under the section even-handedly, extending to non-parties the entitlement to make submissions advocating the enlargement of the duty of care on the same basis as those making opposite submissions. The Article 26 procedure is an obvious precedent of such an even-handed approach.

It is not clear why this controversial power of recruitment of outside submissions should be exercised only by the Supreme Court. If it is a good power, why should it not also be available to the High Court trial judge?

---

[75] Dáil Debates, June 30, 2004, col.763.

The New Rules Relating to Collateral Benefits and Undeclared Income

NEVILLE COX*

INTRODUCTION

Among the various changes introduced by the Civil Liability and Courts Act 2004 ("the 2004 Act") are changes in relation to the manner in which levels of compensatory damages are computed. In this chapter consideration is given to two such changes, namely:

(1) those governing the extent to which collateral benefits (*i.e.* insurance payments, social welfare payments, sick pay, charitable gifts and so on) may be deducted by the court from the overall financial losses claimed by the plaintiff, and

(2) those governing the question of whether, in a situation where a plaintiff provides the Revenue Commissioners with no statement of income or a false statement of income, then the damage suffered by way of loss of income should be assessed by reference to his or her actual income, or the level of income disclosed to the Revenue Commissioners.

In both cases it will be concluded that whereas changes have been effected by the 2004 Act, they are far from substantial and may make comparatively little difference in practice.

*Barrister at Law, Fellow, Trinity College Dublin.

COLLATERAL BENEFITS

In statutory terms, prior to the enactment of section 27 of the Civil Liability and Courts Act 2004 the question of the extent to which benefits (other than statutory benefits) accruing to the victim of wrongdoing were relevant in assessing compensatory damages in any personal injuries action resulting from that action was governed by two statutory provisions, namely section 50 of the Civil Liability Act 1961 and section 2 of the Civil Liability (Amendment) Act 1964.[1] Section 50 deals with a situation where the wrongdoing in question had led to fatal injuries and the action was being brought (under section 48 of the 1961 Act) by the personal representative of the deceased or of his or her dependents. Section 2 on the other hand dealt with a case where the wrongful act did not cause fatal injuries, and hence where the action is being brought by the injured party.

The position arrived at under both these two pieces of legislation is effectively identical, namely that where such a legal action is successful and the question of compensatory damages is being addressed, no account is to be taken of:

(a) any sum payable in respect of the death or injury under any insurance contract, or

(b) any pension, gratuity, or other like benefit payable under statute or otherwise in consequence of the death or injury.

In other words, the normal principle that one receives compensatory damages in order that one can (as far as possible) be returned to the position one was in before the wrongful action is suspended. Instead, because the courts award compensation having no regard to benefits received in mitigation of loss suffered, the victims may well end up in a better financial position *after* the accident than he *enjoyed* before it.

The logic behind these provisions was twofold. First it encouraged thrift on the part of individuals and indeed encouraged them to be financially prepared for any tragedy that might befall them. Secondly it encouraged charity. Moreover, where the donor and the defendant were

---

1 Generally on this see McMahon & Binchy, *Law of Torts* (3rd ed., Butterworths, Dublin, 2000), p.1158 *et seq.*

not the same person, this approach also ensured that the defendant could not seek to reduce his responsibilities for what he had done by relying on the charity of another party.

On the other hand, the downside of this approach is that it can conceivably lead to a situation where an individual victim of a wrongful act would receive "double compensation" for his injuries (as far as special damages were concerned) – a situation of particular concern where it is the defendant who was either paying the pension, gratuity or other like benefit, or who had taken out the insurance contract from which the plaintiff was being compensated. Moreover, it may be suggested that in the current legal climate where the plaintiff in a tort action is arguably regarded less favourably than had previously been the case, this downside has taken on a new significance. Certainly it was a major focus of the Law Reform Commission's consideration of the topic.[2]

To this end, the 2004 Act introduced a change in the law in respect of collateral benefits – albeit one that seems only to cover a very limited set of circumstances. First, section 27 of the 2004 Act amends section 50 of the 1961 Act, such that in the case of a harmful act causing fatal injuries, whereas the old position is retained, it is now also provided that in assessing damages, no account shall be taken of any charitable gift (whether in the form of money or of any other property) made to the plaintiff in consequence of the death of the deceased, unless (a) the defendant is the donor of the gift *and* (b) at the time of making the gift the defendant informed the plaintiff in writing that should the plaintiff recover damages in an action, the defendant would apply to the court for the damages to be reduced by an amount equal to the amount of the gift or the value of the gift. Thus the statutory change does not have any impact in a case where the donor of the gift and the defendant in the action are different persons.

Similarly, section 2 of the 1964 Act is amended such that in the case of an act causing personal injury but not death, assessment of damages should not take account of any money or property paid in the form of a charitable gift unless:

---

[2] Law Reform Commission, *Consultation Paper on the Deductibility of Collateral Benefits from Awards of Damages* (Dublin, 1999) and *Report on the Deductibility of Collateral Benefits from Awards of Damages* (Dublin, 2002).

"(a) the defendant is the donor of the gift, *and*

(b) at the time of making the gift the defendant informed the plaintiff *in writing* that should the plaintiff recover damages in such an action the defendant would apply to the court for the damages to be reduced by an amount equal to the amount of the gift or the value of the gift, *or*

(c) in the case of a plaintiff who is employed by the defendant, the gift consists of a series of payments that resemble, in amount and frequency, the normal remuneration that the plaintiff would be entitled to receive from the defendant in the course of his own employment."

A couple of introductory points should be made about these changes.

First, it is surely the case that the changes as made only have practical application in situations where the defendant is also the victim's employer. It is virtually impossible to conceive of a situation where an ordinary defendant would bother to provide the victim with a charitable gift, yet would also seek, in writing to impose the conditions on the gift that are mentioned in section 27. What seems to be envisaged is a situation where, possibly under pressure from unions, an employer pays an employee some form of sick pay or pays the dependents of a deceased employee some form of payments. Naturally the same employer would not wish to "double-pay" an employee or his/her dependants but would instead want such payment to be factored into any assessment of the level of damage suffered by the victim as a result of the injury, and this new statutory provision ensures that this can be possible.

Once again it should be stressed that the section has no application in a case where the defendant is not also the donor – thus what is involved in reality is a situation where compensation for a workplace injury being is paid in advance of the trial of any action. It should be pointed out that such a procedure seems to have benefits for all parties; the victims have financial support, the employer is acting in line with harmonious industrial relations and the insurance companies who may eventually have to foot the bill in any action will not have to pay what would otherwise amount to compensation to a plaintiff who is not, in this respect, actually out of pocket.

Equally, it is entirely arguable that this section does not relate to situations where an employee is entitled to this form of sick pay as a matter of contract. Such payments, irrespective of the changes made would never have come within the terms either of section 50 or section 2, and would always have been deductible in any assessment of damages.[3] As far as the position under section 27 of the 2004 Act is concerned, it is difficult to see how sick pay provided as a matter of contractual entitlement could ever be regarded as a charitable gift. Furthermore, the effect of section 27(2)(b)(ii) of the 2004 Act is that under the new dispensation no distinction is made between contractual and non-contractual sick pay (*i.e.* both are deductible) provided that the latter is disseminated in a form resembling the former.

Finally, some level of uncertainty arises as to what is meant by the phrase "charitable gift" in section 27. Does it refer to donations that the donor was not obliged to make – in which case it might have been more appropriate to have had recourse to the terminology employed in section 50 and section 2 of "any pension, gratuity or other like benefit …", or does it have a more specific meaning as found for example in the law of equity. It is notable that the phrase "charitable gift" is not defined in the 2004 Act nor in either the 1961 or 1964 Acts, although it is the phrase employed (albeit undefined) by the Law Reform Commission in its treatment of these issues. Could it be argued that, despite the fact that section 27 is designed to be inserted into both section 50 of the 1961 Act and section 2 of the 1964 Act, it deals with matters to which those sections may well not have had any real application in the first place – *i.e.* charitable donations fulfilling one of the four broad categories identified by Lord MacNaughten in *Commissioners for Special Purposes of Income Tax v. Pemsel*,[4] when dealing with charitable trusts namely (i) for the relief of poverty (ii) for the advancement of education (iii) for the advancement of religion or (iv) for other purposes beneficial to the community?[5]

The fact that section 27(2)(b)(ii) refers in its analysis of such charitable gifts to what may effectively be regarded as non-contractual sick pay, suggests that the term "charitable gift" should receive the broad construction. This is the way in which it has been understood in the caselaw on collateral benefits.

---

3 *Honan v. Syntex*, unreported, High Court, Lynch J., October 22, 1990 and *Sturdy v. Dublin Corporation,* unreported, High Court, Lynch J., December 18, 1991.

4 [1891] A.C. 531 at 583.

5 Generally see Delaney, *Equity and the Law of Trusts* (3rd ed., Thomson Roundhall, Dublin, 2003).

In summary then, the changes seem to mean that as a matter of policy, if an employer, under pressure from unions or out of the goodness of his heart, wishes to provide some level of sick pay to an employee or some form of pension relief to the dependents of a deceased former employee, then, either by ensuring that that sick pay resembles in amount and frequency the normal remuneration owing to the plaintiff, or alternatively by making such payment in *any* form while relying on a written statement of the type mentioned in section 27(2)(b)(i), he or she can avoid an effectual "double hit" for compensation. It may be suggested that as a matter of policy, insurance companies will in the future demand of an employer who wishes to engage in such charity that as a matter of course he follows one or other such course.

In order to assess the merits of this approach, however, it is necessary briefly to consider both the former position, and also the comments of the Law Reform Commission in this regard.

Deductibility and Irish law generally

Section 50 of the 1961 Act and section 2 of the 1964 Act represented a deliberate rejection of the old common law position under which in any assessment of damages, all collateral benefits could be deducted. Under the new statutory regime (*i.e.* post-1964) virtually all possible collateral benefits (with the exception of benefits in kind) were covered,[6] and hence there may be said to have been a general principle of non-deductibility. In this respect, the impact of section 50 was arguably greater than that of section 2. It had, after all, been a long accepted rule of common law that where fatal injuries were concerned, a general principle of deduction would apply,[7] although this position was somewhat ameliorated by statute.[8] The position in respect of non-fatal injuries was, however, completely different. Indeed one of the reasons why the 1961 Act only dealt with *fatal* injuries was because of an assumption that at common

[6] In *Murphy v. Cronin* [1966] I.R. 699 the Supreme Court held that both payment equal to the accumulated contributions of the deceased to a superannuation fund and the payment of a sum equal to 25% of such contributions were non-deductible. In addition it would seem that social welfare payments are non-deductible *State (Hayes) v. Criminal Injuries Compensation Tribunal* [1982] I.L.R.M. 210.

[7] *Grand Trunk Railway Company of Canada v. Jennings*, (1888) 13 App. Cas. 800.

[8] Fatal Accidents (Damages) Act 1908 and Fatal Injuries Act 1956 (s.5).

law, the same position existed for non-fatal injuries as had been achieved under section 50.[9] Section 2 of the 1964 Act was therefore merely a consolidation of the existing common law position, and as a result, the Irish courts have concluded that the purpose of section 2 was simply to ensure that an equivalent procedure existed for fatal and non-fatal injuries.[10]

In the case of most charitable payments that an injured party or the plaintiff in a fatal injuries case might receive, this principle of non-deductibility was clear. Thus for example, an invalidity pension or disability benefit was non-deductible,[11] as also was any money paid by an employer to an employee as a matter of statutory obligation[12] and any monies paid as a simple matter of charity.[13] Moreover, it seems clear that where a defendant received sick pay to which he or she is entitled *as a matter of contract* this *was* deductible.

Despite what was until the mid-1980s common judicial practice, it is also clear that in assessing damages for loss of earnings it is the net sum after taxes and so on have been paid that is relevant and not the total amount that the victim earned. Thus for example in *Hogan v. Steele & ESB*,[14] the Supreme Court upheld the finding of Geoghegan J. in the High Court that in a situation where an employer was paying an employee what effectively amounted to sick pay but was deducting PRSI and PAYE from that pay, it was the *net* and not the *gross* pay that was non deductible. In other words, the first named defendant (who in this case was *not* the employer) would not be required to compensate the plaintiff for any more than net loss of earnings.[15]

---

9 *Bradburn v. Great Western Railway*, (1874) L.R. 10 Ex. 1, *Parry v. Cleaver* [1970] A.C. 1 and *Smoker v. London Fire and Civil Defence Authority* [1991] 2 A.C. 502.

10 *Greene v. Hughes Haulage* [1997] 3 I.R. 109 at 117.

11 S.12 of the Social Welfare Act 1984 and *O'Loughlin v. Teeling* [1988] I.L.R.M. 617.

12 *Honan v. Syntex (Ireland) Ltd*, unreported High Court, Geoghegan J., October 22, 1990.

13 *Doherty v. Bowaters Irish Wallboard Mills Ltd*, [1966] I.R. 277 and *McKenna v. Best Travel Limited* [1996] I.E.H.C. 42; [1998] 3 I.R. 57.

14 Unreported, Supreme Court, November 1, 2000.

15 *British Transport Commission v. Gourley* [1956] A.C. 185, *Glover v. BLN Ltd (No.2)* [1987] I.R. 432 and *Cooke v. Walsh* [1984] I.L.R.M. 208.

The Law Reform Commission Report

In its 2002 report on this subject, the Law Reform Commission recognised the inherent ideological tensions in this area.[16] Thus it accepted that there was a strong public policy argument in favour of encouraging "spontaneous acts of social solidarity"[17] and that deducting general charitable benefits from an award for damages might work against this ideal. Moreover, the Commission also accepted that there was a further argument that there was no good reason why a wrongdoer should benefit from the kindness of others – as would happen if the level of money owed by a defendant could be reduced by reference to monies paid to the victim by a kindly third party.

On the other hand, the Commission did feel that a different position would apply where the charitable payments or other benefits were provided by the wrongdoer (the scenario envisaged by section 27 of the 2004 Act), on the grounds that in such a case, "… it may be a disincentive to the tortfeasor to make a timely and useful gesture if he suspects that he will later have to pay again" and furthermore "… when the tortfeasor is the donor, one cannot argue that the wrongdoer is being relieved undeservedly by the donor."[18] Equally the Commission felt that in order to avoid such a "double hit" the donor/wrongdoer could have imposed a condition on the payment of the charitable benefit, to the effect that any such payment would be deducted from any award for damages made in an action. Thus the Commission ultimately recommended that "a charitable gift[19] should not be deducted unless the donor stipulated in writing at the time of the donation, that he or she intended the donation to be deducted from any subsequent award of damages."[20] Moreover, the Commission felt that such recommendation would apply to donors whether or not they were defendants in any tort action.[21] Finally, the Commission further recommended for ease of application, that if the donation emanated from an employer and accorded with the definition

---

[16] Law Reform Commission Report, p.38 *et seq.*

[17] *Ibid.*, p.39.

[18] *Ibid.*

[19] And the commission felt that this should apply irrespective of the form of the charitable gift – that is to say whether it was in money form or as a benefit in kind.

[20] *Ibid.*, p.40.

[21] *Ibid.*, pp.39–40.

of sick pay provided (including any series of payments made by an employer to an injured employee that resemble the employee's regular remuneration in frequency, amount of payment or both) then it should be presumed to be sick pay.[22]

In its specific dealings with sick pay, the Commission recommended that the concept of "double payment" should be avoided as far as possible.[23] Thus where the employer is also the defendant, and is contractually obliged to pay the plaintiff sick play, the Commission felt that such sick play should be deductible.[24] Moreover, there seems little doubt from an analysis of the pre-2004 case law interpreting section 2 of the 1964 Act that such contractually earned sick pay *is* in fact deductible.[25] As a matter of logic, this makes clear sense. After all, in such circumstances, the loss of earnings for which the defendant is claiming is being reduced by payments due under the same contract as that by which he was entitled to earnings in the first place. Allowing him to claim for loss of all earnings in such circumstances offends against the principle that special damages of this kind *are* primarily compensatory, and also, where the defendant is also the employer, it means that the defendant is, in the most blatant and unfair sense facing a double hit.

The Commission further recommended that, in order to further the twin policy ideals of encouraging employers to afford the employee some measure of financial support pending the resolution of the action while reassuring them that they would not face a double hit if they were successfully sued for damages, employers should be informed and encouraged that it is perfectly legitimate for them to insert a term in their contract with employees providing that in situations of this kind, where monies are paid to the injured employee, there is a requirement of repayment of such monies where the plaintiff is successful in an action taken against the defendant.[26] Equally the Commission decided against recommending that there should be a statutory presumption that where sick pay of this kind was being paid that such payment would be presumed

---

22 *Ibid.*, p.42.
23 Generally, *ibid.*, Chap.4.
24 *Ibid.*, p.74.
25 *Henan v. Syntex,* unreported, High Court, Lynch J., October 22, 1990 and *Sturdy v. Dublin Corporation,* unreported, High Court, Lynch J., December 18, 1991.
26 *Ibid.*, p.77 *et seq.*

to be by way of advance or loan.[27] Instead it recommended that the Law Society and employers' organisations consider issuing a circular to bring the option of inserting such conditional clauses into contracts to the attention of their members. The ambition seems to have been to create a culture in which such a procedure became commonplace.

In this respect, the situation recommended by the Law Reform Commission will in all probability be that achieved by the new section 27 – namely one where the norm is for an employer who is also the defendant in any action of this nature, and who wishes, (possibly under union pressure), to give some measure of financial relief to the injured plaintiff, either to do so in the form of what might loosely be termed sick pay (that is to say payments resembling in amount and frequency the normal pay to which the defendant would be entitled) *or* alternatively to do so in any form of his choice while making such payment subject to an undertaking that it is to be repaid from damages earned in any action.

Summary – The impact of section 27 of the 2004 Act

In summary then, what is perhaps most remarkable about the changes wrought by the 2004 Act in this area is that they are remarkably modest – and as the Minister for Justice noted in Dáil debates on this subject, more modest than those contained in the original 2003 draft of the Bill. The Law Reform Commission had recommended more sweeping changes in areas such as pensions, social welfare, insurance contracts and sick pay. Yet in reality few enough of these areas were touched even in theory, and in practice the new section 27 only really has impact on the employer/employee relationship. Effectively it allows any defendant to an action but in reality an employer to make charitable contributions (probably defined as contributions which they were not obliged by statute or contract to make) to an injured employee or the dependants of a deceased employee, in the comforting certainty that, provided that they either ensure that the plaintiff has signed an appropriate undertaking, or alternatively, that such payments are in the specified form set out in the final paragraph of section 27(2), they will be able to offset such payments against any award of compensatory special damages. Moreover, it may well be that whereas the change will have little practical impact it may yet fulfil the ambition

---

[27] *Ibid.*, p.79.

of the Law Reform Commission in creating a culture of awareness on the part of both lawyers and employers' groups that it is possible to provide immediate relief to injured employees or their dependants without facing the risk that in the event of damages being awarded in a personal injuries action it will be impossible to recoup monies provided by way of such relief.

Finally it should be noted that outside of this new statutory regime, an employer who is *not* a defendant to an action may still, if he or she chooses, make such gratuitous payments and yet ensure that they are repaid from any sums awarded by way of damages simply by ensuring that prior to such payment the victim signs an undertaking of the kind that was the subject of the Supreme Court deliberations in *Hogan v. Steele*.[28]

Loss of Earnings and Income Undeclared for Tax Purposes

The issue of whether a victim's loss of earnings should be assessed by reference to the amount of money he actually earned or the amount of money that he earned and which he declared for taxation purposes has received some consideration in recent years in our courts. The issue is after all an important one. It is clear from *Hogan v. Steele* that, in assessing loss of earnings, the relevant figure is the net figure after payment of social insurance and tax. Consider then the case of an individual earning a gross annual salary of €50,000, and assume that, after tax his nett take home pay is €30,000. Clearly it is the latter figure that is relevant under the principle in *Hogan v. Steele* in assessing loss of earnings. However, what if the individual in question only declared €20,000 which would generate, let us say, a net take home pay of €16,000. If that individual is injured by the commission of some tort and seeks special damages for loss of earnings, should the figure for loss of earnings be deemed to be €30,000 – the real level of net earnings – or €16,000 – the amount that the individual pretended was his net level of pay.

[28] See also *McElroy v. Aldritt*, unreported, Supreme Court, June 11, 1955 and *Boyce v. Cawley*, unreported, High Court, Costello J., November 13, 1991. In this respect the decision in *McGuinness v. Reilly*, unreported, High Court, Morris J., November 30, 1992 may perhaps be distinguished on the basis that no mention was made to the judge in this case of the existence of such an agreement.

Of course this question hides a broader policy question, namely should a judge in assessing damages in the context of a specific tort case decide to do the job of the Revenue Commissioners in coming down harshly on someone who has violated the tax code. On one level it might be argued that this represents good public policy; if an individual deliberately flaunts this code, then his flaunting should come back to haunt him whenever the question of his salary is relevant to any element of domestic law. On another level, however, it might be argued in the alternative that whatever course of action the Revenue Commissioners decide to take in respect of the false returns provided by the defendant, this is not a matter for the courts in what is, after all, the trial of a completely different issue. Put simply, a murderer will still be able to avail of the tort of negligence, no matter how awful he is and the judge in the tort case should not be influenced by his conviction for murder. Arguably the latter view is the preferable one, but both have received some degree of favour in our courts.

Fitzpatrick v. Furey and Motor Insurance Bureau of Ireland

The former view was supported in the decision of Laffoy J. in *Fitzpatrick v. Furey.*[29] In this case, the deceased had for some years made returns to the Revenue authorities that were lower than the amount that he earned. Following his death, his widow also made a declaration to the Revenue authorities which she later admitted was false. In the circumstances, counsel for the first named defendant contended that the level of future loss of earnings should be estimated by reference to the figure provided by the deceased to the Revenue authorities. Counsel representing the deceased's widow, on the other hand, conceding that this line of argument might stand some chance of success were the deceased still alive, argued that in the current case a different approach should be taken, in light of the fact that this was a representative action on behalf of the dependents of the deceased. Thus the simple fact was that the wrongdoing of the first defendant had deprived the dependents of the support and lifestyle which they had previously enjoyed, and hence the court should "… find a balance between what was the reality of the situation and the income as declared to the Revenue commissioners."

---

[29] [1998] I.E.H.C. 91 (Laffoy J., June 12, 1998). Generally see Byrne & Binchy, *Annual Review of Irish Law 1998* (Round Hall, Dublin, 1999), pp.658ff.

Laffoy J. admitted that the issue was a difficult one to resolve, not least because of the complete dearth of Irish legal authority in this area. Thus her approach was as follows:

> "I can see the merit of the approach advocated by [counsel for the defendants]. On the other hand I am faced with the fact that the plaintiff, who herself is entitled to the "lion's share" of the dependency claim, has made a declaration to the Revenue Commissioners which she now says is false. I accept that the plaintiff, when making the declaration did the best she could in the circumstances then prevailing. I also understand why she has not been able to address outstanding taxation issues when these proceedings are pending. Nonetheless I have come to the conclusion that public policy considerations preclude me from quantifying the dependency claim on the basis of [the deceased's] declared and undeclared income for the accounting year prior to his untimely death."

In other words, the essential logic of Laffoy J.'s judgment is that there is some public policy concern in punishing tax defaulters by reducing the level of damages available to them, or, where appropriate, to their dependants, in the loss of earnings category by reference to the extent of their violation of the tax code. Indeed this approach is, on one level, consistent with the approach taken in other jurisdictions whereby a court is entitled to scrutinize the source of financial support whose loss is the basis of the fatal accident claim and to decide to award any compensation or limited compensation, if there is some public policy basis for objecting to the source in question. This has arisen for example where the financial support was the result of participation in crime[30] or where the deceased was illegally claiming social welfare payments.[31]

Nonetheless, the decision in *Fitzpatrick v. Furey* has received criticism. Thus it has been suggested that:[32]

> "... it would have been [preferable] to award damages on the net

[30] *Burns v. Edman* [1970] 2 Q.B. 541.
[31] *Hunter v. Butler* [1996] R.T.R. 396.
[32] Byrne & Binchy, *Annual Review of Irish Law 1998*, *op. cit.*, p.664. See also Binchy, "Comment: Tort – Public Policy – Awards in Tort Litigation" (1998) 20 D.U.L.J. 240.

> part of the deceased's *actual*, rather than *declared*, income which benefited the dependents. To proceed on the basis of the declared amount seems a disproportionate penalty, directed at the wrong targets and consequently benefiting a defendant responsible for the full loss of financial benefit. The deterrent effect of a judgment based on the declared income is surely minimal. If it were noticed at all by any member of the public, it would be unlikely to change behaviour in relation to tax declarations to any significant degree."

Whereas the approach of Laffoy J. was understandable in light both of the dearth of Irish case law on the subject and the clear imperative to take tax evasion seriously and to apply a strict *ex turpi causa* logic, nonetheless the criticism more valid. By admitting to the court that both she and her late husband had made inaccurate returns to the Revenue authorities, the plaintiff was in effect leaving herself open to investigation and prosecution *by the Revenue authorities*. On the other hand, the deceased had done nothing illegal in the actual earning of his salary, and given that that was what the case was about, arguably the assessment of loss of earnings should have focused on his actual rather than his declared income.

Downing v. O'Flynn

A different approach to this issue was witnessed in the Supreme Court judgment in *Downing v. O'Flynn*[33] – in which the court appeared to move away from the approach taken by Laffoy J. in *Fitzpatrick v. Furey & MIBI*. Here the deceased operated a small retail fruit and vegetable business prior to his death. He had a mother to whom he paid IR£1,000 per annum and lived with his girlfriend and her three children (in relation to one of whom he was *in loco parentis*) and he contributed IR£150 per week to household expenses. The difficulty was that returns had never been made to the Revenue Commissioners, and, if the accounts prepared after his death (and on foot of which the Revenue Commissioners applied a nil liability) were accurate in their reflection of his income, he would not have been able to make the payments that he had in fact made. In the High Court damages were claimed, *inter alia*, for loss of support by the

[33] [2000] 4 I.R. 383.

mother and the dependant child, and this was opposed on the basis that payment must necessarily have been made out of undeclared income, and hence the same public policy concerns to which the judge referred in *Fitzpatrick* should apply here. McGuinness J. in the High Court, however, awarded such damages, effectively saying that whereas the deceased's accounts were clearly incomplete, this was a not uncommon experience for a small retail business of this kind.

The Supreme Court unanimously dismissed the dependant's appeal. The judges first addressed Laffoy J.'s approach in *Furey v. Fitzpatrick and Motor Insurers Bureau of Ireland*. Each of them expressed their disagreement with it. Referring to what Laffoy J. had stated on the issue, Denham J. was:

> "satisfied that this may not be the correct approach in assessing loss for dependants on declared and undeclared income. Of course the circumstances of each case should be considered. However, in general it would appear appropriate to calculate the loss to the dependants (which has been sustained because of the action of the defendant) on the actual income. If the income, or part of it, has not been declared or taxed then the sum should be analysed to achieve a net figure, net of tax. This net figure would then be the basis on which the loss to the dependants may be calculated."

Murray J. stated his opposition to the approach adopted by Laffoy J. in the following terms:

> "It seems to me that public policy intends that persons who have suffered financial loss as a result of the wrongful act of another be compensated for their actual loss and no more. In my view, therefore the application of the fundamental principle of *restitutio in integrum* is a sufficient basis to exclude, in assessing claims for loss of future income, including those which incorporate an element of undeclared earnings, any element based on gross rather than net income after all lawful deductions."

In short, damages in personal injury or fatal accident cases are, in principle, simply compensation for actual loss and this is particularly evident in the case of special damage. In this context, once liability and actual financial loss have been established the duty in law of the wrongdoer to compensate the injured party by way of damages cannot be negated by the fact that the claim is based, in whole or in part, on undeclared income, once the actual future loss is calculated by reference to the net income after tax.

Geoghegan J. also considered that, in assessing loss of future contributions to dependants in fatal accident litigation, the court should assume that "had the deceased lived he would have probably paid his taxes as and from his death, whatever might have been his conduct before his death." He thought that, in *Fitzpatrick,*

> "both sides wrongly argued it on foot of 'public policy consideration' whereas the true analysis should have been as to whether the trial judge had before her sufficient evidence in relation to undeclared income that she could quantify what would have been the net amount of that income if tax were paid. I think that the learned trial judge should have assumed that the deceased would have paid tax had he survived. Public policy considerations did not dictate that the entire of the £6,000, if properly proved, should be disregarded. It is not necessary for the courts to take such a severe view as apart from anything else it could work great hardship and injustice to other hypothetical cases. The true principle is that a defendant should never have to compensate for alleged loss of monies which ought to have gone to the Revenue Commissioners and should not have been retained by the deceased. But the principle does not go beyond that."

Applying these principles to this instant case, all members of the court were satisfied that McGuinness J.'s award should be sustained. They did so on several grounds. The amount awarded in favour of the child was relatively small. As Denham J. observed, whatever might be said of the figure of £150, it was "difficult to imagine a sum for the child being less than £37.50. On any view [it] would have been available to the child". McGuinness J.'s remarks should, Geoghegan J. thought, be interpreted as indicating a view that there was "plenty of surplus money in reality and that contributions of the amount alleged could have been afforded by the deceased …', rather than involving a finding that they could only have been made out of untaxed income. Denham J. was, moreover, of opinion that the evidence supported a finding that the deceased's business, which was "successful and … growing", would have continued to develop had he survived.

Importantly the decision in *Downing v. O'Flynn* does not reject the *ex turpi causa* defence in tort litigation. It continues to be the case that damages are unrecoverable for loss of illegally obtained earnings.[34] Moreover it is noticeable that the court in *Downing* was influenced by the relatively minor nature of the infringement of the tax code that was at issue. The decision of the court left open the possibility of a different result being reached in the case of a more egregious breach.

Section 28 of the 2004 Act

Section 28 of the Act, arguably in line with the rather restrictive feel of the Act generally, seems to adopt an approach which, while allowing a good deal of flexibility to a judge to have regard to circumstances, nonetheless falls into line with the spirit of the decision in *Fitzpatrick* rather than *Downing v. O'Flynn* (although as it does not apply to actions under section 48 – that is to say actions where a wrongful act has caused *fatal* injuries – the section would not actually have application to either case). The section reads as follows:

> "(1) In a personal injuries action (other than an action under section 48 of the Act of 1961), any income, profit or gain in respect of which—
>
> (a) the plaintiff is making a claim, and
>
> (b) (i) a return has not been made before the hearing of the action in accordance with the Taxes Consolidation Act 1997, or
>
> (ii) the plaintiff has not otherwise notified the Revenue Commissioners,
>
> shall, for the purposes of assessing damages, be disregarded by the court, unless the court considers that in all the circumstances it would be unjust to disregard such income, profit or gain.
>
> (2) This section does not apply to causes of action accruing before the commencement of this section."

Section 28 may be regarded as being a "gentler" statement of law than

---

[34] *Burns v. Edman* [1970] 2 Q.B. 541.

the decision in *Fitzpatrick v. Furey* in that in as much as it only applies in a situation where the tax defaulter him or herself is the plaintiff in an action it prevents a situation where a dependent family, for example, unaware of the nature of the deceased's relationship with the taxman yet used to a certain standard of income does not lose out where he or she suffers fatal injuries as a result of the wrongful act of the defendant. To this extent, therefore, the section seems on a superficial level to work a form of justice – the essential logic being that you, the claimant has cheated the system and now you have been bitten by your own tactics.

Nonetheless on a more holistic analysis, the section is still flawed, and proceeds on an arguably unsophisticated understanding of the nature of the *ex turpi causa* doctrine. The criticisms of the decision in *Fitzpatrick v. Fury* apply that: (a) unless the illegality at issue relates to the manner in which the income was earned then it should concern only the Revenue Commissioners and not the court in a personal injuries action and (b) it allows a defendant to have what is essentially his responsibility lessened by virtue of some entirely unrelated illegality on the part of the plaintiff are still enormously compelling. In other words, the better approach might be to allow recovery on the basis of the actual income of the plaintiff, content that the increasingly active Revenue Commissioners will have been made aware of the plaintiff's tax avoidance propensities.

It should be noted that on one interpretation of the section, it only has application where there has been *no* return rather than where there has been a *false* return. It is perhaps possible that a plaintiff who earned €50,000 from his job but only declared €35,000, could claim that the situation does not have application to his case in that he *did* make a return, albeit a false one. Equally just as legitimate an interpretation (and the one which undoubtedly reflects the purpose of the section) is to say that whereas he made a return on the €35,000 he made no return on the remaining €15,000 and hence in assessing damages for loss of earnings, this €15,000 should be disregarded by the court.

Finally, it should be noted that the new section 28 does not affect the existing rule at Irish law that, in assessing loss of earnings, what is relevant is the net pay (following deduction for income tax, PRSI etc) rather than the gross pay of the victim.[35] Thus as Griffin J. pointed out in *Cooke v.*

[35] *British Transport Commission v. Gourley* [1956] A.C. 185, *Glover v. BLN Ltd (No.2)* [1987] I.R. 432 and *Cooke v. Walsh* [1984] I.L.R.M. 208.

Walsh:[36]

> "... it is the 'take home pay' and not the gross pay that should have been used as the multiplicand. Had the plaintiff been uninjured, he would have to pay income tax on the wages he would earn and PRSI and other deductions would be made from his wages and therefore the sum that would be available to him to spend would be considerably less than [the gross amount]."

---

[36] [1984] I.L.R.M. 208 at 217.

Mediation in Actions for Personal Injury: Is It Good to Talk?

VAL CORBETT*

INTRODUCTION

The Civil Liability and Courts Act 2004 has introduced significant changes in the manner in which personal injury actions are administered in our civil courts. These changes are seen as the Government's latest attack on the so-called compensation culture that apparently exists within the State. However, while procedural reform of our civil justice system is both timely and necessary, the legislature must be careful so that, in its eagerness to eradicate spurious claims, it does not place unreasonable or unnecessary obstacles in the path of citizens who wish to have "their day in court".

One of the more interesting aspects of the legislation is the introduction of mediation as an alternative means of resolving personal injury actions under sections 15 and 16 of the Act. Like much of the legislation, this development could have been a good thing. However, the manner in which mediation has been incorporated into the legislation will severely curtail the effectiveness of the process and represents a lost opportunity to provide litigants with a realistic, efficient and satisfactory alternative to resolving their disputes.

It is the purpose of this chapter to examine the role mediation has played in other common law adversarial civil systems and to propose that while the Oireachtas had the right idea, they erred in its execution.

---

*BCL, LL.M. (NUI); Head of the Law Faculty, Griffith College Dublin.

What is Mediation?

Definition

Mediation is a non-binding process whereby the parties to a dispute meet in private with an independent third party in order to facilitate a solution that is mutually satisfactory to all. In its purest sense participation in the process is voluntary and the parties are free to withdraw at any time.

Moore has defined the process as:

> "... the intervention in a negotiation or a conflict of an acceptable third party who has limited or no authoritative decision-making power but who assists the involved parties in voluntarily reaching a mutually acceptable settlement of the issues in dispute."[1]

Strasser and Randolph have described mediation as a confidential process, consensual in nature whose primary focus is on the needs and interests of the parties rather than on their rights and liabilities.[2]

Thus, the essence of the mediation lies in its consensual nature. The parties control the process and the mediator's primary function is to facilitate the parties in their efforts to reach an agreed solution to their dispute. Unlike an arbitrator, the mediator cannot impose a solution on the parties who are free to walk away from the process if they are of view that a satisfactory solution cannot be discovered. This approach is at odds with the traditional common law adversarial approach to dispute resolution based on the premise that there can be only one winner, the winner being determined by some external body to the dispute. Mediation seeks to bring about a "win/win" situation where both sides are satisfied.

All communications during the mediation are confidential and without prejudice. Neither party can use statements or admissions made during the mediation as evidence at a later trial. Mediation cannot succeed unless the parties feel that they can discuss their dispute candidly by laying all their cards on the table. Thus, the element of high stakes poker, of bluff

---

1 Moore, C.W., *The Mediation Process: Practical Strategies for Resolving Conflict*, (2nd ed., San Francisco: Jossey-Bassy, 1996), 15.

2 Strasser, F. & Randolph, P., *Mediation: A Psychological Insight into Conflict Resolution* (Continuum, 2004), 62–64.

and counter-bluff that usually occurs in other settlement negotiations, is removed from the process.

Finally, mediation centres on the parties' "needs and interests" rather than their "rights or liabilities". In litigation, the primary focus is on what has occurred in the past and proving who was right and who was wrong, rather than focusing energy on how the present dispute can be best resolved looking into the future. An approach based on entrenched positions premised on presumptions of 'rightness' is inherently inflexible and therefore destructive to the relationship between the parties. In contrast the non-binding and voluntary nature of mediation fosters communication and ensures that:

> "Because the process is not real in the sense of binding the rights of the parties, the participants will allow much more serious discussion of needs and interests. Their belief that the mediation will be unenforceable against them in the real world – that the entire mediation and its consequences will disappear when the process ends – allows them to distance themselves from the consequences of open participation."[3]

Why mediation?

The advantages of mediation over other forms of dispute resolution derive from its voluntary and informal nature and may best be highlighted in contrast to more traditional forms of dispute resolution, namely, litigation and negotiation.

As an informal and confidential process, mediation's main attraction is that it is likely to be less costly in that it introduces an early opportunity for settlement of the dispute.[4] Even if the mediation fails to resolve the dispute, it may succeed in narrowing some of the issues involved thereby saving costs at any subsequent trial. In 2001, an evaluation report commissioned by the Ontario Ministry of the Attorney General in Canada

---

3 Smith, G., "Unwilling Actors: Why Voluntary Mediation Works, Why Mandatory Mediation Might Not", *Osgoode Hall Law Journal*, Vol.36 No.4 (1998) 847 at 859.

4 As part of a survey, when asked what they considered the benefits, if any, of mediation in resolving disputes, 61% of companies responded that the less expensive nature of the process was determinative (CEDR Commercial Mediation Statistics 2000/01) at p.21.

analysed, *inter alia*, the cost effectiveness of a mediation program introduced in that jurisdiction on a trial basis in 1999[5] and found that in a survey of Ottawa lawyers that:

> "In general, there was a consensus that the mediation process does result in a decrease in overall costs. Costs are most likely to be decreased in the simpler cases; for example, those that deal with quantum of damages rather than establishing liability. It was generally agreed that even for cases that did not settle at mediation, there is an increased likelihood that cases will then settle either at a settlement conference or at judicial pre-trial. It is very difficult to put an actual dollar value of the costs saved by settling earlier at some point in the overall process, as this is somewhat intangible, but there was general agreement that there is a cost saving."[6]

Parties prefer mediation as a method of resolving their dispute, as they are active participants in the process. This empowerment generates better communication and encourages the parties to speak openly and honestly. The role of the lawyer in this process is advisory, allowing the parties to express their feelings directly to the other side rather than through intermediaries and gives parties the feeling that "they have been listened to". This approach generates an atmosphere where creative and tailor-made solutions can then be developed.

Mediation also has the advantage of being an entirely private process. This means that only the parties to the dispute and the mediator are aware of the details of the dispute and any subsequent settlement. Thus, if the parties would prefer not to wash their "dirty linen" in public for fear of the possible damage that could be caused by the bad publicity of any litigation, mediation is an attractive alternative.

If the parties are in a continuing relationship as in the case of an employer and employee for example, mediation may be a preferred option to litigation. A resolution reached from the input of both parties is more likely to ensure the continued preservation of such a relationship into the future.

---

5 *Evaluation of the Ontario Mandatory Mediation Program (Rule 24.1): Final Report – The First 23 Months*, March 12, 2001.

6 *Op cit.*, p.56.

Negotiated settlements present the client with many of the same difficulties and pitfalls that exist with litigation. Negotiation usually takes place lawyer-to-lawyer with little direct input from the client. In many cases, the parties do not even meet. In such a land, the bluff is king. As Strasser & Randolph have noted:

> "The motivating factor for each solicitor in putting forward an 'extreme' offer is the fact that they are involved in representative bargaining, acting as champions for their clients. They would like to achieve a result that is better than the client expected; this they believe will earn them respect, gratitude and admiration – and further work."[7]

Mediation guarantees the parties a "settlement event" where they can meet face to face and discuss the difficulties that exist between them. This informal setting fosters a more conciliatory atmosphere and is more likely to be devoid of bluff, allowing the parties to focus on solving the issues which divide them.

The presence of a mediator facilitates the conciliation process. The parties are free to concentrate on the issues in dispute. Through careful management, the mediator can guide the parties from impasse to a mutually satisfactory conclusion. Within the mediation, the mediator can meet with the parties individually and privately (also known as a "caucus"). In this environment, the mediator can learn even more about the party's case, what result he she is hoping for from the process, what they would accept as a minimum settlement etc. This information can be imparted to the mediator in full confidence. Armed with this knowledge, the mediator can guide the parties to a resolution which both find acceptable simply because he is the party in the room with the most information regarding the dispute.

Mediation in an adversarial world

So, is mediation a good thing? Given the success of mediation in resolving violent and political conflicts in Bosnia, Rwanda and Northern Ireland, is it fair to assume that it could be equally successful at resolving non-

---

7 Strasser, F. & Randolph, *op.cit.*, p.71.

violent conflicts that arise in litigation? After all, the process is empowering, inexpensive (in comparative terms) and more efficient. On principle, therefore, mediation should be promoted as a means of dispute resolution although not necessarily in the form envisaged in the Civil Liability and Courts Act 2004.

How does one go about promoting the use of such a process? Traditionally, mediation as a method of resolving legal conflict in this jurisdiction has been limited to situations where the parties to the dispute hoped to preserve their legal relationship.[8] People, and in particular lawyers are cautious by nature and are slow to change. In a utopia, the option of mediation as an alternative to litigation would be entirely voluntary and all parties involved – including their lawyers – would at the very least always seriously consider the option as a solution. However, the creation of such a utopia would require a complete change in mindset from both lawyers and Irish society generally. The alternative, preferred by the Minister for Justice, Equality and Law Reform, is to institutionalise the mediation process by blending it into the litigation system.[9]

Unfortunately, the primary difficulty with the institutionalisation of mediation lies in the adversarial nature of our legal system. In litigation, the parties are opponents involved in a battle to prove who is right and wrong, seeking to establish blame for some past event. According to Professor Wangerin, this system is based on the premise that human beings are self interested and competitive. These characteristics shape our conduct, which in turn, leads to an environment of competitiveness where one party must win and the other must lose.[10] Mediation on the other hand is almost everything litigation is not. The process empowers the parties, is focused on creative problem-solving, focuses on the future and is not concerned with past events and who was right or wrong. In Professor Wangerin's view, this approach to dispute resolution is centred on the notion that human beings are by nature co-operative and altruistic which gives rise to a collaborative approach to problem solving.[11]

How does one weave the mediation process into the litigation system

---

8 Such as s.78 of the Employment Equality Act 1998.

9 S. 15(1) of the Civil Liability and Courts Act 2004.

10 See generally, Wangerin, P., "The Political and Economic Roots of the "Adversary System" of Justice and "Alternative Dispute Resolution", 9 Ohio ST.J. on Disp. Resol. 203 (1994).

11 *Ibid.*

when both processes seem entirely incompatible? Experience of other common law jurisdictions would lead one to the conclusion that three options are available. First, mediation can be made mandatory, *i.e.* the parties are compelled to enter the process prior to the trial of the action. Failure to do so will leave the recalcitrant party subject to sanctions usually in the form of an order for costs.[12] Second, the parties can be strongly "encouraged" to take part in mediation; unreasonable refusal to do so could also leave the offending party subject to similar costs' sanction.[13] Third, mediation can be mandatory only where one party to the action requests that the dispute be subject to mediation;[14] failure by the other side to take part could leave them liable to a costs' sanction.[15] It is this latter approach that has been incorporated into the Act of 2004.

All of these methods involve a certain amount of abrogation of the individuals' right to self-determination within the mediation process. They all involve an element of compulsion, cajoling or coercion. Each attempts to bring the horse to water. The question is which represents the best opportunity of making him drink?[16]

It would appear that the policy makers' motivations in institutionalising mediation are inextricably linked to the likelihood of its success as an alternative means of dispute resolution. Where the predominant or only motive of the legislature in introducing mediation to the litigation process is simply to reduce the cost of litigation and to lighten the courts' workload, the effectiveness of the overall mediation process is somewhat neutered and party satisfaction with the outcome diminished. This approach fails to consider that the greatest advantage to mediation in conflict resolution lies in the party satisfaction it generates. Jurisdictions preoccupied with saving costs and time develop systems of mediation which compel the parties to undertake mediation irrespective of their preference. Such systems remove the choice of participation from the parties, taking the integral element of control from them, leaving them somewhat disenfranchised and unlikely to be in a conciliatory mood when meeting

---

[12] See for example, r.24.1 of the Ontario Court Rules for the Ontario Superior Court of Justice, Canada.

[13] See for example, r.1.4(2)(e) of the Civil Procedure Rules 1999 (England & Wales).

[14] *Supra.*, n.9.

[15] S.15(3) of the Civil Liability and Courts Act 2004.

[16] Boettger, "Efficiency Versus Party Empowerment – Against A Good Faith Requirement in Mandatory Mediation", 23 *Rev. Litig.* 1.

the other side. Ireland is now one such jurisdiction. The Minister for Justice, Equality and Law Reform's zealousness in attacking the costs of litigation is evidenced in the following comments made during the Seanad Debates on the Bill:

> "The Bill also provides for major procedural changes in personal injury actions to reduce the time taken and the costs involved in processing such actions … the Bill aims to streamline the procedure in personal injuries actions so as to reduce litigation costs. These costs are quite simply too high relative to the quantum of compensation."[17]

This preoccupation with reducing costs fails to recognise the underlying psychology of mediation. Can a process built upon principles of conciliation, agreement and voluntariness ever operate efficiently where the parties to the process are forced to the table? Is there a better way of encouraging the parties to partake in such a process that can have so many positive benefits, but which would not shear the parties of their autonomy?

Mandatory mediation – The Canadian experience

Proponents of mandatory mediation argue that while it does deprive the parties of the right to choose, it does not mandate that the parties must reach a settlement nor does it impose a settlement on them. In fact, once ordered to mediate it is argued, control is returned to the parties who can then decide themselves whether an appropriate settlement can be reached. As Dr Boettger has opined:

> "Mandatory mediation decreased self-determination by transferring the decision to engage in mediation from the parties to the court. On the other hand, the refusal of parties to go to mediation often was caused by a lack of information about the process itself, about the role of the mediator, and about the benefits available from mediation. Lawyers were not the proper counsellors to teach parties about mediation, and sometimes the lawyers' interests in increasing

---

[17] Seanad Debates, March 11, 2004, vol.175.

> their fees by taking cases to trial and in the personal gratification of winning cases prevented mediation. From this perspective, mandatory mediation was an opportunity to get parties in touch with a mediator and to educate the participants about their powers as parties. Despite the harm that was done to the self-determination of the parties by taking away the initial decision to participate, mandatory mediation actually increased self-determination and education of the parties when compared to trial procedures. The parties were given back the power to resolve their own disputes."[18]

It is argued that the advantages of mandatory mediation outweigh any potential pitfalls. It concentrates the minds of the parties towards an early resolution of the dispute and it educates litigants and lawyers on the value of mediation by compelling them to use a process they may not have otherwise considered. Further, mandatory mediation in dispensing with the parties' consent will involve savings both in time and money.

In 1999, a programme, which mandated mediation for non-family civil case-managed cases in the Ontario Superior Court of Justice in Ottawa and Toronto, was introduced on a trial basis. The continuation of this pilot programme beyond 2001 was dependent upon the conclusions of an evaluation report conducted by an independent evaluator.

In March 2001, the final evaluative report on the Ontario Mediation Program was published.[19] It strongly recommended the continued use of mandatory mediation within the Ontario civil litigation system. The report concluded that:

- mandatory mediation has resulted in significant reductions in the time taken to dispose of cases;
- mandatory mediation resulted in decreased costs to the litigants;
- mandatory mediation resulted in a high proportion of cases (roughly 40% overall) being completely settled earlier in the litigation process – with other benefits being noted in many of the other cases that did not completely settle;

---

[18] *Supra.*, n.16.

[19] *Evaluation of the Ontario Mandatory Mediation Program (Rule 24.1): Final Report – The First 23 Months* submitted by Robert Hann and Associates Limited, March 12, 2001.

- in general, litigants and lawyers expressed considerable satisfaction with the mediation process under Rule 24.1.[20]

The pace of mediated litigation

The report concluded that cases were settled earlier when they were part of a mandatory mediation programme.[21] This conclusion was based on evidence gathered which compared the settlement rate of cases which were subject to the mandatory mediation programme as against cases which were brought prior to the introduction of mandatory mediation. The report found that a greater number of cases that went to mandatory mediation were settled than those that did not (see extract of table below).[22]

% of cases disposed within different follow-up periods after 1st defence

Total Cases		0–3 months	0–6 months	0–9 months	0–12 months
	Control Group	7.0	15	23	*34*
	Mandatory Mediation	7.6	25	38	*49*

In analysing these findings, the report found that most participants in the process believed that it resulted in earlier disposition as it forced counsel to concentrate on the issues in dispute at an earlier stage. Further, the report discovered that the process allowed the parties an input in the resolution of the dispute at a much earlier stage which enhanced the prospects of early settlement.[23]

The cost of mediated litigation

It was the conclusion of the report that when cases were settled either at mediation or shortly after, the parties made significant financial savings. Research conducted by the authors of the report established that 72% of

[20] *Ibid.*, p.2.
[21] *Ibid.*, p.34.
[22] *Ibid.*, p.38.
[23] *Ibid.*, p.39.

lawyers surveyed in the Ottawa and Toronto regions reported substantial savings to clients. Indeed, the authors estimated that in 343 cases sampled as part of the survey, civil litigants had saved over $3 million in costs because of the mediation programme.[24]

The impact of mandatory mediation on dispute resolution outcomes

Perhaps the most interesting results produced by the report arise from the authors' analysis of the outcomes of mediated cases. Statistics gathered for the report found that approximately 40% of cases in Ottawa and Toronto were settled at or within seven days of mediation.[25]

In response to the statement, "I was satisfied with the overall mandatory mediation experience", 80% of Ottawa and 59% of Toronto lawyers agreed. 82% of Ottawa and 65% of Toronto litigants agreed.[26] Interestingly, when asked whether they believed the mediation process had served justice, 61% of Ottawa and 43% of Toronto lawyers agreed. 61% of Ottawa and 39% of Toronto litigants agreed.

Ontario's experience of mandatory mediation has been rather mixed to date. Certainly, in cases where mediation was successful, significant savings on cost and time were made. However, the analysis of the outcomes of mediation was somewhat under whelming, with 60% of cases failing to settle at or within seven days of mediation. In addition, only 52% of lawyers and 50% of litigants declared that they were of the opinion that they believed justice had been served.

Criticisms of mandatory mediation

Critics of mandatory mediation argue that the very term itself is oxymoronic.[27] How can a voluntary process ever work if it is made mandatory? Parties who are compelled against their wishes into mediation are unlikely to be in a conciliatory frame of mind once there. As Smith has pointed out, in mandatory mediation, "the unwilling parties will always be conscious of their compulsion. Consequently, they will never

---

[24] *Ibid.*, p.61.
[25] *Ibid.*, p.66.
[26] *Ibid.*, p.96.
[27] Smith, G., "Unwilling Actors: Why Voluntary Mediation Works, Why Mandatory Mediation Might Not", *Osgoode Hall Law Journal* (Vol.36 No.4, 1998), 847.

experience the kind of commitment to the process which produces the theatrical effects of distancing and denial."[28]

Professor Kovach contends that the ADR profession, in order to promote the use of mediation within the adversarial system, encouraged the courts and legislature to compel litigants to take part by promising that significant cost savings would accrue to the litigants and the courts as a result. Thus, mandatory mediation was "sold" on the basis that it was cheaper.[29] However in making mediation mandatory one simply creates another procedural step in the litigation ladder. It becomes part of the process and is not seen as an alternative conflict resolution mechanism and as such becomes subsumed into the adversarial system. This form of mediation has become known as "litigation lite" because it is said to have all the attributes of litigation but minus the fat, *i.e.* less cost and formality.[30]

What effect does "litigation lite" have on mediation? Traditional negotiation settlements outside of mediation are set against the background of the adversarial system. Hence, the parties adopt what has been identified by Fisher & Ury as "bargaining positions."[31] Both parties take a series of positions which they may or may not give up during the course of negotiations, and which may or may not, ultimately, lead to the conclusion of an agreement between the parties. Such an approach has its drawbacks:

> "When negotiators bargain over positions, they tend to lock themselves into those positions. The more you clarify your position and defend it against attack, the more committed you become to it. The more you try to convince the other side of the impossibility of changing your opening position, the more difficult it becomes to do so. Your ego becomes identified with your position. You now have a new interest in "saving face" – in reconciling future action with past positions – making it less and less likely that any agreement

---

[28] *Ibid.*, p.875.

[29] Kovach, K., Symposium: "New Wine Requires New Wineskins: Transforming Lawyer Ethics For Effective Representation in a Non-Adversarial Approach to Problem Solving: Mediation", 28 *Fordham Urb. L.J.* 935.

[30] Sabatino, J., "ADR as "Litigation Lite": Procedural and Evidentiary Norms Embedded Within Alternative Dispute Resolution", 47 *Emory L.J.* 1289 (1998).

[31] See generally Fisher R., & Ury W., *Getting To Yes – Negotiating an Agreement Without Giving In* (Random House Business Books, 1982).

> will wisely reconcile the parties' original interests. ... As more attention is paid to positions, less attention is devoted to meeting the underlying concerns of the parties. Agreement becomes less likely."[32]

Mediation in its purest form is based on what Fisher & Ury have called "principled negotiation." According to the authors, this form of negotiation involves separating the people from the problem, focuses on interests and not positions and generates a number of options making this approach to negotiation much more likely to be successful in producing a mutually satisfactory result for the parties.[33]

Because mandatory mediation has taken on board many of the characteristics of litigation, it is unlikely to be very effective in producing creative solutions satisfactory to the parties. One, or both, of the parties, will resent having to take part in the mediation, which they will simply view as a step on the road to trial. This reluctance will manifest itself in the negotiation stance adopted by that party which in turn will often have a negative effect on the outcome. As a consequence, any gains or advantages that mandatory mediation may have had for the parties in terms of savings of cost and time will be lost. The parties will have wasted time and, in doing so, will have increased the costs of the action.

Finally, the mandatory use of mediation raises issues of procedural justice. Mediation is informal in nature and hopes to achieve "substantive justice" between the parties. However, in the absence of procedural safeguards how can such justice be guaranteed? Fiss has been severely critical of ADR mechanisms for this very reason:

> "Settlement is for me the civil analogue of plea-bargaining: consent is often coerced; the bargain may be struck by someone without authority; the absence of a trial and judgement renders subsequent judicial involvement troublesome; and although dockets are trimmed, justice may not be done. Like plea-bargaining, settlement is a capitulation to the conditions of mass society and should be neither encouraged nor praised."[34]

---

[32] *Ibid.*, p.5.
[33] *Ibid.*, p.11.
[34] Fiss, O., "Against Settlement", *The Yale Law Journal*, Vol. 93: 1073 (1984) at p.1075.

The author points out that ADR process (such as mediation) tend to assume equality between the participants. However, in many disputes there exists an imbalance in power between the parties. For example, one party may be in a much better financial position than the other. In such a scenario, this imbalance in power may lead to unfair resolution. The 'weaker' party may feel obliged to settle for a lesser amount at mediation because they may not have the resources to fund the trial of the action or because they are in need of compensation immediately and cannot wait until the case comes before the courts.[35] While the author's comments could apply to voluntary mediation, they are magnified in the case of mandatory mediation where the litigants never had the option of refusing mediation in the first place.

Court-encouraged mediation – The English and Welsh experience

In 1995 and 1996 Lord Woolf published two reports on the system of English civil procedure.[36] Lord Woolf considered that the then current English system was defective in many ways. In particular, he concluded that it was expensive,[37] was procedurally complex[38] and the adversarial culture created a hostile and aggressive culture in litigation.[39] Lord Woolf proposed changes to the rules of civil procedure whose aims were to, *inter alia*, make civil justice more accessible to the ordinary members of the public and to encourage early settlement of disputes. Thus, the overriding objective of the changes brought about to the English civil procedure system was, unlike the Irish position, to improve the ordinary person's access to, and satisfaction with, civil justice. Lord Woolf recommended that these changes would be implemented by the development of a judicial case management system where responsibility for civil litigation would be transferred from the litigants and their lawyers to the courts.[40] The principles from Lord Woolf's Reports were codified

---

[35] *Ibid.*, p.1076.
[36] Lord Woolf, *Access to Justice*, Interim Report (1995) and *Access to Justice*, Final Report (1996).
[37] Lord Woolf, *Access to Justice*, Interim Report (1995), Chap.3, paras 12–8.
[38] *Ibid.*, para.4.
[39] *Ibid.*, paras 3–11.
[40] *Ibid.*, Chap.4, p.18, para.2.

in the form of the Civil Procedure Rules (CPR) 1998, which took effect in April 1999.

When managing cases under this system, the overriding objective of the courts is to deal with cases justly.[41] This duty also extends to the parties involved in litigation. In this regard, Rule 1.4(2)(e) defines active case management to include:

> "Encouraging the parties to use an alternative dispute resolution procedure if the court considers that appropriate and facilitating the use of such procedure."

In addition, a party may make a written request for the proceedings to be stayed while the parties try to settle the case by alternative dispute resolution.[42] More controversially, the court may, of its own initiative, direct that the proceedings be stayed for one month [43] or until such a date as it considers appropriate.[44] Failure to adhere to the court's directions may leave the offending party open to a costs' sanction. Rule 44.5(3) provides that when assessing the amount of costs, the court will have regard to a number of factors including:

> "(a) the conduct of all the parties, including in particular—
> (i) conduct before, as well as during, the proceedings;
> and
> (ii) the efforts made, if any, before and during the proceedings in order to try to resolve the dispute."

Lord Woolf's approach towards the institutionalisation of ADR mechanisms in the English civil justice system has much to commend it. Rather than compulsorily requiring the parties to enter mediation, Lord Woolf favoured an approach which "robustly encouraged" the parties to try alternative means of resolving the dispute. Unlike mandatory mediation programmes and the Irish legislation,[45] a party would not be subject to

---

[41] CPR (1998), Pt 1, r.1.1(1), CPR (1998).
[42] *Ibid.*, Pt 26, r.26.4(1).
[43] *Ibid.*, Pt 26, r.26.4(2).
[44] *Ibid.*, Pt 26, r.26.4(3).
[45] S.16(3) of the Civil Liability and Courts Act 2004.

sanction simply because he declined to take part in mediation. Rather, the conduct of the parties before and during the trial of the action would be taken into consideration when making an order for costs. In the context of mediation, only where one of the parties unreasonably refused to participate would they be penalised with an order for costs. Dyson L.J. in *Halsey v. Milton Keynes General NHS Trust*[46] explained the rationale behind the rules as follows:

> 'It is one thing to encourage the parties to agree to mediation, even to encourage them in the strongest terms. It is another to order them to do so. It seems to us that to oblige truly unwilling parties to refer their disputes to mediation would be to impose an unacceptable obstruction on their right of access to the court. ... If the court were to compel parties to enter into a mediation to which they objected, that would achieve nothing except to add to the costs to be borne by the parties, possibly postpone the time when the court determines the dispute and damage the perceived effectiveness of the ADR process."[47]

Refusal to mediate

In what circumstances, then, would a party's refusal to mediate lead to sanction from the courts? It would seem that while the choice to participate remains with the parties, where a court directs that they should consider mediation, the parties would be foolish to ignore such advice without good reason. Certainly, a point blank refusal to mediate from one side could attract sanction from the courts as occurred in *Dunnett v. Railtrack plc.*[48] In that case, the claimant was in occupation of property adjoining a railway line. There was an accommodation crossing across the railway line and a gate from the claimant's field led to the crossing. The gate was replaced with a new one by the defendant. The gate opened and three of the claimant's horses which had been grazing in the field and had wandered onto the railway track were killed by an express train. The claimant alleged, *inter alia*, that the defendant had breached its duty of care to her

---

46 [2004] E.W.C.A. Civ. 576.
47 *Ibid.*
48 [2002] 2 All E.R. 850.

when its employees had wrongly told her that it was illegal to allow the gate to be locked and/or in failing to act on her request to keep the gates locked. Having failed in her claim at first instance, the claimant was granted leave to appeal to the Court of Appeal.

The court suggested to the claimant under Rule 1.4 of the CPR, that she explore the possibility of ADR to resolve the dispute. The claimant referred the suggestion to the defendant, who flatly refused it. Instead, the defendant offered the claimant a sum of £2,500 inclusive of interest and costs. The claimant did not find this offer to be either reasonable or fair and rejected it. The case proceeded to trial where the claimant ultimately failed in her action. However, the court declined to make any order on the defendant's application for the costs of the appeal. The court, applying CPR Part 44, found that the defendant's behaviour in refusing to consider ADR was unreasonable. The defendant had argued that it had refused to consider ADR because they felt it would have necessitated payment of a sum over and above what they had already offered. In the opinion of Brooke L.J. the defendant's view was based on a misunderstanding of the mediation process:

> "A mediator may be able to provide solutions which are beyond the powers of the court to provide. Occasions are known to the court in claims against the police, which can give rise to as much passion as a claim of this kind where a claimant's precious horses are killed on a railway line, by which an apology from a senior police officer is all that the claimant is really seeking and the money side of the matter falls away."[49]

Where does the decision in *Dunnett* leave parties who genuinely believe that the other side's case has little chance of success? Must they still participate in mediation with that other side or run the risk of being saddled with costs? The court's power to recommend mediation robustly, and the dangers of ignoring such a direction were recently examined and clarified by the English Court of Appeal in *Halsey v. Milton Keynes General NHS Trust*.[50] In that case, a widow brought a claim against the hospital where her elderly husband had died. The coroner's finding as to the cause of

---

[49] *Ibid.*, para.14.
[50] [2004] E.W.C.A. Civ. 576.

death was inconclusive. The claimant made a number of offers to resolve the action rather than go to trial including an offer to settle the case for £7,500 plus costs. The defendant rejected these overtures. The claimant's action was dismissed and she appealed the judge's decision to award the defendant its costs since it had refused offers to mediate. The court found that as the general rule is that "the costs follow the event" the burden rests with the unsuccessful party to justify a departure from this rule. Such a departure, the court stated, would be justified where the successful party unreasonably refused to agree to mediation or other alternate methods of dispute resolution.[51]

In deciding whether a party had acted unreasonably in refusing mediation, the court found that the following factors would be relevant:

(a) nature of the dispute – while the vast majority of disputes are suitable for ADR, the court recognised that in certain situations such an approach may not be suitable e.g. issues of law or construction under a contract which require clarification by the parties, cases where it would be considered that a binding precedent would be useful, or where injunctive relief is essential to protect the position of one of the parties;

(b) merits of the case – whether a party reasonably believes that his case is strong will be relevant. Otherwise, as the court pointed out, claimants could use the threat of costs sanctions to extract a settlement from the defendant;

(c) other settlement methods have been attempted – if one party has made other attempts to settle the case then this may indicate that while one party is making efforts to settle the other has unrealistic views of the merits of the case;

(d) costs of mediation would be disproportionately high – this factor will be important where the amounts litigated over are very small. Mediation is not without its costs and as the fees will usually be borne by both parties, the fact that an abortive mediation will add expense to the whole process cannot be ignored;

(e) delay – if the mediation is not suggested until late in the action this may cause the delay of the trial of the action.

---

[51] *Ibid.*, *per* Dyson L.J. at para.13.

(f) whether the mediation had a reasonable prospect of success – the unsuccessful party must show that there was a reasonable prospect that mediation would have been successful;

(g) ignoring court encouragement – the successful party's refused to agree to ADR despite the court's encouragement would be a factor taken into consideration as to whether the refusal was unreasonable.[52]

Having applied each of these factors to the case before them, the court held that while the case was not inherently unsuitable to mediation, the fact that, *inter alia*, the defendant believed he had a strong case (which later proved right), the costs of mediation would have been disproportionate and the claimant could not show that the case had any reasonable prospect of success required the court to dismiss the claimant's appeal as to costs.

Is there any real difference between the approach to institutionalised mediation adopted in Canada and the modified approach taken in England? Are not both approaches essentially the same with only cosmetic differences existing between them? After all, both strongly encourage and promote the use of ADR mechanisms within their civil litigation systems. The only difference being that in Canada, use of mediation is mandatory whereas in England it is "strongly encouraged". However, these apparently minor differences, will have a dramatic effect on the outcome of the mediation process.

The CPR reflects the spirit of Lord Woolf's Reports with its overriding objective to ensure that both the courts and litigants deal with cases justly thereby improving access to the courts. With this in mind, the parties are encouraged, where possible, to consider the merits of ADR. Crucially, parties are not compelled by the courts to attend mediation; rather they are 'robustly' encouraged to consider the option where it is appropriate to their case. This difference has significant consequences. The parties still retain control over the decision as to whether to participate in mediation. True, this decision may be heavily guided by the courts, but critically, it remains their decision. In such circumstances, the parties enter the mediation in a more flexible frame of mind greatly increasing the prospects of a successful outcome. Further, the courts will only

---

52 *Ibid.*, paras 17–23.

penalise the successful party on costs where it can be proven by the unsuccessful party that his refusal to mediate was unreasonable. While not mediation in its purest sense, the CPR has managed to institutionalise and weave mediation into the fabric of the English civil justice system with limited erosion of the parties' autonomy thereby guaranteeing the greater effectiveness of the process.

Mediation under the Civil Liability and Courts Act 2004

Section 15(1) of the legislation formally introduces mediation into our civil justice system. It provides:

> "Upon the request of any party to a personal injuries action, the court may—
>
> (a) at any time before the trial of such action, and
> (b) if it considers that the holding of a meeting pursuant to a direction under this subsection would assist in reaching a settlement in the action,
>
> direct that the parties to the action meet to discuss and attempt to settle the action, and a meeting held pursuant to a direction under this subsection is in this Act referred to as a 'mediation conference'."

Interestingly, section 15(1) provides that mediation can only be initiated by one of the parties to the action. Should neither party request the holding of a meeting the court cannot compel the parties to consider the option.

However, once a party makes such a request then, irrespective of the views of the other side, the court, if it considers that such a meeting would assist in reaching a settlement, can direct the parties to meet. Thus, the use of mediation under the Act is neither mandatory, in the sense that it is not initiated by the direction of the court, nor is it voluntary, in the sense that both parties agree to participate in the process.

Unfortunately, section 15(1) represents a missed opportunity by the Oireachtas.

By choosing an approach whereby the power to initiate mediation rests with one of the parties, irrespective of the views of the other side, the legislature has created a significant power imbalance in the relationship between the parties, which will cause grave difficulties for the mediation process.

What will happen where one party requests mediation and the other side clearly does not want to meet? Is it likely that an agreement will materialise ? In such circumstances, a mutually satisfactory outcome might never be reached. Parties subject to such a direction would resent their own presence at the meeting because it was not of their choosing. This feeling of resentment would only be worsened where their presence at the meeting was the direct result of the direction – through the court – of the other party to the action. Such resentment will manifest itself in the bargaining position taken by the compelled party. He or she is likely to enter the meeting in an adversarial manner and prepared for a fight, a situation hardly conducive to creative problem-solving. To rub salt into the wounds, if such scenarios did present themselves, the introduction of section 15(1) would only serve to increase the costs of litigation, as parties would now be forced to pay for a failed mediation conference that they never wanted to attend in the first place.

Alternatively, section 15(1) could produce a stalemate between the parties considering mediation. In the current adversarial climate, a request to mediate could be perceived as weakness or a lack of confidence in the merits of the case by the other side. In such circumstances, either party would not want to be seen to "blink first" with the result that very few, if any, cases would go to mediation.

Also, section 15(1) could make defendants vulnerable to less-than-genuine claims, the very thing the entire legislation was designed to eliminate. Potentially undeserving plaintiffs could use section 15(1) as a legal tactic by forcing the defendant to meet with them in the hope that a settlement of the claim could be extracted from the defendant. However, it is hoped that such a scenario will not materialise as section 15(1)(b) provides that the court will only order a meeting between the parties where such a meeting "would assist in reaching a settlement in the action." If this provision is interpreted in accordance with the principles laid down by the English Court of Appeal in *Halsey v. Milton Keynes General NHS Trust*,[53] then the danger highlighted will be greatly diminished, as only claims that have a potential for resolution would be ordered to mediation.

[53] [2004] E.W.C.A. Civ. 576.

Finally, section 15(1) assumes an equality of bargaining power between the parties, a characteristic it shares with mandatory mediation programmes.[54] One could envisage scenarios where one side with significantly greater financial resources such as the Government or multinational corporations could compel litigants to take part in a mediation process against their will. Fiss argues that in such circumstances their financial resources would "invariably infect the bargaining process"[55] making the other side vulnerable to making an agreement they may not otherwise have made. He notes that such a resource disparity could effect the negotiations in three ways:

> "First, the poorer party may be less able to amass and analyse the information needed to predict the outcome of the litigation, and thus be disadvantaged in the bargaining process. Second, he may need the damages he seeks immediately and thus be induced to settle as a way of accelerating payment, even though he realises he would get less now than he might if he awaited judgement. ... Third, the poorer party might be forced to settle because he does not have the resources to finance the litigation, to cover either his own projected expenses, such as his lawyer's time ...".

Vesting the power for initiating mediation in either party, regardless of the views of the other side, will only serve to strangle the mediation process at birth. If used at all, this lop-sided approach will only serve to alienate the parties to the dispute further resulting in a high number of failed mediation conferences and increased costs to the parties by adding another layer to the civil litigation process. This in turn will colour the litigants' view of the benefits of mediation thereby lowering the numbers of litigants who actually consider it as a viable alternative to litigation.

The mediation conference

The specific wording of the provisions of the legislation relating to mediation requires further analysis.

---

54 *Supra*, n.34.
55 *Ibid.*

Who must attend the conference?

Section 15(1) provides that the court may "direct that the parties to the action meet to discuss and attempt to settle the action." This provision raises a number of questions as to its practical operation. Does this impose an obligation on the litigants to meet personally at such a conference or can they send their legal advisors on their behalf? The only logical interpretation of the section is that it imposes a requirement on the parties themselves, with or without a legal advisor, to attend such a meeting. Any other interpretation would lead to an absurdity and defeat the purpose of mediation. The success of mediation lies in the fact that the litigants have an opportunity to communicate face-to-face. If this provision were interpreted as being satisfied by the parties sending their legal representatives on their behalf the mediation conference would simply move the war to a different battlefield.

Should the legislation have included a further requirement that "the parties" ordered to meet have the authority to settle the action? Such meetings may involve parties who are representing an institution or organisation such as an insurance company. It would be most frustrating, not to mention a waste of time and expense, if after meeting and negotiating a settlement, the other party then left the table to confirm whether the settlement was suitable with his other employers/principal only to return with the news that he or she had no authority to settle and the agreement was "off the table." As Strasser and Randolph have commented:

> "Too many mediations flounder at the final stage, when one of the parties 'disappears' in order to check with his or her board, or executive, or partner, or spouse, or superiors, or the insurers, as to whether the proposed settlement is acceptable."[56]

Duration of the mediation conference

Where the court orders the parties to meet, section 15(3) provides that a mediation conference will take place "at a time" and place agreed by the parties or where the parties do not agree "at a time" and place specified

---

[56] Strasser, F. & Randolph, P., *op. cit.*, p.82.

by the court. Such language would indicate that the legislation only envisages a single meeting, rather than a series of meetings. This would appear to be a further erosion of the autonomy of the parties in dealing with their own dispute. Should it not be the participants' choice as to whether further meetings are required to resolve an impasse? That said, it has been the Canadian experience that cases with more than one mediation session are rare with only 3% of completed mediations requiring more than one session.[57] Strasser & Randolph comment that it is debatable whether imposing time limits on such negotiations is productive:

> "Some believe that if all parties are aware that at, say, 6 pm the mediation will terminate, with or without settlement, it serves to concentrate the mind and precipitate agreement. For as the deadline approaches, the parties are more likely to make concessions, in their desire not to leave without settlement. Others consider that such strictures are not conducive to settlement, and prefer an open-ended stipulation as to duration. Many mediators with experience of the Court Pilot Mediation Schemes, where mediations are conducted strictly between 4.30 pm and 7.30 pm, will argue that the poor settlement rates encountered there are due to these difficulties of time."[58]

The reference to "a time" as opposed to "times" must be deliberate. It is possible that the drafters of the legislation were concerned that to allow for a number of sessions would only increase the costs of litigation. In reality, this restriction may possibly decrease the likelihood of agreement. Without the possibility of meeting again, parties are forced back on the litigation highway, with their costs increased because of their short detour in mediation.

Confidentiality of the mediation process

Section 15(5) of the Act provides:

> "The notes of the chairperson of a mediation conference and all

---

[57] *Supra*, n.56 at p.61.
[58] *Supra*, n.58 at p.102.

communications during a mediation conference or any records or other evidence thereof shall be confidential and shall not be used in evidence in any proceedings whether civil or criminal."

The guarantee of confidentiality is essential to the mediation process. It encourages better communication between the parties who may freely make admissions, or offer concessions, in the knowledge that any such communications could not be used as evidence against them at any subsequent trial of the action.

Section 15(5) states confidentiality applies to all communications made during the mediation conference. It would be wrong to interpret this section as being absolute and where it is in the public policy to do so, exceptions will be recognised. The English Court of Appeal identified some of these exceptions in *Unilever Plc v. The Proctor & Gamble Co.*,[59] as arising where the parties have waived the right to privilege, the claim is not *bona fide* or situations where one of the parties is trying to conceal some reprehensible behaviour.[60]

It is clear that the cloak of confidentiality attaches to admissions made during the mediation conference. However does confidentiality extend to documents or other materials which exist independent of the mediation process? In other words, can one party subsequently seek the discovery of objective material of which he only became aware during mediation? This very issue has been raised in other jurisdictions. In the Australian case of *AWA Ltd v. Daniels*,[61] the plaintiff company commenced proceedings against its auditors (the defendants). The defendants cross-claimed against the former directors of the company. Mediation was ordered.

During the mediation the plaintiff disclosed the existence of an indemnity in which the plaintiff accepted the denial of each director that he was negligent in carrying out his duties in relation to the action commenced by the plaintiff and indemnified them in respect of any such claim. When the case resumed after the failed mediation the defendants sought to obtain a copy of the deed. The plaintiff refused to produce on

---

[59] [1999] 2 All E.R. 691.
[60] *Ibid.*, p.701, *per* Laddie L.J.
[61] (1992) 7 A.C.S.R. 463.

the grounds that, *inter alia*, it was confidential. This raised the question whether an objective fact revealed during mediation could be deemed confidential, and therefore inadmissible, simply by virtue of the fact that it came to the attention of the other side during mediation? In this particular case the issue was somewhat moot as the court found that the defendants and their solicitors were aware of the possibility of the existence of the indemnity in the meeting and thus the issue of confidentiality did not arise. However, Rogers C.J. did take the opportunity to comment on the admissibility of objective fact material revealed during mediation:

> "If the fact that the other side has absolutely no inkling of some matter, which, if known about is capable of being established by objective evidence, but which would not ordinarily come to the knowledge of the other side in the normal progress of litigation and its existence is revealed only by a statement made in the course of, and for the purposes of, the mediation, I would hesitate long before concluding that the objective evidence so revealed is admissible. It is of the essence of successful mediation that parties should be able to reveal all relevant matters without an apprehension that the disclosure may subsequently be used against them. As well were the position otherwise, unscrupulous parties could use and abuse the mediation process by treating it as a gigantic, penalty free discovery process".[62]

Does the element of confidentiality extend to materials compiled as evidence for the purposes of the action and which is revealed at mediation? If such evidence is of objective facts, can the other side seek its disclosure after mediation?

This issue came before the Supreme Court of California in *Rojas v. Los Angeles County Superior Court*.[63] The petitioners were tenants in an apartment complex owned by a third party and which various contractors had built. Prior to the action brought by the tenants, litigation had commenced between the owner of the complex and the contractors. The owner alleged that the complex contained a number of construction

---

[62] *Ibid.*, pp.467–468.
[63] 125 Cal. Rptr. 2d 97 (2002).

defects. In preparation for litigation, the owner compiled evidence of the defects including photographs, videotapes, test results for mould caused by dampness, writings giving the opinions of various experts on the defects etc. A confidential settlement of the action was subsequently reached between the parties.

In the case before the court, the petitioners had brought an action against both the owners of the apartment complex and the contractors who had built it. They alleged that the construction defects in the property had allowed dampness and microbes to infest the building which in turn caused the tenants to suffer ill health. As part of their action, they sought production of the evidence gathered by the owner and which was produced in the earlier mediation with the contractors. The owners argued that all such information was privileged.

In interpreting the relevant legislation,[64] the court found that privilege from disclosure did not apply to "evidence'" or "raw data." The court was of the view that the statute was designed to protect the substance of mediation such as communications and admissions between the parties. Therefore, any evidence of such communications would not be admissible. However, the court distinguished material objects introduced as evidence of the existence or non-existence of certain facts. Such evidence was admissible by virtue of its existence independent of the mediation. In examining whether the other information compiled by the owners of the complex would be privileged, the court drew an analogy with the Californian "work product doctrine." This doctrine provides that material which reflects a lawyer's work, his opinions etc. during preparation for litigation is privileged. The doctrine does not protect factual material *per se* however. In applying the principles of this doctrine, the court decided that:

> "To the extent any of the materials sought are part of a 'compilation' prepared for the mediation are put together in such a manner that it discloses the attorney's or parties' evaluations of the strengths and weaknesses of the case or discloses their negotiation posture, if it can be reasonably detached from the compilation, it must be protected. Thus, photographs in a book labelled 'defects' would be

---

[64] Ss. 1119 and 1120 of the Evidence Code of California.

> removed from the book and given to petitioners singly … test data that in any fashion indicates the attorneys' or parties' evaluation of the case or their negotiation posture, it is protected. However, to the extent such test data may be extrapolated from the chart and given to petitioners, it must be produced."[65]

In conclusion, section 15(5) of the Act, protects the confidentiality of the mediation process. It is in the public interest that this should be so in order to encourage frankness between the parties that will aid the early settlement of disputes. However, both the parties and their legal advisors must be on their guard when making revelations during a mediation conference. Examination of the wording of section 15(5) and case law from other jurisdictions, indicates that it may only be the substance of the mediation that will be privileged. Parties revealing anything, other than their feelings, may find such revelations being used against them at a later trial should the mediation fail.

Mediator's report

If section 15(1) of the Act represents the legislature's attempt at bringing the horse to water, section 16 is its effort to make him drink. It provides that a person appointed as chairperson of the mediation conference shall prepare and submit a report to the court which shall set out:

> "(a) where the mediation conference did not take place, a statement of the reasons as to why it did not take place, or
> (b) where the mediation conference did take place—
> (i) a statement as to whether or not a settlement has been reached in the personal injuries action concerned, and
> (ii) where a settlement has been entered into, a statement of the terms of the settlement signed by the parties thereto."

This provision could have significant implications for the parties to the litigation. Does section 16 place an obligation on the parties to negotiate in good faith? Can the obdurate conduct of one of the parties during the

---

[65] *Supra*, n.63 at p.110.

mediation be reported by the mediator to the court, notwithstanding the confidential nature of the proceedings? How far does this obligation go? Do the parties have to be seen to be 'bending over backwards' to accommodate the other side during negotiations?

Certainly, it would appear that the legislation expects at least a minimum standard of participation from the parties. This standard has been described as the "minimal meaningful participation" standard and would not impose too onerous a duty on the parties:[66]

> "The minimal meaningful participation standard does not direct a comprehensive presentation of the case but, rather, requires little more than the parties briefly discussing their positions as to the relevant issues, listening to the other side, and reacting to the other side's positions."[67]

Thus, it would seem that any party who did not bother to turn up for the mediation, or sent their legal representative instead, could be deemed to have not properly engaged in the process leaving the offending party open to a costs' sanction under section 16(3). It is even possible that a party who sends a representative who does not have "the authority to settle" the dispute could be deemed not to have complied with the direction of the court to mediate.[68]

Moreover, the wording of sections 15 and 16 indicates that the conduct of the parties during the mediation could be the subject of the mediator's report notwithstanding the confidential nature of the mediation process. Section 15(5) states that only "communications" during a mediation conference are privileged. The provision does not include the "conduct of the parties" within the ambit of this privilege. It would therefore appear, that should a party attend the meeting and refuse to take part in any meaningful way, such conduct could be cited by the mediator to the court as one of the reasons why the mediation conference failed.[69]

Not only does the legislation provide for the potential compulsion of

---

[66] Sherman, E., "Court-Mandated Alternative Dispute Resolution: What Form of Participation Should be Required?", 46 *SMU L. Rev*. 1079 (1993).

[67] *Supra*, n.29 at p.965.

[68] *Gee Gee Nick v. Morgan's Foods Inc*., 270 F.3d 590 (8th Cir. 2001).

[69] *Foxgate Homeowners' Association v. Bamalea California Inc*., 25 P.3d 1117 (2001).

one of the parties into mediation, with or without their consent but, once present, he or she is further compelled to participate in the process. Of course, there would be little point in compelling the parties to attend mediation if when present there was no obligation on them to communicate meaningfully with the other party. However, compelling the parties to participate weakens the process. It leads to the further erosion of the parties' self-determination and removes yet another element of control from their grasp. Needless to say, no such requirement would be necessary if the parties were allowed the choice of entering mediation in the first place. That said, it is hoped that when interpreting whether the parties have complied with the court's direction regarding mediation, the "minimal meaningful participation" standard will be applied. To require any more of the parties would place too onerous a burden on their shoulders and could lead to situations where a party feels compelled to reach an agreement, and may accept a settlement which is less than he or she deserves, simply because of a feeling that, if it is refused the conduct would be viewed as being in breach of the court's direction.

Access to justice

Section 16(3)(b) of the Act provides that if the court may:

> "(b) if satisfied that a party to the action failed to comply with a direction under section 15(1).
>
> make an order directing that party to pay the costs of the action, or such part of the costs of the action as the court directs, incurred after the giving of the direction under section 15(1)."

Under this section the court may compel an otherwise unwilling party to participate in mediation before the trial of the action. Should that party refuse to follow the court's direction in this regard, the court may direct such a party to pay the costs of the action. Effectively, section 16 places a restriction on the parties' right of access to the courts, or perhaps more accurately, their right to litigate[70] guaranteed under Article 40.3 of the Constitution and Article 6 of the European Convention on Human Rights.

---

[70] *Tuohy v. Courtney* [1994] 3 I.R. 1.

The right to litigate has been defined as:

> "the right to achieve by action in the courts the appropriate remedy upon proof of an actionable wrong causing damage or loss as recognised by law."[71]

Article 40.3 of the Constitution is not an unfettered right and is subject to such qualifications that are in the public interest. For example, the court has the inherent jurisdiction to manage the litigation process and under the rules of civil procedure it may strike out claims which are frivolous or are considered by the court to be an abuse of process.[72] It has been held that orders for security for costs against a plaintiff may amount to a restriction on the party's right of access to the courts. In *Malone v. Brown Thomas & Co. Ltd.*,[73] Hamilton C.J. warned that, "no unnecessary monetary obstacle should be placed in the path of those who seek access to the courts."[74]

Article 6(1) of the European Convention on Human Rights guarantees the individual's right of access to the courts which includes a right to bring civil proceedings. The European Court of Human Rights has held in *Deweer v. Belgium*[75] that while this right of access may be waived by the parties, any such waiver should be carefully reviewed in order to ensure that it does not unduly constrain the party's right of access. In that case, the plaintiff had waived his right to litigate under an arbitration agreement. The court upheld the validity of the clause as such clauses were necessary for the administration of justice and "did not in principle offend against the Convention."[76] However, the court did state that:

> "Nevertheless, in a democratic society too great an importance attaches to the "right to a court" for its benefit to be forfeited solely by reason of the fact that an individual is a party to a settlement reached in the course of a procedure ancillary to court proceedings.

---

[71] *Ibid.*, p.45.
[72] See generally; Hogan G. and Whyte G. (eds), *Kelly: The Irish Constitution* (4th ed., Lexis Nexis, Dublin, 2003), pp.1446–1464.
[73] [1995] 1 I.L.R.M. 369.
[74] *Ibid.*, p.373.
[75] [1980] 2 E.H.R.R. 439.
[76] *Ibid.*, pp.460–461.

> In an area concerning the public order of the Member States of the Council of Europe, any measure or decision alleged to be in breach of Article 6 calls for particularly careful review".[77]

Certainly, Dyson L.J. in the English Court of Appeal in *Halsey v. Milton Keynes General NHS Trust*,[78] was convinced that court-ordered mediation was in breach of Article 6 arguing "that to oblige truly unwilling parties to refer their disputes to mediation would be to impose an unacceptable obstruction on their right of access to the court."[79] If, according to Dyson L.J. when referring to the *Deweer* decision, "that was the approach of the European Court of Human Rights to an agreement to arbitrate, it seems to us likely that compulsion of ADR would be regarded as an unacceptable constraint on the right of access to the court and, therefore, a violation of Article 6."[80]

It is clear that a direction by the court under section 16(3) where the party would rather to go to trial is a restriction on his right to achieve, through the courts, an appropriate remedy. The English Court of Appeal is of the view that court-enforced mediation is capable of breaching Article 6, hence their reluctance to compel parties against their will into mediation.[81] If this is the case, can such a restriction be justified? It would seem that there would have to be strong reasons for doing so. It could certainly be argued that it is in the public interest that ADR mechanisms be used where possible in order to bring about the early resolution of disputes. This would have the added benefit of saving costs and easing the workload of an already overburdened court system. However, whether the restriction in section 16(3) could be justified on this basis is open to debate.

Conclusion

There can be no doubt that encouraging mediation of personal injury disputes is a very good thing. The advantages of the process as a method

---

[77] *Ibid.*
[78] [2004] E.W.C.A. Civ. 576.
[79] *Ibid.*, para.9.
[80] *Ibid.*
[81] *Supra*, n.78.

of resolving disputes are clear. By encouraging the parties to meet in a mediation forum where the issues between them can be discussed openly and frankly, an earlier and perhaps more satisfactory solution to the dispute can be achieved. However, it is clear that the advantages of mediation as a dispute resolution mechanism are diminished when it is statutorily enforced in an adversarial civil justice system.

Mediation is by very definition a voluntary and non-adversarial process. The question then becomes how does one introduce mediation into an adversarial justice system without its developing the characteristics of that system?

To make mediation mandatory at the behest of the court involves too great a dilution of the parties' autonomy. By depriving the parties of the right to choose whether to go to mediation, it greatly diminishes the likelihood of its success. In such circumstances, it is likely that the parties will resent their own presence at the meeting and the atmosphere will not be conducive to settlement. Proponents of mandatory mediation see it primarily as a method of reducing costs or freeing up the courts' docket. In their view, such goals justify the creation of a mandatory system. Unfortunately, this approach is so blinkered by the benefits of mediation as a cost and time saving device it fails to consider that the other critical feature of mediation lies in providing party satisfaction.

The better approach would be to support the promotion of mediation by the courts. While a direction from a court 'encouraging' the parties to mediate could be interpreted as an order, from the parties' viewpoint there is a qualitative difference. Under such a system the parties would feel that the choice to mediate still rests with them. While there may be some erosion of their self-determination, it will not be as significant as in the case of mandatory mediation. In such circumstances, the parties would enter the mediation in a more conciliatory frame of mind, thereby increasing the chances of a satisfactory outcome.

Instead of making the process mandatory at the instigation of the court, the Oireachtas vested the power to initiate mediation with one party under section 15. This is the worst of both worlds. The party compelled to mediation will resent being called to the meeting and this feeling of resentment will only be magnified where it is the other party to the dispute who is responsible for his presence at the meeting. In such a situation, it is probable that the compelled party will 'dig their heels in' and will not interact with the other side in any meaningful way. While section 15 will herald the greater use of mediation in personal injury actions initially at least, it will also result in a high number of failed mediations and ironically – when one considers the purpose of the legislation – the system will only serve to increase the cost of litigation for all concerned.

It would seem that not only can the court compel a party to attend a mediation conference, but that, once there, it can also compel the parties to make some effort at resolving the dispute. Section 15(5) provides that all communications during the conference are confidential. It is noticeable that the legislation does not include the conduct of the parties within the ambit of that confidentiality. Thus, when a mediator is providing the court with a report as to the reasons why the mediation failed, it would seem likely that the conduct or misconduct of the parties during the mediation could be divulged to the court. It would also seem that should a party send their legal advisor to the meeting in his or her place, or if an organisation or institution sends a representative without authority to settle the matter, this could also be construed as a failure to engage in the process and could be the subject of the mediator's report to the court as to the reasons why the mediation failed. The obligation to engage in the process should be interpreted liberally; otherwise it could place an onerous burden or expectation on the party to settle, or face the wrath of the court at the end of the trial.

Finally, the constitutionality of imposing a costs' sanction for failing to follow the direction of the court under section 15 is questionable. Effectively, the provision penalises a party for exercising his right to litigate. The requirement to meet and engage in a mediation conference unduly fetters this right and it is questionable that it can be justified solely on the grounds that it is in the public interest to settle disputes between private parties as early and as inexpensively as possible.

In conclusion, the promotion of the use of mediation to resolve actions for personal injury is to be welcomed. However, it should not be advocated as a replacement for litigation and it should not be seen as a panacea for the perceived difficulties of our current adversarial system. Mediation is a private informal process concerned with "substantive" rather than "procedural" justice. Litigation contains procedural safeguards designed to protect the rights of the parties whereas no comparable safeguards exist in mediation.

Proponents of court-enforced mediation tend to equate costs' savings with party satisfaction and this is reflected in legislation that has been subsequently enacted. The court-enforced mediation system provided for in the Act threatens litigants' rights to procedural justice. Further, a system which drags one of the parties to the table is unlikely to be very successful in resolving the parties' differences. In practice, mediation could then just become another procedural step or detour on the way to trial. Such a development would only increase costs for the litigants, thereby defeating the purpose of the legislation.

That said it is good to talk and there is room within our civil justice system for a mediation programme. The benefits to the parties and to society as a whole cannot be denied and where appropriate the process is preferable to the trauma and expense of going to trial. However, in order to take full advantage of the benefits of mediation the parties must be willing participants. Of course, an entirely voluntary process may never gain a foothold in the traditional adversarial world of civil litigation. Therefore a court-encouraged system as used in England would be the better option. Such a system would leave as much autonomy to the individual parties as voluntary mediation and while not directing the parties to undergo mediation, would push them towards considering it. Unfortunately, the Oireachtas has missed a wonderful opportunity to introduce a viable alternative to dispute resolution in our civil justice system. In the eagerness to reduce the costs associated with litigation they have produced a somewhat flawed piece of legislation which, rather than promote mediation, will bring it into disrepute with both litigants and lawyers alike.

The Impact of the Act on the "Compensation Culture": Big or Small?

RAY RYAN*

INTRODUCTION

There is a widely held perception that Ireland is in the grip of a "compensation culture," which has profoundly impacted upon Irish society, and not for the better. Professor Binchy has remarked that "Tort law is now in a state of crisis", whilst observing that "a strong spirit of hostility to the old 'compensation culture' is abroad."[1] There is, it seems, across the board support for the idea that this culture requires to be tackled for, in the words of the late Fine Gael TD, Jim Mitchell, it is "a runaway train which must be stopped."[2] The Taoiseach, Mr. Ahern, has described this compensation culture as "an enormously serious problem,"[3] whilst the Minister for Justice, Equality and Law Reform, Mr. McDowell has vowed to "drive a stake into the heart"[4] of this compensation culture. The political orthodoxy has been to present the Personal Injuries Assessment Board Act 2003 and the Civil Liability and Courts Act 2004 as "represent(ing) the Government's legislative response to the crisis caused by the compensation culture."[5] Arguably what characterised the

---

*Scholar, Trinity College Dublin; Barrister. Thanks to Des Ryan for his helpful comments.

1 Binchy, "Recent Developments in the Law of Torts" (2004) 4 (1) *Judicial Studies Institute Journal* 8.
2 Coghlan, "Panic as claims may shred the Budget sums", *Irish Times,* May 6, 1998.
3 *Dáil Debates*, December 15, 1999.
4 Cullen, "Proposed law would cut fraudulent injury claims", *Irish Times*, July 5, 2003.
5 "McDowell publishes Civil Liability and Courts Bill 2004," www.justice.ie/pressreleases.

passage of the Civil Liability and Courts Act 2004 through the various stages in the Oireachtas[6] was the prevailing orthodoxy that this compensation culture had for too long gone unchecked, and needed to be addressed. It seems fair to say that the overwhelming majority of those who articulated views on the merits of the new Act were entirely *ad idem* with the members of the Alliance for Insurance Reform, who have spoken of the "out of control Irish Compensation Culture."[7] Political muscle is behind a campaign to tackle our "blame culture" and it is predicted that the worst excesses of our "compo culture" will be the first casualty of this campaign.[8] In launching this Act, its main architect, the Minister for Justice, Equality and Law Reform, was adamant that it is a major assault on the "compensation culture." Mr. Michael McDowell, said:

> "The Civil Liability and Courts Act 2004 is a major plank in this government's efforts to tackle insurance costs and insurance fraud and I believe that it will dramatically change the way in which personal injury actions are processed. In a very real way, the Act tackles the 'compensation culture' that has developed in this country."[9]

This chapter is concerned with the accuracy of this assertion. This description of the Act by its sponsors has prompted speculation that it may herald the demise of this claims culture in Ireland.[10] Does the Act really represent a full-scale attack on the compensation culture? The question seems one worthy of attention not least because it seems to have been taken for granted that the Act does indeed tackle the perceived compensation culture. But does it do so in any meaningful way? What do we mean when we speak of "tackling the compensation culture"? And, insofar as the development of the law of torts in recent times has been characterised by an acute awareness of what we might term "the societal downside of tort liability", does the 2004 Act provide yet further evidence of a marked shift in the Irish outlook on a claims culture?

---

6 See www.feargalquinn.ie/debates.
7 www.insurancereform.ie.
8 O'Halloran, "Compo culture under fire" *Business and Finance*, February 13, 2003.
9 www.justice.ie/pressreleases ("Minister signs order to bring Civil Liability and Courts Act 2004 into operation").
10 "Is Compo Culture in Danger of Dying Out?", *Irish Independent*, February 21, 2004.

The Compensation Culture – What is it all about?

The term "compensation culture" is not used to describe a society where people are able to seek compensation. Rather a "compensation culture" implies that a decision to seek compensation is wrong. "Compensation culture" is a pejorative term and suggests that those that seek to "blame and claim" should be criticised. It suggests greed, rather than people legitimately enforcing their rights. Few would oppose the principle that if people's rights are infringed, appropriate action should be available to the injured party to gain compensation from the guilty party.[11]

The 2004 Act has been hailed as a considered response to the pernicious effects of a claims culture that has spiralled out of control. It is noteworthy that the current government had taken the trouble to set out such an objective in its programme for government. Intuitively, such an aim seems sensible and desirable. At least, it is scarcely the case that a government would set out as one of its aims to preserve the status quo regarding the compensation system. The very term "compensation culture' conjures up all sorts of negative connotations. These follow all the more readily from the uniquely Irish term "compo culture." On a close analysis, however, precisely what it is that those who rail against this "compo culture" want to eliminate becomes difficult to ascertain. Is there dissatisfaction with the very idea of seeking compensation in respect of injuries suffered as a result of the want of care by another party? Certainly, any attempt to deny such an opportunity raises major difficulties, not least from a constitutional perspective.

Moreover, a real danger with this type of hostility to compensation claims is that it is insensitive to perhaps the great merit of a claims culture – that it is the most effective way to encourage individuals to be solicitous of the bodily integrity of other individuals. The suspicion persists that it has been all too easy for large business groups to complain about the outrageous spectre of liability in Ireland next to other countries, whilst deflecting attention from a health and safety record that does not compare favourably with those same neighbouring countries.[12] These observations

[11] Better Regulation Taskforce Report, May 2004, available at www.brtf.gov.uk/taskforce. *See* Arculus, "Common sense and the claims culture" *The Times Law Supplement*, November 16, 2004.

[12] Armstrong, "Safety management key to tackling 'compo' culture" *Irish Times*, November 24, 2000.

are made at the outset not to colour the analysis that follows, but simply to demonstrate that in a climate where certain interest groups have great clout, and where populist ideas of blitzing our "crazy compo culture" are employed, there is a danger that the pendulum may swing too far the other way.

As the UK Better Regulation Taskforce recently observed:

> "It has got to be right that people who have suffered an injustice through someone else's negligence should be able to claim redress. What is not right is that some people should be led to believe that they can absolve themselves from any personal responsibility for their actions and then expect someone else to pick up the pieces when something goes wrong, regardless of whose fault it was."[13]

Indeed, one might contend that the history of the 2004 Act itself demonstrates the competing needs that require to be served. It is to be recalled that there was considerable momentum behind reducing the Statute of Limitations to just one year. It seems that the concerns voiced to the effect that such a reduction would create manifest injustice – leaving certain individuals without a remedy – prevailed upon the drafters. The Act reduces the limitation period to two years. This serves as a salutary reminder of the tension that exists between a clampdown on a so-called "compo culture" and the need to facilitate appropriate redress for genuinely aggrieved claimants with meritorious claims.

But what of this term, "compo culture"? Is it more perception than reality? Interestingly, a recent UK study into the "compensation culture" in that jurisdiction concluded that "compo culture" was little more than a myth.[14] Litigation is not easy. Plaintiffs have many hurdles to cross. However, even in disposing with entirely frivolous claims, scarce resources are utilised which could be better employed elsewhere. Media hype, the proliferation of rights talk[15] and an erosion of a sense of individual responsibility have all been attributed to the increase in

---

13 www.brtf.gov.uk/docs/pdf/betterroutes.

14 www.brtf.gov.uk/pressreleases/2004/compoculture.asp.

15 American scholar Mary Ann Glendon has memorably captured this "rights talk" phenomenon. Speaking of the US experience, she concludes that this "American rights dialect promotes unrealistic expectations, heightens social conflict, and inhibits dialogue"; moreover, it fosters "a climate that is inhospitable to society's losers" (p.14).

frivolous claims. That these claims are not sustained in the courts is no answer to those disenchanted by the "compo culture." The mere increase in spurious claims has put a drain on public sector resources; it may make businesses and other organisations more cautious for fear of litigation; it contributes to higher insurance premiums and it clogs up the system for those with indisputable claims. For reasons of efficiency and economic expediency, settlements may be reached notwithstanding that claims are without substance or foundation. This in turn fuels the perception held by certain members of the public that the "compo culture" is alive and well. Thus the *perception* becomes reality. It is this perception that needs to be addressed,[16] and that arguably will be addressed to an important extent by the 2004 Act.

The New-Found Hostility to the Claims' Culture

For many, the relentless rolling of the compensation bandwagon has served to foster in a not insignificant minority a mean-spirited, opportunistic mindset. Trivial and exaggerated claims for compensation are made, and all too often resources are allocated to plaintiffs whose claims are in reality almost entirely unmeritorious. Legislative impatience with Ireland's compo culture is of a relatively recent vintage. Some observers might say that it followed inexorably from the Army deafness litigation. Hailed by senior politicians as "immoral" and "the result of a cancer which is eating at the heart of our society",[17] that litigation is estimated to have

In short, Glendon argues that America is the land of the "lone rights bearer" – "helmetless and free on the open road" (p. 46) – who treats rights as entitlements and who uses them as the ultimate weapon: a trump against opponents in which the "winner takes all and the loser has to get out of town" (p.9). (Glendon, *Rights Talk: The Impoverishment of Political Discourse* (New York, Free Press, 1991)).

[16] This ideology, produces the mentality denounced by an English Law Lord in the 1980s:

> "The pleading assumes that we are all neighbours now, Pharisees and Samaritans alike, that foreseeability is a reflection of hindsight and that for every mischance in an accident-prone world someone solvent must be liable in damages"

CBS Songs Ltd v. Amstrad plc [1988] A.C. 1013 at 1060 *per* Lord Templeman. *Cp* the comment of Lord Steyn in *Gorringe v. Calderdale MBC* [2004] U.K.H.L. 15 at [2] that: "the courts must not contribute to the creation of a society bent on litigation, which is premised on the illusion that for every misfortune there is a remedy."

[17] Brennock, "Smith says deafness claims are wrong and immoral", *Irish Times*, December 11, 1997.

cost the exchequer some €300m. There appears to be widespread cynicism about a tort law system that all too frequently allows opportunistic, unmeritorious plaintiffs to board the compensation gravy train. Now, if the popular response to a current controversy is a reliable indicator, this general disenchantment with what is seen as a compensation gravy train is widespread indeed. Consider the coverage given to the news that inmates past and present of Irish prisons have instituted proceedings against the State seeking damages for violation of their human rights suffered through having to "slop out" in their cells.

The prisoners allege that forcing them to slop out in their cells has amounted to a violation of their human rights for which they are entitled to damages. What has characterised the popular response to this issue has not been concern that, in a country that strives to offer the highest standards of human rights protection, such degrading and inhuman treatment is still accepted practice.[18] Arguably it has been the widespread hostility to the claims, and the reference to the pervasive effects of Ireland's perceived "compo culture." In the view of Mr. John Minihan, Chairman of the Progressive Democrats, these claims amount to "an absolute scam" and a "blatant attempt to rip off the Irish taxpayer." Pledging that his party would advocate strong resistance to these claims, Mr. Minihan condemned these claims as "rip-off Ireland at its worst."[19]

This political assault on that culture – purportedly demonstrated by, *inter alia*, the 2004 Act – mirrors developments in other jurisdictions. In Britain, the Conservative Party has been particularly vocal on the need to crack down on the compensation culture there.[20] Further, the appellate courts in England have delivered judgments of late that are quite clearly

---

[18] Cf the Scottish case of *Napier v. The Scottish Ministers*, *The Times*, May 14, 2004, (Outer Session) per Lord Bonomy: "I am entirely satisfied that the petitioner was exposed to conditions of detention which, taken together, were such as to damage his human rights, his human dignity and to arouse in him feelings of anxiety, anguish, inferiority and humiliation. There was no doubt that the appellant was being held "in accordance with law" but the fault was to hold him in conditions which were not proportionate to the need to detain him securely. Such conditions could not be said to be necessary in a democratic society." See Clissmann, "Degrading Treatment in Prison" [2004] *Law Society Gazette* (October) 10.

[19] Brady, "State Confident of Beating Jail Slop-out Claims", *Irish Independent*, September 16, 2004.

[20] Sparrow, "Tory Proposals would Tackle 'Deeply-Rooted' Compensation Culture that is Costing the Country £10bn a Year", *Daily Telegraph*, August 20, 2004.

policy-driven and seek to limit the scope of liability.[21] In May 2004, the BRTF Report examined at length the scale of the "compensation culture."[22] And in Australia, debate has raged –and major legislative developments have arrived– in the wake of the report on the law of negligence authored by Justice David Ipp of the New South Wales Court of Appeal.[23]

The emergency allegedly arising out of the claims culture is presented as being an issue of "distributive justice." Interestingly, when the Supreme Court employed that precise term last year in the course of its landmark judgment in the *Fletcher* case,[24] the court's decision was warmly

---

[21] A landmark decision was that of the House of Lords in *Tomlinson v. Congleton Borough Council* [2004] 1 A.C. 46, where a unanimous court bemoaned the blame culture and routed the idea that compensation for injury could be awarded independently of an assessment of its broader effect on society. This decision has been applauded as recognising "the societal downside of tort liability": see Mullis and Nolan, "Tort" in [2003] All E.R. *Annual Review* 349. Interestingly, a recent Supreme Court decision on the Occupiers' Liability Act 1995, reversing the High Court's decision to impose liability on the occupier, and dismissing the plaintiff's claim, appears to approve of the sentiments expressed in the *Tomlinson* case: *Weir-Rodgers v. The SF Trust Ltd*, unreported, Supreme Court, January 21, 2005 (Murray C.J., Denham and Geoghegan JJ.). See generally Ryan and Ryan, "Trespassers (and Recreational Users) Beware: The Supreme Court decision in *Weir-Rodgers v. The SF Trust Ltd* (2005) 23 *I.L.T. (n.s.)* 56.

[22] *See* n.14, *supra*.

[23] Although any extensive analysis of the Australian position is beyond the scope of this discussion, it is salutary to note the similar disenchantment to a claims culture that has emerged in that jurisdiction. Australia experienced an explosion of litigation in the 1990s, with a succession of class action claims funded with contingency fees, but this boom was brought up short in 2001 when the second largest insurer went bust. The result in Australia has been a retrenchment of both substantive and procedural law, with caps on liability. The most dramatic change is a requirement for a claimant lawyer to certify that the claim he brings is valid. The Civil Liability and Courts Act 2004 doesn't go as far as this (During the debate of the Bill in the Dáil, the leader of the Labour Party, Mr Pat Rabbitte TD, complained that this was a weakness in the Bill) but the tenor of the Act is clearly the same. The Ipp Review's terms of reference asserted that the damages awards for personal injury had become "unaffordable and unsustainable as the principal source of compensation for those injured through the fault of another." It stated: "It is desirable to examine a method for the reform of the common law with the objective of limiting liability and quantum of damages arising from personal injury and death." See *Review of the Law of Negligence*, Second Report, Canberra, September 2002, (available at http://revofneg.treasury.gov.au/content/review2.asp). Further, see Ipp, "Policy and the Swing of the Negligence Pendulum" (2003) 77 Australian Law Journal 732.

[24] *Fletcher v. Commissioner of Public Works* [2003] 1 I.R. 465; [2003] 2 I.L.R.M. 94 (SC).

welcomed in the Dáil by the then Minister for Finance, Mr Charles McCreevy. Mr McCreevy described *Fletcher* as "a major step in reversing the compensation culture which has become endemic in this country in recent years."[25] In a time when the liability pendulum has arguably swung too far in plaintiffs' favour, judges have grown impatient with attempts to extend further the boundaries of tortious liability. The evidence of this trend at Superior Court level has been discussed elsewhere.[26] A shift too has been evident at Circuit Court level of late. There have been repeated instances in the last few years of Circuit Court judges seemingly taking a firmer stance on compensation claims.[27] The Circuit Court's President, Mr Justice Smyth, said of a plaintiff in one case that he was "one of a number of people suffering from a disease present in the Irish legal system, the symptoms of which are concoction and exaggeration."[28] And just prior to his retirement, Judge Liam Devally spoke in the course of dismissing a compensation claim of "a rabid disease which was spreading like wildfire." This disease, for Judge Devally, was "a mental disease that will challenge the lexicographers of medical dictionaries to define, a mindset which I can only describe as compensationitis."[29]

Insofar, then, as the target of those railing against the "compo culture" is this *mindset*, the impact of legislative measures is treacherously difficult to predict. However, and sensitive to Professor Hedley's caution that the 2004 Act "should properly be regarded as the beginning of the fight, not the end"[30] – the Act does bring reforms to the "system" that can be seen as an effective response to the compensation culture. In the analysis that

---

[25] Newman, "McCreevy Hails Asbestos Judgment", *Irish Times*, February 22, 2003.

[26] See Ryan and Ryan "Some Comments about Caution: Emerging Trends in Irish Negligence Law" (2004) 7 *Trinity College Law Review* 114. See also Byrne and Binchy, *Annual Review of Irish Law 2001* (Thomson Roundhall 2002); Binchy "The PIAB Act: Implications for Tort Law and Practice" in Binchy and Quigley, *The Personal Injuries Assessment Board Act 2003: Implications for Legal Practice* (Firstlaw, Dublin, , 2004).

[27] See, e.g, Healy "Judge Says Day of Suing Council for Fall on Path is Over", *Irish Times*, March 12, 2004.

[28] See McDonald, "Tables Turn on Personal Injury Claims" *Sunday Times*, December 1, 2002.

[29] "'Compensationitis' attacked", *Irish Times*, December 16, 2000.

[30] Hedley, "The Rise and Rise of Personal Injury Liability: A Temporary Difficulty or a Permanent Crisis?" Inaugural Lecture, University College Cork, January 22, 2004 at www.ucc.ie/law/faculty/hedley_text.doc (accessed October 17, 2004), reproduced later in this publication.

follows, it will be suggested that this is so not least because the 2004 Act, arguably for the first time, symbolises a societal intolerance of a culture of advancing claims for monetary compensation that are frivolous, exaggerated and generally without merit.

The climate in recent times, then, has been one of a definite hardening in attitude – judicial, political, societal – to the relentless rolling of a compensation bandwagon. It is against this background that the Civil Liability and Courts Act 2004 was enacted.

Debate surrounding the compensation culture has been heated, with an absence of authoritative statistical data and a certain amount of mudslinging between various interest groups such as the legal profession, the insurance industry, trade unions and business groups. Accordingly it seems opportune to commence the analysis with what is almost universally accepted – that mechanisms to weed out fraudulent and vexatious claims are necessary, timely and welcome.

The 2004 Act and Fraudulent Claims

Perhaps the feature of the Act which has attracted most attention is the provision dealing with fraudulent and exaggerated claims. This is certainly true in respect of those commentators who have sought to present the Act as an attack on the compensation culture.[31] The scourge of fraudulent claims and problems of proof have been exercising the courts of late in formulating the law in crucial liability issues.[32] Section 26(1) of the 2004 Act provides that:

> "If … a plaintiff in a personal injuries action gives … evidence that:
>
> (*a*) is false or misleading, in any material respect, and

[31] Dowling, "Liars Face Jail in Bid to Crush Compo Culture", *Irish Independent*, July 5, 2003.

[32] *Pace* Kearns J. in *Cuddy v. Mays*, unreported, High Court, November 28, 2003: "Should not the possibility of exaggerated, or even fraudulent claims, in this area not weigh heavily with judges whose sympathies may all too easily be won over by horrifying accounts of such accidents and their aftermath?" See also Geoghegan J.'s sentiments in *Fletcher*, whilst noting "public policy considerations which have been put forward in other cases and, indeed, were put forward by counsel for the defendants in this case are the dangers of fraudulent claims and problems of proof": [2003] 1 I.R. 465 at 514.

> (*b*) he or she knows to be false or misleading,
> the court shall dismiss the plaintiff's action unless, for reasons that the court shall state in its decision, the dismissal of the action would result in injustice being done."

The section equally applies this to plaintiffs who have knowingly sworn by affidavit evidence which is misleading.[33]

The requirement that plaintiffs supply an affidavit attesting the veracity of their claims is set down in section 26(2) The importance of this introduction ought not to be underestimated, not least because it is the provision of an affidavit that would make the securing of a conviction for the provision of misleading evidence readily attainable.[34]

The penalties for providing such misleading evidence are swingeing indeed: section 29 sets out that a person convicted of having furnished such evidence "shall be liable ... to a fine not exceeding €100,000 or imprisonment for a term not exceeding 10 years, or to both."

It is clear that the shadow of fraudulent claims loomed large in the framing of the 2004 Act. Any economic analysis of a compensation system such as that operating in Ireland acknowledges that, over time, certain distortions are engendered by the system. One such distortion of any system where compensation is available is that some individuals will feign injury and advance false claims in order to secure compensation. The problem of dishonest claims has received considerable attention of late. It was the subject of an RTÉ *Prime Time* documentary in 2002, after which it was reported that insurance companies were engaging the services of private detectives to investigate suspect claims. CCTV footage from a Supermacs restaurant which clearly showed a number of individuals staging a slip and fall "accident", has been broadcast. The Irish Insurance Federation (IIF) estimates that fraudulent and spurious claims cost insurers – and therefore Irish policyholders – some €100 million annually. And the "pick-pocket" radio advertisements used to discourage exaggerated

---

[33] S.26(2).

[34] Note the views of the former Chairman of the Bar Council, Mr. Conor Maguire SC: "If you had a verifying affidavit being sworn by the plaintiff as to the truth of all his evidence, it would be much easier to ground a prosecution where the actual evidence turns out to be very different. All you would need would be a change in the rules of court and legislation to cover the nature of the affidavit, its contents, the consequences and the penalties.": O'Halloran n.8, *supra*.

compensation claims – emphasising that you and I are left to pick up the tab – appear to have been highly effective in highlighting the cost of dishonest claims to the community as a whole.

But prosecutions for perjury following the tendering of false evidence in a civil case were virtually unheard of, and the absence of any emphatic legislative deterrent to those minded to make false claims was seen as a lacuna in the law. At a symbolic level then, the attempt to crack down on such claims is important. Further, the sentiments behind the enactment of these provisions are entirely consistent with an impatient approach to exaggerated/concocted claims that has manifested itself at Supreme Court level of late.[35]

Welcoming the new penalties for fraudulent claimants, an IIF spokesman said that "This legislation is the big stick that we have been seeking to finally deal with fraudulent compensation claims."[36]

But, whilst this tough new stance on fraudulent claims commands – and deserves– overwhelming support, can we say with any degree of confidence that it will have any significant effect on our compensation culture? Given the controversy over the extent to which such fraud exists, any change in this regard is likely to be difficult to monitor.[37] Concededly, the long term impact of, say, a number of high profile prosecutions involving those charged with making false claims – in terms of chipping away at a culture of exaggeration and concoction – ought not to be underestimated. But given the uncertainty surrounding the extent of this

---

[35] *Pace*, e,g, Hardiman J. in *Shelley-Morris v. Dublin Bus* [2003] 1 I.R. 232 at 258: "It must not be thought that a falsehood in respect of one aspect of a claim will, at worst, lead to that particular part of the claim being reduced or disallowed. The Courts have a power and duty to protect their own processes from being made the vehicle of unjustified recovery. In a proper case this will be done by staying or striking out the plaintiff's proceedings." See also *O'Connor v. Dublin* Bus [2003] 4 I.R. 459 (SC).

[36] See Dowling, n.32, *supra*.

[37] Professor Hedley remarks that: "*Perhaps* the new provisions on fraud will deter some of the more outrageous lies and fabrications. But while everyone knows that there is fraud, nobody really knows how much there is, or how easy it will be to detect; it is not obvious, therefore, how great a reduction in claims can be achieved by this method." Hedley, "The Rise and Rise of Personal Injury Liability: A Temporary Difficulty or a Permanent Crisis?" Inaugural Lecture, University College Cork, January 22, 2004, at www.ucc.ie/law/faculty/hedley_text.doc (accessed October 17, 2004) (emphasis in original).

problem,[38] the likelihood that the great majority of cases in which fraud, or at least exaggeration/embellishment is present never see the inside of a courtroom, and the presumably thick skin of those disposed to make false claims, the suggestion that this measure alone will somehow blitz the compensation culture seems wildly overstated. This is not to suggest that these provisions will have *no* effect or will make a negligible contribution: it is simply to emphasise that their impact is likely to be far less dramatic than some commentators have predicted.

The Minister for Justice has insisted that these provisions will result in fraudulent claims being much more heavily contested by insurers, since insurance companies will now have the incentive that if they can show that any material portion of a claim is brought in bad faith, the claim in its entirety will be struck out. While this is unimpeachable *in theory*, in practice, will insurers really be willing to resist a far higher percentage of claims than at present, to the point of fighting them in court? Does it not seem plausible to suggest that in a great number of those very cases where the suspicion of fraud exists, the insurers will know that any order for costs they may secure against the plaintiff would be virtually worthless, in terms of actually seeking to enforce it? Insurance companies – not being in the habit of throwing good money after bad – will not suddenly be defending far more cases in court, where there is a reasonable suspicion of fraud. This is not to criticise the effectiveness of the new provisions. Rather it is an acknowledgment of the mundane reality that, even assuming Minister McDowell is correct about the "incentive" he has given to insurers, it is dwarfed by one of the greatest incentives of them all – avoiding the enormous costs of litigation. This lamentable state of affairs has recently been described by the second most senior judge in England and Wales, as the system of blackmail at the root of the compensation culture.[39]

The Master of the Rolls, Lord Phillips, has complained of the daily occurrence where, even where the plaintiff's claim seemed somewhat weak and unlikely to be sustained in a court, the costs of fighting the case would have been so entirely disproportionate to the sum that would secure

---

[38] See Humphreys, "Insurance Body Study Challenges Perception of 'Compo' Culture", *Irish Times*, January 27, 2003.

[39] See Driscoll, "Judge Risk – It Dares You to Live on the Edge", *Sunday Times*, August 15, 2004.

a settlement, or even to the level of damages payable were the plaintiff to succeed,[40] that vigorously defending even suspect claims was simply not an option. Opportunistic, unscrupulous individuals make claims in respect of personal injury, which would be virtually impossible to disprove. They do so secure in the knowledge that the temptation to throw them a sum of money that is modest in comparison to potential litigation costs, in full and final settlement, may well prove too great for the defendant to resist ("the ransom factor"). On one view this is *the* great inefficiency of a system such as ours: simple cost considerations leading to the early settlement of "nuisance" cases that could be successfully defended.

In the final analysis on this particular feature of the Act then, it would be too much to imagine that these new sanctions and deterrents will bring an end to fraudulent claims. However, these measures are an important statement of intent with regard to the activity of making a fraudulent claim. The idea that the plaintiff who fabricates a story or greatly exaggerates it is some sort of "likeable rogue", who is merely getting a windfall from some faceless insurance company must be abandoned. Such dishonesty is entirely unacceptable, and ultimately involves the distribution of resources in a most antisocial manner. All, presumably, would endorse the hope of the Minister for Justice that these anti-fraud measures will "mark a significant watershed in our efforts to combat those unscrupulous individuals who embark on legal actions for compensation on a fraudulent or exaggerated basis in order to enrich themselves at the expense of the wider community."

Previous "Form" of the Plaintiff: The Effect of Section 11

Much was made in the Dáil debates of the 2004 Act's innovation that plaintiffs will now have to disclose to defendants, information regarding previous compensation claims they have made. This is seen as an effective deterrent to those individuals who would be minded to claim compensation repeatedly for "injuries" suffered, often in similar circumstances.

---

[40] Or, of course, the cost in real terms where the insurer had no prospect of enforcing an order for costs against the plaintiff.

Anecdotally, at least, this phenomenon was quite conspicuous when the "compensation culture" first emerged in Ireland. For example, when Dublin Corporation began to find itself subject to an increasing number of claims, many of those claims –reportedly at least– were made by the same families, who were well used to having recourse to litigation. Of late, Tralee Town Council has taken to publishing the names of those who have sued for compensation, apparently leading to a reduction in the number of claims.[41]

The legislative response to those who make repeated claims for compensation is to be found in section 11 of the 2004 Act. Section 11 provides, *inter alia*, that

> "(1) Upon the request of a defendant in a personal injuries action, the plaintiff shall provide the defendant with—
> (*a*) particulars of any personal injuries action brought by the plaintiff in which a court made an award of damages,
> (*b*) particulars of any personal injuries action brought by the plaintiff which was withdrawn or settled."

Failure by the plaintiff to comply with such a request could be fatal to his or her claim, with the court enjoying a discretion under section 11(3)(a)(ii) to dismiss the plaintiff's action, where it considers that the interests of justice so require. The impact of section 11 is a matter of conjecture. Certainly it will not be welcomed by those who have a "track record" of claiming– and presumably receiving– compensation. Nobody suggests, of course, that a plaintiff who has had the misfortune to have been injured in the past because of the unlawful behaviour of another should be in any way prejudiced by that past experience. But, frankly, there are cases on record where individuals have been awarded compensation, and it is their twenty fifth compensation award in the last six years. To borrow a phrase from the law of evidence: "The man who wins the lottery once is envied; the one who wins it twice is investigated."[42]

Doubtless insurance companies welcome this aspect of the 2004 Act. Evidence of a claims history will be grist to the mill of counsel for the

---

[41] Lucey, "Claims Drop as those who Sue are Named", *Irish Times*, August 14, 2003.
[42] *United States v. York*, 933 F.2d 1343 (7th Cir. 1991), at p.1350.

defendants in their cross-examination of the plaintiff. It seems reasonable to conclude that in many cases such evidence will be influential; in some it will be determinative in causing the claim to be struck out. Again, this measure is a welcome one since it simply *should* be more difficult for the plaintiff with a long history of seeking compensation to recover than for the plaintiff who is advancing his or her first claim for compensation. In any event, the plaintiff's prior "form" is relevant information which defendants may have been denied heretofore. Inasmuch as the deficiencies which the 2004 Act purports to address were seen as skewing the system in favour of plaintiffs, a measure such as section 11 serves to level the playing field.

However, although section 11 is to be welcomed, a caveat must be entered. The goal is balance, and section 11 must not be used as a blunt instrument to deny a plaintiff appropriate compensation merely because of the fact that that plaintiff has been awarded compensation on a previous occasion. The following words of caution from O'Toole carry considerable weight:

> "If a plaintiff receives a six-figure sum arising out of a personal injuries action some years earlier, then subsequently brings a claim arising out of an accident where he actually suffered less serious injuries that are not affected by the earlier injuries, why should a court have regard to the earlier award or settlement when such regard will only have the effect of reducing its award to benefit the insurers?"[43]

Reducing the Statute of Limitations

Will the reduction of the Statute of Limitations in cases of personal injury to two years – contained in section 7 of the 2004 Act – impact to any appreciable extent on the compensation culture? Presumably the thinking behind this initiative – and remember that initially it was proposed to reduce the limitation period to just *one* year – was to ease the plight of defendants, and to result in fewer claims being made. As a matter of

---

[43] O'Toole "Why we should fight the PIAB Tooth-and-Nail" [2004] *Law Society Gazette* 18.

logic, it seems axiomatic that more claims will be barred when the period is two years as opposed to three. But, as against this, we note Professor Hedley's view that:

> "*Perhaps* reducing the limitation period will reduce the number of claims, but equally it may have the reverse effect: lawyers will know that if they do not sue quickly they will not be able to sue at all, and so perhaps they will issue a summons where they might earlier have let matters ride."[44]

What can be said with confidence is that the reduction in time is consistent with the overall tenor of Part 2 of the Act, and has been introduced to redress a perceived imbalance in personal injury litigation that was unduly benevolent to plaintiffs. But if it brings any change, the reduction is more likely to manifest cases of injustice than it is to make any noticeable impression on the culture of seeking compensation. That is, while *bona fide* plaintiffs agonizing over what steps to take in respect of a wrong that may be life-altering in its impact may fall victim to the change in section 7, it may be that those disposed to make frivolous, opportunistic claims for compensation find that two years is ample time in which to do so.

The novel requirement in section 8 of the Act that the plaintiff furnish in writing to the defendant details of the alleged wrong within two months falls to be considered in this context. Presumably the legislative thinking here is that this requirement supplements nicely the reduction of the limitation period in the preceding section, acting as a filtering device: there is a certain logic to the thinking that those disposed to advance spurious claims are less likely to comply with the two month deadline. Of course, failing to comply with this two month deadline will not mean automatic dismissal of the case. It will be interesting to monitor the willingness with which the courts exercise their discretion under section 8 with regards to the plaintiff's costs. Is section 8 manifestly anti-claimant? Certainly, it was not introduced to make things easier for *plaintiffs*. Insofar as the 2004 Act might be regarded as representing a shift in favour of defendants, sections 7 and 8 are undoubtedly important elements of that shift.

---

[44] Hedley, *op. cit.*, n.37 *supra*. Emphasis in original.

DAMAGES IN PERSONAL INJURIES CASES:[45] THE IMPACT OF SECTION 22

A concern that damages awards in personal injury cases are too high is discernible in the legislative initiative provided in section 22. As a preliminary point here, that the level of damages is an important variable when considering a so-called compensation culture. Robert Pierse noted six years ago that there was "a crisis in quantum" which called for new initiatives; and that a damages-fuelled compensation culture posed considerable sociological and legal problems.[46]

By any standards, section 22 of the 2004 Act brings an important change to the law. Under section 22(1) "the court shall, in assessing damages in a personal injuries action, have regard to the Book of Quantum." The Book of Quantum created by the PIAB Act 2003, of course, sets out threshold levels of damages to be awarded for different categories of injury. The highest amount to be awarded in the Book of Quantum is €300,000. Will the practical effect of section 22 be to keep awards in personal injury cases reasonably in line with the Book of Quantum figures?[47]

What is the significance of this section, it might be asked, in an analysis of the impact of the Act on the compensation culture? Two points might be in order. First, in seeking to address a distortion that is contributing to the claims culture (presumably in this instance the unpredictability of awards, and what is perceived as their overgenerous nature) the pendulum may swing too far the other way (just as it would have had the statute of limitations been reduced to *one* year[48]). Secondly – and relatedly – even if section 22 has the effect of reducing the overall damages bill which defendants face,[49] it is a neat point whether this in any sense amounts to

---

45 For valuable discussion, see Pierse, "Guessing Damages in Personal Injury Cases- A Practitioner's View" (2005) 23 *Irish Law Times* (*n.s.*) 43.

46 See Newman, "Warning on Crisis in Injuries Awards", *Irish Times*, April 6, 1998.

47 Cf s.22(2)(1) which provides that this " shall not operate to prohibit a court from having regard to matters other than the Book of Quantum when assessing damages in a personal injuries action."

48 For compelling argument to this effect, *see* Burke, "Why Bad Law is not the Answer to Rising Insurance Costs", *Irish Times*, February 20, 2004.

49 Note O'Dwyer's view that s.22 of the Act is "already causing problems for *defendants* as plaintiffs now expect to receive the damages specified in the Book (of Quantum), which many observers believe to be quite generous (€14,400 for a whiplash injury to

an attack on the compensation culture. Without wanting to be overly pessimistic, at this juncture, there are broadly echoes of the earlier sentiments expression in relation to the effect of the reduction of the limitation period. Were a reduction in damages awards to materialise, it is possible that this would be no real disincentive to those of the "look for compensation" mentality referred to, but it may well produce cases of hardship where those who have suffered serious injury perhaps go under compensated.

Intervention in a Personal Injuries Action: The Effect of Section 22

The 2004 Act provides for a novel process in the course of a Supreme Court hearing of an appeal in a personal injuries action. Section 21(1) of the Act merits careful attention:

> "The Supreme Court may, upon an appeal to it in a personal injuries action, invite such persons as it considers appropriate to make submissions to the court—
>
> (*a*) in relation to any matter concerning either liability or damages that it considers to be of exceptional public importance,
>
> and
>
> (*b*) if the action belongs to a class of causes of action in which the same or a similar matter arises."

Here there is a legislative aspiration to ensure that in a test case with major ramifications for a particular area of liability, as well as for the public purse, the Supreme Court will be made fully cognizant of the policy concerns that surround such a claim. Interestingly the Dáil exchanges in this regard focused on the recent Supreme Court decision in the *Fletcher* case. It seems that *Fletcher* is precisely the type of litigation that the drafters of the 2004 Act had in mind.[50] This was a classic test case, with

---

the neck from which the plaintiff has substantially recovered within twelve months is one example that is often quoted): O'Dwyer, "New Procedures for Personal Injuries Claims" (2004) 9 *Bar Review* 199, at 204 (emphasis added).

[50] See Nolan, "The Civil Liability and Courts Act 2004"(2004) 9 *Bar Review* 181.

many millions of euro riding on the result. In ruminating on the legislative outlook in publishing the 2004 Act, and on the possible path which lies ahead for Ireland's compo culture and section 21 of the 2004 Act, it is worthwhile to record what Minister McDowell had to say in the Dáil about *Fletcher:*

> "When I was Attorney General, a series of such cases was brought against the State by State employees. The claims were not made on the basis of having suffered asbestosis or any of its symptoms, but because those involved, who now realised they had been exposed to asbestos in the course of their work, claimed to have suffered psychological trauma as a result. A raft of cases was brought against the State and substantial damages – between €30,000 and €60,000 – were awarded in the High Court in the first instance as a result of the alleged psychological damage. The Supreme Court eventually reversed the judgment in one of the cases, which was good. The Attorney General and I want to introduce a system whereby his office can intervene at an early stage in such cases to point out that they may cost about €200 million to the State or about €100 million to Irish employers. The question of whether such cases are reasonable should be examined at an early stage."[51]

For the architects of the 2004 Act, then, *Fletcher* is the type of litigation in which the judicial response must be based on political and economic pragmatism. The only option is to strike out such claims, because that is the outcome rooted in public policy. Such plaintiffs are mountebanks, looking for a meal ticket at the taxpayers' expense for "harm" that is trivial, and "damage" that has been concocted.

Or are they? Aren't we after all speaking of *Fletcher*, the case in which the State had, in egregious dereliction of its duty, needlessly exposed its servants to asbestos, the substance which we now know has been quietly killing many thousands of people for the last thirty years or so? Is not *Fletcher* the case where the plaintiff was found by the High Court to *bona fide* have been haunted by fear having learned of his exposure to

---

[51] Address to Oireachtas Committee on Enterprise and Small Business, July 22, 2003 (at www. irlgov.ie/oireachtas/ Committees-29th-Dáil/jcesb-debates/jesb220703.rtf.

asbestos, and was found to be suffering with an anxiety neurosis disorder by an eminent consultant?

The plaintiff in *Fletcher* was a worthy plaintiff, and an unlucky loser.[52] The point for present purposes, however, is that saving the Exchequer's money in these test cases might one day prove to be the falsest of false economies. There is something to be said, surely, for a legal system that vindicates the rights of vulnerable individuals who have been exposed to asbestos.

The key point for present purposes is that section 21 might *possibly* – and one oughtn't put it any more firmly than that – result in the politicisation of high profile liability cases where there would be heavy fiscal implications in the event of the plaintiff is being allowed to recover. Certainly it seems reasonable to speculate that in such litigation the State, in seeking to resist the claim, will inevitably be deploying arguments about distributive justice and the wider societal implications of allowing recovery. Possibly then, section 21 – which may have seemed one of the less important initiatives – takes on a good deal of significance. Moreover, the section, at a symbolic level, gives legislative backing to, and legitimises, the idea that it is perfectly permissible – nay, necessary – to take cognizance of broader societal concerns in these test cases. Will the asbestos litigation, the army deafness claims, or dare one say it, the prison slop out cases ever be the same again?

Conclusion

Accordingly, and by way of conclusion, the 2004 Act can indeed be seen as an important attack on the compensation culture. This chapter has sought to emphasise that the impact of the Act on the compensation culture

---

[52] Cf *Grieves v. FT Everard & Sons*, Q.B.D., February 15, 2005, Holland J. where *Fletcher's* case was considered but distinguished. Insurers had sought to argue they were not liable to pay compensation for "pleural plaques" (benign scarring of the lining of the lung) on the basis, *inter alia*, that sufferers developed psychological rather than physical symptoms. Holland J rejected this contention, and stated – persuasively – that: "I cannot myself regard as minimal the presence of asbestos within the body that is permanent, raising a possibility (albeit no higher than that) of the future onset of asbestosis or the even more daunting mesothelioma. Vivid from the trial is the impact of that possibility upon impressive, far from hysterical claimants, notwith-standing consistent medical reassurance."

must not be assessed in isolation but must rather be viewed against the backdrop of a deeper change in attitude towards civil liability generally. The Act – through welcome initiatives such as the crack down on fraudulent claims in section 26 – targets in a forceful way some of the worst spin-offs of our claims culture. In other respects, such as the provisions in section 10,[53] and the reduction of the statute of limitations in section 7, the legislation can be seen to be positively "pro-defendant" Analogous to the earlier argument about how the perception of a compo culture feeds into the system, causing that culture to become a reality, perhaps a clearly stated disenchantment with that culture is an important development in its own right – regardless of its effectiveness. Time may yet come to record that the fact that the growing intolerance of a claims culture discussed earlier reached its zenith in 2004 with a piece of legislation heralded as the first meaningful assault on that culture was *in itself* something of a turning point. Professor Hedley has commented that:

> "The problem of too many tort claims is not a temporary little difficulty which can simply be removed by some legislation. Whatever we do to patch it up for now will only take the pressure off for a short while. The law's expansionist tendencies mean that there is a permanent crisis, which we will always need to keep an eye on."[54]

The 2004 Act is the starting point in a war on the compo culture. It represents the first real legislative hostility to that culture. The battle will not be won overnight. It will fall to society as a whole to carry on the prosecution of a war on our compo culture that has commenced with the enactment of the Civil Liability and Courts Act 2004.

The goal, however, ought to be to prosecute such a 'war' whilst simultaneously ensuring that the pendulum does not swing too far towards defendants. In reflecting on what type of "system" of civil liability our society aims for, it seems opportune to end with the following observation

---

[53] S.10, creating the "personal injuries summons," is an important feature, and a response to what was described in the Dáil debates as the phenomenon of "trial by ambush." It is seen as a levelling of the playing field, and a measure that ensures defendants will have every opportunity to defend effectively a claim by having full access to the particulars at an early stage.

[54] Hedley *op. cit.*, n.37 *supra*.

from the Chief Justice of Canada:

> "Tort law is about compensating those who are wrongfully injured. But even more fundamentally, it is about recognising and righting wrongful conduct by one person or a group of persons that harms others. If tort law becomes incapable of recognising important wrongs, and hence incapable of righting them, victims will be left with a sense of grievance and the public will be left with a feeling that justice is not what it should be."[55]

[55] Beverly MacLachlin, "Negligence Law – Proving the Connection" in *Torts Tomorrow, A Tribute to John Fleming*, eds Mullany and Linden (LBC Information Services 1998) 16.

Successful Mediation

HONORABLE MICHAEL J. GALLAGHER* and JOHN V. SMITH II**

The Civil Liability and Courts Act 2004 includes a provision for a mediation conference. An analysis of the specific details for the mediation conference is already well discussed elsewhere.[1] Our goal is to provide the reader with a description of the impact of mediation in the Circuit Court of Cook County, located in Chicago, Illinois, which is the largest independent court system in the United States. Although there are other areas with a larger combination of court systems, the Circuit Court of Cook County is the largest judiciary system in the world. It has a large volume of litigation including a system for mandatory mediation that can be ordered by any particular trial judge.

In analysing whether a mediation program will succeed or fail, the successes and failures from our jurisdiction serve as a useful test laboratory for the analysis of mediation as set forth by the 2004 Act. It is the view of these authors that mediation is a very helpful process to the system of litigation and will succeed in Ireland. We have found that mediation becomes more and more successful in almost every area where mediation is introduced. We appreciate that the litigation environment in Cork County is radically different from that in Ireland. The centrality of the jury in tort litigation certainly affects how cases are settled. But the process of settlement involves human characteristics that are universal.[2] Haggling can be expected in many, perhaps most, cases as the trial approaches trial."

The clear advantage of mediation is that the negotiations take place

*Justice Michael J. Gallagher, Appellate Court Justice, Illinois. Prior to his elevation to the Appellate Court, Justice Gallagher served as a judge in the Circuit Court of Cook County, where he was responsible for overseeing settlements and negotiations in many cases that appearted before him.

**John V. Smith II is an Equity Partner in the law firm of Pretzel & Stouffer, and is a Trial Attorney in Cook County. He is a certified mediator in the Circuit Court of Cook County and is also a member of the International Association of Dispute Resolution.

1 See Corbett, *supra*, pp.103 *et seq.*
2 Dáil Select Committee, July 6, 2004, Cols 1243–1245.

in a more organised process rather than on the courtroom steps or in the Round Hall. Litigants are better served if their decisions are made in a thoughtful manner rather than in the crucible of pressure that occurs immediately before trial begins. Our experience is that the mediation programmes in the United States, especially in the Circuit Court of Cook County, have created an atmosphere for some cases that allow a successful resolution of complex issues.

The Reasons why Mediation will be a Useful Settlement Tool in Ireland

Mediation is no more than a tool that can be employed to resolve certain types of litigation. Mediation has been found to be most useful in several situations. First, mediation is helpful when both parties prefer to maintain the appearance that they will never give an inch regardless of how long it will take justice to prevail. Opposing counsel may confess, confidentially, that the attempt to negotiate a settlement is a fine idea, but there is no way to raise the issue without appearing weak or conciliatory to the opponent. Court ordered mediation allows both sides to appear "reluctant" to move forward with the negotiations even though both parties may secretly welcome the chance.

A second type of litigation that is ripe for mediation is the case where one counsel or the other is extremely unreasonable in his or her settlement position. The advantage of mediation is that both sides to the litigation usually come to some type of agreement on the identity of the mediator. In Cook County, a practice has developed of "co-mediators" with one mediator typically representing plaintiffs and the second mediator typically representing defendants. This team of "co-mediators" often has significant success with litigants and counsel who take an unreasonable settlement position. The reason for this success is that the counsel who take the arguably unreasonable position is confronted by counsel who often is "on the same side."

A third area where mediation is often successful involves the party with unrealistic expectations. Where the neighbour or cousin has created unreasonable expectations, a counsel often has difficulty convincing his own client that the client has unrealistic expectations. Since counsel will not disclose to his or her opponent that he disagrees with his or her client's position, a mediator is often the needed third party who provides sound advice to the client. The mediator can strongly express opinions that might bruise the relationship between the counsel and his or her client if the counsel pushed "too hard" to bring the client to a more reasonable position.

A final area where mediation in similar types of litigation has proven successful are those cases where there are a group of defendants who agree that settlement is best, but cannot agree on the settlement amount or on the percentage of contribution to the settlement for each defendant. A friendly colleague usually has more success in persuading a counsel with an unreasonable demand to face reality. A "preliminary mediation" among the defendants is often very useful in sorting out the disagreements among the defendants who then resolve their differences through mediation. When the preliminary mediation has resulted in an agreement among defendants, the defendants then move forward to the primary mediation as a united front.

There are many other areas where mediation creates a very successful result; both authors here have served as counsel during mediation and as mediators. Although there are certainly mediations that result in disappointing results, mediation usually provides some degree of success and, more often than not, leads to a resolution of the lawsuit.

THE KEYS TO SUCCESSFUL MEDIATION

There are several factors that will statistically increase the likelihood of a successful mediation. Our experience is based on the culture and personalities present in both the Circuit Court of Cook County and the Appellate Court of the State of Illinois. Nevertheless, the human psychological factor that is common to litigants and counsel as they approach trial means that some of the keys to success in the area of Chicago may also translate to successful mediation in Ireland.

Let us now explore some of the principles that lead to a successful mediation result. The most important decision is the identity of the mediator or co-mediators. In the mediation programme in place in the Circuit Court of Cook County information relating to the mediators is readily available. Training as a mediator, trial experience and certain types of litigation experience, and even the rate of success from prior mediation efforts is described in good detail. An important consideration is identifying a mediator who is well-respected by your opponent. A mediator should also have significant experience in the type of litigation that is the focus of the dispute. There are often certain "key times" during the mediation when the mediator can provide an opinion that the mediator's experience does or does not support a position held by either counsel. Then, there is the human factor. Some individuals are simply better at mediation than others. A mediator must be respectful to both parties, but also firm in his or her position relating to important issues in the case. A firm statement by a mediator often moves the case forward in a way that makes a fair agreement inevitable.

The second important factor in a mediation is the actual physical presence of those individuals who have the "decision making authority." It is strongly recommended that the individual who is bringing the claim attend the mediation conference in person. Likewise, the individuals who control the "purse strings" should also attend. Attendance by the individuals with decision making authority increases the likelihood that a capable mediator will achieve a successful settlement. A seasoned mediator is often able to bring the negotiations to a successful conclusion if he is better able to understand the true interests of the parties.

A third factor that increases the likelihood of a successful mediation is thorough preparation for the mediation by the parties to the lawsuit and the mediator. This is usually accomplished by requiring all parties to submit a "statement of the case" to the mediator. This statement of the case includes the facts surrounding the litigation and an analysis or argument made by counsel relating to the litigation. Particularly helpful to the mediator is a description of any prior settlement negotiations and an inclusion of any important documents that will be discussed at the time of the mediation.

An additional factor that increases the likelihood of a successful mediation is a reasonable time limit. Many mediations are conducted in a way that allows for a full day for the mediation. When all parties are aware of the termination point for the mediation, all parties are pressured to make their best settlement offer as the deadline approaches.

The Sequance of Events for a Mediation Conference

The sequence of events at a mediation conference has an impact on the likelihood of success. The initial stages of the mediation conference are particularly important. The conference usually begins with the mediator welcoming all participants and emphasising the theme that the participants have the opportunity to reach a decision relating to the outcome of the case rather than allow the unpredictable risk of a decision by the court or a jury. The mediator usually brings a Mediation Agreement to the conference. The Mediation Agreement usually includes an agreement that all discussions during the mediation are inadmissible in any future legal proceedings.

An "Opening Statement" is usually made by counsel for each of the parties. The first opening statement is typically made by the claimant or plaintiff. The opening statement usually requires no more than thirty minutes for each party. As part of the opening statement, counsel is able to present exhibits or other documents that support the highlights of his party's position. After each party has made an opening statement, the mediator will usually separate the parties and their counsel by placing each group in a separate conference room. The mediator then begins "shuttle diplomacy" by speaking with the parties and their counsel individually. The mediator usually begins with the plaintiff and his or her attorney.

An effective mediator will tell each party and their counsel that any information disclosed to the mediator will be kept confidential unless the mediator is told that he or she can disclose the information to the other side. This confidentiality agreement is one of the most important factors involved in a successful mediation. If the mediator can learn the "true range" at which the party will agree to a settlement, the mediator can often determine that the "true range" for the various parties overlaps. These confidential discussions with each party require time to evolve. Confidence in the mediator is not gained immediately. Typically, a mediator will have several discussions with each group before any party and their counsel feel more comfortable with the mediator's approach to the settlement negotiations.

If no settlement negotiations have occurred, the mediator will encourage the plaintiff to make his or her initial "demand." If the demand seems unreasonable, the mediator can provide advice to the plaintiff relating to the initial demand.

Before returning to the defendants (either together as a group or individually in separate conference rooms) the mediator will often obtain some additional information from the plaintiff to accompany the initial demand. The plaintiff and his or her counsel can often provide information to the mediator relating to the defendants' vulnerabilities in the litigation.

When the mediator first meets with the defendants, the mediator will have a fresh demand from the plaintiff along with issues raised by the plaintiff that may affect the settlement negotiations. At this point, the mediator often serves as an advisor to not only the defence counsel, but also to the person with settlement authority accompanying the defence counsel to the mediation. A mediator with significant experience can advise the parties as to whether the verdict is likely to be in the range of the plaintiff's demand or the subsequent defendants' offer. The advantage of a very experienced mediator is that the representative with settlement authority must often contact a superior for additional authority. The presence and experience of a seasoned mediator is a significant assistance to the defendant's representative with settlement authority (often an insurance claims representative) who must seek additional authority from a superior.

After receiving the information from the mediator, the defendants' group usually has a private discussion in order to determine the amount of the offer that they will make in response to the plaintiff's demand. It can go back and forth like this for several sessions until some consensus is reached. A mediator may make a recommendation as to an appropriate "range" of settlement.

It is very typical during the initial steps of the mediation to leave the impression that the case will never reach a settlement. Nevertheless, there is a high number of mediations where most of the movement relating to settlement occurs towards the end of the mediation, usually at the end of the day.

Predicting the Likelihood of Success of a Mediation

One of the key components of predicting the success of a mediation is an analysis of similar cases with their historic settlement value or verdict value. Personal injury actions often leave a trail of settlements and verdicts that can be analysed in order to obtain the likely range of a verdict.[3]

---

[3] In Ireland, the Book of Quantum will be likely to have some use in this context but of its nature will lack the degree of specificity to assist the parties fully.

Armed with the probable range of a verdict, the parties are better able to identify the "fair" range based on other similar cases.

The mediator is often provided with some of this settlement or verdict information which has an impact on his or her opinion as to the value of the litigation. A mediator with experience will have his or her own opinion relating to the value of this particular lawsuit which is certainly influenced by the underlying facts of the litigation, the impression that the witnesses will make at trial, and the quality of any expert testimony provided.

Costs of Mediation

The cost of a mediation conference can be a significant factor in determining whether a mediation conference should proceed. The cost for the time of the mediator, including the mediator's time to read the "Statement of Facts" sent by each party, the cost of the preparation by each party prior to the mediation and the time involved in the mediation itself is a factor that must be considered by all parties. Nevertheless, a mediation that occurs at a point before significant trial preparation costs have occurred usually results in two significant benefits. The first benefit is the overall savings in litigation costs that would have been incurred if the case had gone to trial. The second benefit is the removal of risk for all parties to achieve an acceptable settlement and remove the risk of a verdict.

Conclusion

The vast majority of lawsuits involve some settlement negotiations at some point. If the settlement negotiations occur in the "panic mode" that often accompanies parties who are heading toward the courtroom door to begin trial, there is a significant likelihood that one side or the other will settle for an unjust amount to avoid the pressure or risk of trial. In a mediation conference, the discussions relating to settlement are presented in a more organized manner with the assistance of a mediator who can guide each party to a more just result. Thus, the salutary effect of mediation as a useful tool for litigators cannot be overstated.

Counsel's Fundamental Right to Client: Constitutionally Cementing Lawyers into Personal Injuries Compensation?

PAUL QUIGLEY*[1]

> The problem with any unwritten law is that you don't know where to go to erase it.
>
> *Glaser and Way*

This chapter will consider the judgment of McMenamin J. in *O'Brien v. Personal Injuries Assessment Board.*[2] Here, the High Court found that the Personal Injuries Assessment Board (PIAB) policy of corresponding directly with claimants was *ultra vires* the statutory powers of the PIAB. It will be argued that the court failed to consider the economic rationale of the PIAB policy it struck down. It will also be argued that the application of the right to legal representation was inappropriate to the PIAB procedure, which protects the interests of claimants through other means.

This discussion is divided into four sections. First, it restates the economic rationale and methodology of recent reforms of the tort system introduced by the Personal Injuries Assessment Board Act 2003 ("the 2003 Act") and the Civil Liability and Courts Act 2004 ("the 2004 Act"). Second, it briefly summarises the *O'Brien* judgment. In the third section, this decision is criticised for failing to consider the goals and context of the PIAB reform in considering the scope of the right to legal representa-

---

*Hugo Grotius Fellow and LL.M. Candidate, New York University School of Law; Scholar of Trinity College Dublin.

[1] Thanks to Julian Moore, Jim Quigley, and David Fennelly for proofreading and valuable suggestions.

tion. An alternative approach to constitutional supervision of the PIAB is proposed. The final section considers whether expansive interpretation of certain principles of Irish administrative law may preclude reform of civil litigation, while not necessarily protecting any substantive rights.

1. The PIAB and the Civil Liability Act: Economic Rationales

The recent reforms of the personal injuries compensation system have been inspired by the belief that Ireland is suffering from a "compensation crisis."[3] When Ireland is compared with other European countries, this belief seems reasonable. Irish motor insurance premiums, public liability insurance, and employer's liability insurance are among the highest in Europe, and, in 2003, were the highest in several categories.[4] Large insurance overheads add to the cost of employment, making Ireland less attractive for foreign investors, and increasing costs for domestic businesses.[5]

Over the past nine years, government and private sector investigations of the compensation problem failed to identify any single cause for Irish insurance rates.[6] The Motor Insurance Advisory Board (MIAB) made

---

2 *O'Brien v. Personal Injuries Assessment Board*, unreported, High Court, McMenamin J., January 25, 2005.

3 96% of Irish people surveyed in a November 2002 poll said that car insurance was either "expensive" or "very expensive", MIAB, *MIAB Report, 2004* (Department of Enterprise, Trade and Employment, 2004), p.13. Only 5% of people surveyed disagreed with the statement "people make fraudulent claims." Many newspaper articles documenting the perceived crisis are cited in Ray Ryan's chapter in this book, *supra*, pp.138 *et seq.*

4 MIAB, *The Final Report of the Motor Insurance Advisory Board* (Department of Enterprise, Trade and Employment, 2002); MIAB, *MIAB Report 2004*, *op. cit.* n.3, p.25. "Irish insurance premiums double European norm", *Irish Times*, April 10, 2002.

5 The cost of personal injuries tort actions was estimated to be between 1.6% and 1.95% of 2002 GDP. MIAB, *MIAB Report 2004*, *op. cit.*, n.3.

6 See The Department of Enterprise, Trade and Employment, *The Second Report of the Special Working Group on Personal Injury Compensation* (Dublin, 2001); The Competition Authority, *Competition Issues in the Non-Life Insurance Market (with particular reference to Motor, Employers' Liability, and Public Liability Insurance)* (Dublin, 2004); IBEC Research and Information Services, *IBEC National Survey of Personal Injury Claims 2000* (Dublin, 2001); MIAB, *The Final Report of the Motor Insurance Advisory Board*, *op. cit.*, n.4.

no less than 67 distinct recommendations to be implemented by the government, the Irish Insurance Federation (IIF), the Law Society, the Irish Business and Employers' Confederation (IBEC), the Competition Authority and the Courts Service.[7] One of the principal causes of high insurance premiums was found to be large sums being paid out to persons alleging personal injuries. This was attributed to (i) an increase in the frequency of personal injuries claims (more claims), (ii) escalating sums paid in individual settlements and awards (bigger payouts), and (iii) the overall expense of the personal injuries system (high delivery costs). Almost all of the reforms brought in by the 2003 and 2004 Acts may be seen as responses to these three, distinct factors.[8] The following descriptions demonstrate how these three factors are addressed by the two acts.

1.1 Reducing the number of claims

The first "compensation crisis" factor identified is the number of personal injuries claims. The 2004 Act addresses this on several fronts, with the overarching policy of discouraging exaggerated or fraudulent claims. Most controversially, it reduces the statute of limitations for personal injuries claims to two years.[9] This is intended to reduce the incidence of older claims, which are perceived as more difficult to defend, and more likely to be based on questionable grounds. Also, the Act requires speedy service of a letter of claim by the claimant this must be within two months of the "date of the cause of action."[10] The rationale is that defendants receive notice of claims while accidents will still be fresh in memory, and evidence may still be preserved.[11] According to statistics from 1994 to 1997, in

[7] MIAB, *Final Report of the Motor Insurance Advisory Board: Annotated version of the Recommendations* (Department of Enterprise, Trade and Employment, 2003).

[8] Also, almost all of the reforms may be traced to the recommendations of the MIAB, *Ibid.*

[9] Civil Liability and Courts Act 2004, s.7.

[10] *Ibid.*, s.8. The penalty for failing to comply with the deadline is that the judge may "draw such inferences from the failure as appear proper" and may make appropriate costs awards. Presumably, this discretion will not threaten litigants who are delayed in good faith or through no fault of their own.

[11] On the remarkable statistical unlikelihood of successfully defending a claim in the High Court, see MIAB, *MIAB Report 2004, op. cit.*, n.3, p.24.

this jurisdiction claimants wait an average of 230 days after an accident before filing a claim; the comparable figure for England is 75 days.[12]

The 2004 Act requires claimants to swear affidavits verifying the "assertions or allegations" on which their claim is based, and introduces criminal liability for those who knowingly lie or exaggerate in making a claim.[13] This provision is expected to discourage false claims. The creation of court-appointed expert witnesses is presumably also designed to identify claims based on questionable evidence.[14] Arguably, the PIAB procedure could also discourage false claims, as the PIAB process requires the claimant to submit the details of the alleged injury, thereby making vague claims more difficult.[15] The creation of a register of personal injuries actions should also discourage false claims, as it will identify serial litigants.[16]

Elsewhere in this book it is demonstrated how all of the changes may result in injustices in some circumstances.[17] However, it should be noted that the changes seem to be directed at addressing the pathologies of personal injuries litigation rather than reshaping its substance. The burden of proof has not been changed, damages have not been capped or fixed, and no impediments have been placed on access to the courts (other than the PIAB procedure itself). Some valid claims may be compromised by the new requirements, but the intended targets are false or exaggerated claims.

1.2 Reducing size of payouts

The second means of reducing the costs of personal injuries is to reduce the amounts of compensation paid in each award or settlement. Reducing, or at least stabilising, levels of compensation is a goal that the Oireachtas

---

[12] Greenford, "The Handling of Personal Injuries Claims by Insurers in England and Ireland", Appendix 3 of *The Second Report of the Special Working Group on Personal Injury Compensation* (Department of Enterprise, Trade and Employment, Dublin, 2001)

[13] Civil Liability and Courts Act 2004, s.14.

[14] *Ibid.*, s.20.

[15] Personal Injuries Assessment Board Act 2003, s.11. A requirement for specific detail in pleadings is also found in s.13 of the 2004 Act.

[16] Civil Liability and Courts Act 2004, s.30. The courts have also played a role in discouraging false claimants. *Vesey v. Bus Éireann* [2001] 4 I.R. 192.

[17] See Binchy, *supra*, pp.44 *et seq.*

has approached indirectly, through the creation of a book of quantum (created by the PIAB), to which the courts must "have regard" when assessing personal injuries damages.[18] The 2004 Act also envisages the creation of actuarial tables that courts must "refer to" in assessing damages in respect of future financial loss.[19] These measures are directed at harmonizing personal injuries awards in our courts, which, when compared with other jurisdictions, are very high.[20] It is debatable whether the measures will have the effect of reducing awards (or whether this is desirable), but presumably they will act as a force against further escalation of the amounts of awards, and perhaps be a damper against exemplary awards of damages. Another means of reducing quantum of awards is the change in the rules relating to collateral benefits and undeclared income. Section 27 of the 2004 Act amends section 50 of the Civil Liability Act 1961 and section 2 of the Civil Liability (Amendment) Act 1964, two provisions which prevent courts from taking various collateral benefits into account when calculating damages.[21] Following this reform, certain collateral benefits may now be deducted from personal injury awards. But it has been convincingly argued that, in practice, such deductions will have little impact, and even then, possibly only in the context of the employer/employee relationship.[22]

1.3 Reducing delivery costs for personal injury awards

The biggest focus of the recent reforms is not in reducing levels or numbers of awards; it is in reducing their delivery costs. Statistics from insurers indicate that legal expenses add approximately 40–56% to the amount of personal injuries settlements. This money goes to the claimant's solicitors, barristers, expert witnesses and others involved in the adversarial process.[23] Barristers play a role in 76.2% of personal injuries claims in

---

[18] Civil Liability and Courts Act 2004, s.22; The Book of Quantum is prepared and published by the Personal Injuries Assessment Board.

[19] *Ibid.*, s.23.

[20] On the quantum of Irish awards, see Greenford, "The Handling of Personal Injuries Claims by Insurers in England and Ireland", *op. cit.*, n.12. See, also, MIAB, *MIAB Report 2004*, *op. cit.*, n.3, p.24.

[21] Civil Liability and Courts Act 2004, s.27.

[22] See Cox, *supra*, pp.84 *et seq.*

[23] The total cost of injury claims (compensation only) in 2000 was approximately €1.05 billion. An additional €440 million was spent on legal costs. *IBEC National Survey*

Ireland; in England this figure is only 2.9%.[24] The creation of the PIAB is designed to remove the need for two sets of legal professionals in reaching settlements, by replacing them with a single assessor equipped with a book of quantum. If it works as expected, the PIAB will also arrange awards in a fraction of the average time taken by the adversarial process.[25]

The 2004 Act also seeks to reduce delivery costs by providing for mediation.[26] Additionally, it creates an incentive for early settlement by creating a formal offer process. If no reasonable formal offer is made, or if one is rejected, a court may take this into account in making orders for costs.[27] This incentive should operate to lower legal costs by encouraging settlements. Having linked the major reforms introduced by the new acts to their three basic economic rationales (reducing litigation, keeping awards in check, and reducing delivery costs), the *O'Brien* decision will be set out.

2. The *O'Brien* Decision

This is intended to be a very brief synopsis of the judgment in *O'Brien v. Personal Injuries Assessment Board*, and as such many details have been excluded. First, the facts and backgrounds are set out (2.1). This is followed by an overview of the submissions of the applicant, Mr O'Brien (2.2), the Law Society (2.3), and the respondent, the PIAB (2.4). Finally, the consideration of the issues by McMenamin J. is summarised (2.5).

---

of Personal Injuries Claims 2000, *op. cit.*, n.6. See comparable statistics from the period 1997–2000 in MIAB, *The Final Report of the Motor Insurance Advisory Board*, *op. cit.*, n.4.

24 Greenford, "The Handling of Personal Injuries Claims by Insurers in England and Ireland", *op. cit.*, n.12.

25 According to the Greenford Report, *ibid.*, the *average* time between a claim and a settlement is just over two years, seven months. The PIAB procedure is intended to deliver an assessment in a maximum of nine months, with a possible extension to 15 months. Personal Injuries Assessment Board Act 2003, s.49.

26 Civil Liability and Courts Act 2004, s.15. However, see Corbett, *supra*, pp.103 *et seq.* and Binchy, *supra*, pp.94 *et seq.*

27 *Ibid.*, s.17.

2.1 Facts and background

The applicant, Declan O'Brien, was a boner in a meat factory who alleged that he was injured in a workplace accident on November 5, 2001. On August 12, 2004, he travelled to Newbridge, Co. Kildare, to meet with a solicitor, Mr Boland. Mr Boland notified the PIAB of the claim and began making arrangements for a medical report to accompany an application to the PIAB. As the statute of limitations was due to expire on the claim in less than three months (on November 4, 2004), Mr Boland wished to register the claim as soon as possible.[28] However, there was a delay with obtaining the medical report that must accompany the claim at registration, and initially the PIAB insisted that the claim would not be registered without the report.[29] Later, the PIAB made it clear that the claim could be registered without the report if it was not ready.[30]

Shortly after a dialogue had been initiated with the PIAB, Mr Boland furnished a document to the applicant entitled "Confirmation and Authority". The applicant signed the document, dated August 16, 2004, which purported to give Mr Boland authority "solely to deal with all correspondence on behalf of Mr O'Brien."[31] Even after this document was furnished to the PIAB, the Board continued to deal directly with the applicant, but copied the solicitor on all correspondence.[32] On September 7, 2004, the applicant initiated judicial review proceedings in the High Court, seeking two principal remedies: (i) an order of mandamus directing the respondent to record and register the applicant's claim, and (ii) an injunction directing the applicant to cease interfering with the solicitor-client relationship by corresponding directly with the applicant.[33]

After these proceedings were initiated, the PIAB wrote to the claimant's solicitor, stating that, "[i]f you remain unable to obtain a

---

[28] The 2003 Act forbids instituting personal injuries actions without first obtaining authorisation from the PIAB (s.12) and this authorisation cannot be granted unless the claim is registered with the PIAB (s.32). Registering a claim with the PIAB stops the Statutes of Limitations, so Mr. Boland wished to register it before November 4, 2004.

[29] *O'Brien v. Personal Injuries Assessment Board*, n.2 *supra*, p.3 of the unreported judgment.

[30] *Ibid.*, p.4.

[31] *Ibid.*, p.3.

[32] *Ibid.*, p.4.

[33] *Ibid.*

transcription of your clients medical records by 31/10/04 we will register the claim and we will proceed to arrange an independent medical examination through our nationwide panel. Or we can immediately arrange such an independent medical examination and again we will register the claim by 31/10/04." The letter also stated that the PIAB would continue to correspond directly with the claimant, but would copy the solicitor – who the PIAB viewed as an "advisor" – on all correspondence.

Proceedings began before de Valera J. on October 4, 2004, and concerned the order for mandamus compelling the PIAB to register the claim. However, the medical report finally materialised and the claim was registered on October 22, 2004.[34] Curiously, the medical report, though dated September 3, 2004, was signed on October 1 of that year.[35] Before McMenamin J., the issues cemented into a simple, but different, question; whether the PIAB, in declining to act in accordance with the authorization of August 16, 2004, and by corresponding directly with the applicant and copying such correspondence to his solicitor acted in breach of: (a) section 7 of the Personal Injuries Assessment Board Act 2003, or (b) the applicant's constitutional rights.[36] The Law Society appeared as *amicus curiae* in the case.[37]

2.2 Applicant's submissions

Relying on Irish and European Court of Human Rights precedents, counsel for the applicant stated that all individuals have a constitutional right of access to the courts.[38] It was submitted that "hindering the effective exercise of a right" may amount to a breach of that right, and that interfering with the solicitor client relationship has such an effect.[39] The difficulties that the applicant faced in registering the claim were adduced as evidence that the PIAB may not have had the "interests of the claimant at heart."[40] It was argued that the limitation of the right to counsel in the

---

[34] *Ibid.*
[35] *Ibid.*, p.7.
[36] *Ibid.*
[37] *Ibid.*
[38] *Ibid.*, p.13, relying on *Murphy v. Greene* [1990] 2 I.R. 556, *R.B. v. A.S.* [2002] 2 I.R. 428, and *Golder v. UK* (1979–1980) 1 E.H.R.R. 524.
[39] *Ibid.*, p.14.
[40] *Ibid.*

situation was not proportionate, and that it was not "introduced or effected" in a constitutionally sustainable manner.[41] Furthermore, it was submitted that the power of the Board to make rules concerning its claims procedure could not be interpreted to alter, diminish or interfere with a right of constitutional or common law character. Such a power would be contrary to the reservation of the legislative power to the Oireachtas, as enunciated in Article 15.2.1 of Bunreacht na hÉireann.[42] Hence, the policy or practice was claimed to be *ultra vires* the enabling provisions of the 2003 Act.

2.3 Submissions of Law Society

The Law Society made submissions regarding the importance of the solicitor/client relationship as a professional privilege.[43] "[B]y reason of the complexity and difficulty of our law", it argued, litigation requires professionals.[44] It was claimed that the PIAB process was just such a difficult and complex process.[45] The Law Society noted that claimants may be out of the country, or wish to have their privacy respected, and hence should be able to nominate a legal representative.[46] Convenience aside, the Law Society argued that there was an equality-of-arms issue. The PIAB corresponds directly with respondents too, the Law Society admitted, but these respondents will frequently have in-house counsel who will provide respondents with professional legal advice.

The Law Society argued that abrogating the solicitor-client relationship by allowing a statute-created body to specify the means by which "legal advisors" should be copied in correspondence would require specific powers which the Board did not receive from the 2003 Act.[47] It noted that the solicitor-client relationship is important for protecting certain categories of client (such as those with poor literary skills), and for protecting the privacy of individuals. It was also submitted that, at any

---

41 *Ibid.*

42 *Ibid.*, p.15. Article 15.2.1 states: "The sole and exclusive power of making laws for the State is hereby vested in the Oireachtas: no other legislative authority has power to make laws for the State."

43 *Ibid.*, at pp. 18–19.

44 *Ibid.*, p.18.

45 *Ibid.*, p.19.

46 *Ibid.*

47 *Ibid.*, p.21.

rate, the goals of the 2003 Act would not be undermined if solicitors acted as legal representatives, as claimants would not be permitted to recover legal costs within the PIAB procedure. The submissions of the Law Society also invoked the constitutional right to "fair procedures of an even handed nature."[48] As the PIAB procedure involved the potential of a substantial benefit accruing to a successful claimant, it was argued that the Board must observe fair procedures which include legal representation. The dicta of Ó Dálaigh C.J. in *In re Haughey* were cited as support for the proposition that a right to fair proceedures extends beyond the sphere of the courts.[49]

The Law Society argued that the fact that a cheque is sent to the client, rather than the client's solicitor, undermines the policy of solicitors giving undertakings to financial institutions on behalf of clients. The Law Society acknowledged that statutory corporations must be regarded as having powers that are incidental to, or consequential upon, their legislatively defined goals.[50] However, it submitted that there was no basis for finding the policy of the Board to be incidental or consequential upon its functions.[51] The Law Society also dealt with the possibility that the power to deal directly with individuals was, in fact, granted to the PIAB, and argued that, if it was, its use where the claimant wished to appoint a legal representative was unreasonable.[52]

2.4 Respondent's submissions

The PIAB argued that it was not required to correspond with solicitors, but stated that it would do so in certain situations. The Board claimed that the power to make this determination was within its discretion.[53] It was submitted that the PIAB is not a court of law, and hence the PIAB policy does not interfere with access to any court.[54] It was also argued

---

48 *Ibid.*, p 22.
49 [1971] I.R. 217.
50 *O'Brien v. Personal Injuries Assessment Board*, n.2, p.23 of the unreported judgment, citing *Howard v. The Commissioners of Public Works* [1994] 1 I.R. 101, *Attorney General v. Great Eastern Railway Company* (1880) 5 App. Cas. 473.
51 *Ibid.*
52 *Ibid.*, p.21.
53 *Ibid.*, p.12.
54 *Ibid.*, p.16.

that the PIAB is not a body that makes determinations of legal rights or obligations, and hence the rights recognised in *In re Haughey*[55] are inapplicable.[56] Counsel for the Board submitted that section 7(2) of the Act shows that there is no right of legal representation before the Board, and that if the Oireachtas wished to create one, it would have been specified in the legislation.[57]

The Board claimed that there was no evidence that the applicant had been hindered in any way in his right to obtain legal advice.[58] It was also argued that the contractual relationship between the solicitor and the claimant could not decide how the Board conducts its business.[59] The Act, according to the PIAB, made provision for vulnerable persons, but reserved the discretion as to how to advise or deal with such persons to the Board.[60] The submissions of the applicant related to rights before a court, and the PIAB it argued, is not a court. For this reason, counsel argued that *Murphy v. Green*[61] and *A.S. v. R.B.*[62] (cases cited by the applicant) were not relevant, and neither were the decisions of the European Court of Human Rights, as these referred to rights of access to courts.[63] The Board also challenged the applicant's *locus standi*, stating that the Board had been flexible, and supplied the applicant's solicitor with copies of correspondence as requested.[64]

2.5 Consideration of the issues

The consideration of the issues was brief.[65] McMenamin J. opened by finding that the applicant had *locus standi*: the procedures had identifiable consequences for the applicant's relationship with his solicitor. He then identified the primary question to be addressed as that of *vires*.[66] The

---

55 [1974] I.R. 217.
56 *O'Brien v. Personal Injuries Assessment Board*, *op. cit.*, n.2, p.16.
57 *Ibid.*, p.16.
58 *Ibid.*, p.15.
59 *Ibid.*, p.17.
60 *Ibid.*, p.16, relying on s.29 of the 2003 Act.
61 [1992] 2 I.R. 566.
62 [2002] 2 I.R. 428.
63 *O'Brien v. Personal Injuries Assessment Board*, n.2, p.17 of the unreported judgment.
64 *Ibid.*, p.18.
65 *Ibid*, pp. 24–29.
66 *Ibid.*, p.24.

court then considered two cases, *Maguire v. Ardagh*[67] and *Re Commission to Inquire into Child Abuse*,[68] and noted that both of these cases involved the protection of the rights to legal advice and legal representation in adjudicative inquiries. Particular attention was paid to the decision of Kelly J. in *Re Commission to Inquire into Child Abuse*. There, the Commission's attempt to impose a restriction on the number of lawyers who might act by being present was struck down as *ultra vires*, as the general powers given to that Commission could not be interpreted as allowing such a "novel and far reaching power."[69]

Having established that the right to counsel could be relevant to administrative proceedings outside the courts, McMenamin J. reduced the issue to two questions. The first of these was whether there was a specific power set out in the 2003 Act to adopt the policy at issue.[70] He found that there was not. He then addressed the second question: whether the policy could be "necessary, expedient or incidental" to the functions of the Board so as to come within section 54 of the Act of 2003, which reserves such powers to the Board.[71] In determining whether the policy was expedient, the court explicitly rejected the argument, submitted by counsel for the Board, that the policy of the PIAB would save money for all involved.[72] The court stated that:

> "the question of legal costs is not affected one way or the other by the policy adopted by the Board. The Board is not empowered to award legal costs and expenses. Any legal costs incurred by a claimant, therefore, can only be deducted [from the award] made by the Board to the claimant."[73]

Therefore, in the eyes of the court, there was no economic rationale for the interference. The court continued to state that it could not find any basis for labelling the practice of direct client communication

---

[67] [2002] 1 I.R. 385.
[68] [2002] 3 I.R. 459.
[69] *O'Brien v. Personal Injuries Assessment Board*, *op. cit.*, n.2, p.26, citing [2002] 3 I.R. 459 at 478.
[70] *Ibid.*, p.27.
[71] *Ibid.*
[72] *Ibid.*
[73] *Ibid.*

"expedient."[74] Furthermore, the court found that "[w]ere it the intention that lawyers should be excluded from dealings between claimant and the Board the Act might have said so."[75] Thus, the court concluded that the policy of the Board of dealing directly with claimants was *ultra vires* the Act of 2003.[76] The judge summed up the issues that had led him to this conclusion. These were (i) the fact that the matters before the Board were of substance, (ii) the inflexible aspects of the Board's power to prescribe the manner in which it communicates with claimants and their solicitors, (iii) the absence of an express statutory authority permitting the policy of direct communication, (iv) the recognition of the right to legal advice in the Act, and (v) the gravity of the consequences of the procedures for the claimant.[77] The judgment concluded by citing two American cases; *Powell v. Alabama*,[78] and *Mosley et al v. St. Louis South Western Railway*.[79] McMenamin J. made some *obiter* comments on how the right to legal representation can be essential in certain administrative procedures, and suggested that the Board is such a procedure.[80]

3. Critiquing the *O'Brien* Decision

There are three principal argumens in the critique of the reasoning of the *O'Brien* decision. First, contrary to the findings of the court, the PIAB policy of direct communication was vital to reducing costs in personal injuries compensation (3.1). This goal of reducing costs was "necessary or expedient for, or incidental to, the performance of [the PIAB's] functions" (3.2, 3.3.3).[81] This conclusion is reinforced by teleological statutory interpretation and by reference to the intent of the legislature. Secondly, as a matter of constitutional law, the right to legal representation effectively functions as an enabling right, necessary to protect the substance of other rights or interests in adversarial procedures. Therefore,

---

[74] *Ibid.*
[75] *Ibid.*
[76] *Ibid.*, p.28 of the unreported judgment.
[77] *Ibid.*
[78] 287 U.S. 45 (1932).
[79] 634 F.2d. 942 (1981) (Fifth Circuit Court of Appeals).
[80] *O'Brien v. Personal Injuries Assessment Board*, n.2, p.29.
[81] Personal Injuries Assessment Board Act 2003, s.54(2).

the full protection of the right to legal representation is unnecessary in the PIAB procedure (3.3).

3.1 The economic rationale for the policy of direct communication

In the *O'Brien* decision, McMenamin J. stated that he could not find any economic rationale for the PIAB policy of dealing directly with claimants.[82] This led to the conclusion that the policy was not "necessary, expedient or incidental" to the functions of the Board. In order to test this a simple method is used. First, the financing of legal costs in the PIAB process pre-*O'Brien* is described. Then, this is contrasted with the financing of legal costs (and the size of these costs) in a situation where the PIAB must deal directly with legal representatives, as required by the *O'Brien* decision.

3.1.1 The PIAB procedure before O'Brien

After suffering an injury and deciding to make a claim for damages, the vast majority of claimants will consult their solicitor.[83] This first step has deep cultural roots and is unlikely to change in the near future, even with a popular, functional, and well-publicized PIAB. The solicitor will outline the procedure for registering a PIAB claim. The claimant then initiates the PIAB procedure. He may receive legal advice and procedural and substantive assistance through the PIAB national helpline and the independent medical panel. The claimant may arrange for as much, or as little, legal advice as he wishes from his solicitor. Following the submission of a medical report and claim, the respondent decides whether to accept liability for the assessment. If it does, the PIAB completes and issues an assessment, which the claimant and respondent either accept or refuse, probably in co-operation with their respective legal advisors. The process is not removed from the claimant by the intervention of a solicitor. If the PIAB provides a fair assessment (which it should, as its awards are designed to be commensurate with those of the courts), there will be no reason to reject the award.[84] As the claimant will have largely arranged

[82] *O'Brien v. Personal Injuries Assessment Board*, n.2, p.29.

[83] According to the Greenford Report (*op. cit.*, n.12), claimants seek legal advice or representation in 95.2% of personal injury insurance claims.

[84] Personal Injuries Assessment Board Act 2003, s.20(4).

the claim himself, the legal expenses incurred should be much less than if the solicitor had handled the entire case. If the award is accurate and acceptable, it will be accepted, and the claimant will pay the legal expenses himself.

Such a well-functioning situation should, in theory, become self re-enforcing. If claimants must pay their own legal expenses, there will be less incentive to rely heavily on a solicitor in making a claim, especially if a solicitor's involvement makes no difference to the quantum of the award made. At present, people immediately turn to solicitors for personal injuries disputes, but the existence of a smoothly functioning, speedy, and claimant-friendly PIAB procedure may de-mystify the personal injuries compensation process.

The PIAB is designed to interact directly with individuals. The claim form can be ordered or downloaded.[85] The draft guide to how the PIAB procedure works was drawn up with the assistance of the National Adult Literary Agency,[86] and the PIAB Helpline is designed to assist applicants with every stage in the process.[87] The PIAB can arrange for a medical assessment if the claimant cannot.[88] Most importantly, the interests of the PIAB are aligned with those of claimants. The institution will only succeed if its assessments are accepted by claimants, and these assessments will only be accepted if they are fair and accurate.[89] Of course, not all persons will be in a position to handle their claim themselves, but the 2003 Act explicitly protects the right to legal advice,[90] and makes special provision for vulnerable parties that may include legal representation.[91]

---

[85] The claim form may be downloaded from www.piab.ie, the PIAB website.

[86] Dowling, "The Personal Injuries Assessment Board: A Win Win Solution", in Quigley & Binchy (eds.), *The Personal Injuries Assessment Board: Implications for Legal Practice* (Firstlaw, Dublin, 2004), 32, p.34.

[87] *Ibid.*

[88] In fact, the PIAB offered to do so for Mr. O'Brien, the applicant in the decision under discussion. See the letter of September 17, 2004 from the PIAB to Mr. O'Brien's solicitor, *O'Brien v. Personal Injuries Assessment Board*, n.2, p.5.

[89] If PIAB awards are not accepted, the Board may become a superfluous additional layer in the litigation process. See Maguire, "The Personal Injuries Assessment Board Act 2003: A Barrister's Perspective" in Quigley & Binchy (eds.), *The Personal Injuries Assessment Board: Implications for Legal Practice* (First Law, Dublin, 2004), p.22.

[90] Personal Injuries Assessment Board Act 2003, s.7(1).

[91] *Ibid.*, s.29.

3.1.2 The PIAB procedure after O'Brien

The following narrative outlines how the PIAB procedure may unfold after the *O'Brien* decision, which mandates that the PIAB may not communicate directly with a claimant if he appoints a legal representative. As before, a claimant will generally first approach a solicitor when making a personal injuries claim.[92] The solicitor, following the Law Society position on the PIAB and rationally pursing his own economic interest, will advise the claimant against trusting the PIAB procedure without legal representation.[93] Relying on the *O'Brien* ruling, the solicitor will adopt complete control of the process, as was the norm before the creation of the PIAB. The solicitor will fill out the claim form and correspond with the PIAB, presumably having regular meetings with the client to determine particulars relating to the application. The PIAB will correspond with the solicitor, who will receive the final damages assessment. The solicitor will then advise the claimant on whether or not to accept it.

In handling the claim, arranging meetings, completing the claim form, and corresponding with the PIAB, the claimant's solicitor will accumulate substantial legal expenses.[94] In advising his client with regard to these expenses, he will be presented with two options. He can either (i) advise the claimant to accept the settlement and pay the legal fees out-of-pocket, or (ii) advise the claimant to reject the PIAB assessment, and, armed with the objective PIAB assessment of the claimant's damages, demand the damages *and* legal fees from the respondent.

The first option, deducting the legal fees from the settlement, has obvious negative financial consequences for the claimant, whose interests

---

92 As noted above, the Greenford Report (*op. cit.*, n.12), found that claimants seek legal advice or representation in 95.2% of personal injury insurance claims.

93 On the Law Society's position on PIAB, see Murphy, "The PIAB: A Solicitor's Perspective" in Quigley & Binchy (eds.), *The Personal Injuries Assessment Board: Implications for Legal Practice* (First Law, Dublin, 2004), 13. "The Personal Injuries Assessment Board (PIAB) should be called 'the inequality tribunal… .' The Law Society opposed this unfairness on grounds of principle. We were right to do so."

94 Studies indicate that fees incurred by claimants' solicitors in processing personal injury claims are substantial; for every €100 awarded in personal injuries settlements in 2002, an additional €42 was paid in claimant's legal fees. MIAB, *MIAB Report 2004*, *op cit.*, n.3, p.55, see also: The Greenford Report, *op. cit.*, n.12. MIAB, *Final Report of the MIAB*, *op. cit.*, n.4. Litigation costs, as a percentage of awards, have risen steadily for the past decade; in 2004, the claimant's legal fees on each settlement amounted to an average of 46% of the settlement. MIAB, *MIAB Report 2004*, p.57.

the solicitor will wish to protect. This alone should mean that solicitors and clients might choose to reject the assessment, and seek damages and legal expenses from the respondent. Also, it can be argued that if the claimant makes decisions regarding his legal representation based on the expectation of having to pay the legal expenses himself, these decisions will be contrary to the solicitor's economic interests. Claimants will attempt to avoid paying substantial legal fees by completing the PIAB process by themselves. Even if claimants did need some legal help, if fees will eventually come from the pocket of the person who is selecting the solicitor (the claimant), potential claimants will have an incentive to "shop around" and identify which solicitor will deduct the least from their eventual award.[95] This could engender price competition amongst solicitors, an outcome which individual solicitors may not wish to encourage. Thus, accepting the PIAB assessment after legal expenses have been incurred through legal representation is inimical to the interests of both claimant and his solicitor.

The second option for the solicitor is to advise his or her client to seek damages *and* legal fees from the respondent. The means of doing so are simple. First, the PIAB assessment is rejected.[96] The PIAB then issue an authorisation to proceed with the claim.[97] Thanks to the PIAB, the claimant has an objective assessment of the fair value of the damages suffered, and the claim is still valid.[98] The claimant's solicitor will have an assessment of the value of the legal services he provided. These two sums can be combined and submitted to the respondent (i.e. an insurance company, public authority, or employer), who, following historical precedent, will probably pay the full amount.[99]

---

[95] As assisting with filling out a PIAB claim form could become a standardized service, it may be more susceptible to price competition than most other legal professional services. Competition between service providers becomes more acute the more interchangeable the services are perceived as being.

[96] The assessment may be refused in accordance with s.30 of the 2003 Act. On the PIAB procedure generally, see Quigley & Binchy, "Navigating the PIAB Procedure", in Quigley & Binchy (eds.), *The Personal Injuries Assessment Board Act 2003: Implications for Legal Practice* (First Law, Dublin, 2004).

[97] Pursuant to s.32 of the 2003 Act.

[98] Refusing to accept a PIAB assessment has no negative consequences on one's right of action. Personal Injuries Assessment Board Act 2003, ss.12 and 30.

[99] The insurance industry has been criticised by one of the High Court Taxing Masters for "blindly consenting" to all-embracing orders for legal costs. MIAB, MIAB Report 2004, *op.cit.*, n.3, p.55.

Thus, in a situation where the claimant has legal representation, he has an economic incentive to reject the assessment as he or she then receives full damages without having to deduct legal fees. The advantage to the solicitor is that he or she will receive substantially larger legal fees as a representative (handling all aspects of the claim), than would be available as a legal advisor (merely offering guidance or advice). Furthermore, the solicitor is not forced to reduce the amounts charged for providing personal injuries services in order to attract clients, because the quantum of legal expenses ceases to be a factor for the claimant in choosing a solicitor. At the end of the action, the respondent will pay the legal expenses. Thus, the spectre of inter-solicitor price competition is dispelled.

3.1.3 Potential economic effects of the O'Brien *decision*

A scenario in which legal professionals are extensively involved in the PIAB process is not economically optimal for society. Assuming that the PIAB will safeguard the interests of the claimant whether or not he has legal representation (the basis for this assumption is set out below),[100] the claimant will receive the same amount of damages with or without legal representation. Hence, no economic benefit emerges from the representation to any member of society other than the solicitor.[101] For everyone else, insurance premiums will stay higher than they would without any legal professional involvement, with negative consequences for employment, business and investment. Funds of public authorities must be diverted from welfare-generating projects (for instance, public works), or taxes must be raised.

The finding that the right to legal representation precludes the PIAB from insisting on dealing directly with claimants will also affect its evolution as an institution. As established, it will be rational (and therefore should be expected) that solicitors will advise their clients to exercise

---

[100] See below, *Section 3.3.2: Claimant Protection in the PIAB Procedure.*

[101] This conclusion in based on the assumption that a solicitor's input will not change the amount awarded by the PIAB. The assumption on which this discussion proceeds is that the PIAB will award the correct quantum of damages to an applicant; the involvement of a solicitor does not change this. However, some marginal benefit may accrue to the claimant as he no longer has to spend time filling out the PIAB forms.

their right of legal representation. This will stop a dialogue, and trust, building up between the PIAB and the public, preventing it from becoming the institution it was designed to be. Nonetheless, the PIAB remains of value. As the sum awarded for personal injuries damages is determined by the PIAB, there will be less point in involving two sets of barristers and solicitors in the negotiation of damages. A reasonable, fixed sum will already be on the table. As noted, barristers are involved in 76.2% of Irish personal injuries claims (compared with 2.9% in England).[102] Reduced barrister involvement in the process will probably lead to overall savings, notwithstanding the *O'Brien* decision.

3.1.4 The role of the solicitor in protecting the interests of claimant

The most glaring objection to the economic narrative above is that it excludes the role of the solicitor in protecting the claimant's interests, and ignores the role of the solicitor in maximising the value of his client's claim. The reason for this exclusion is the assumption, already noted, that the PIAB will fairly determine the quantum of damages in all claims which it accepts.[103] If the PIAB do so with or without the intervention of counsel, then counsel's contribution to the process becomes irrelevant. This is, of course, a debatable assumption, and the arguments that underpin it are considered below.[104]

3.1.5 The direct communication policy was not "inexpedient"

As noted, McMenamin J. found that "the question of legal costs is not affected one way or the other by the policy adopted by the Board."[105] This conclusion was based on the fact that the Board does not award legal expenses. Thus, it was presumed, the expenses incurred by the claimant will be paid by the claimant, and will not be passed back over to the respondent.[106] The court seemed to accept the argument that the policy was, in fact, "inexpedient".[107] The argument that the policy of the Board

---

[102] Greenford, *op. cit.*, n.12.

[103] The Board has discretion not to arrange for an assessment in certain complex or sensitive cases, as outlined in s.17 of the 2003 Act.

[104] Section 3.2.2: Claimant protection in the PIAB procedure.

[105] *O'Brien v. Personal Injuries Assessment Board*, n.2, p.27.

[106] *Ibid.*

[107] *Ibid.*, p.28.

was inexpedient was made in the *amicus curiae* submissions of the Law Society.[108] The idea was that by corresponding with two parties instead of one, a succession of extra contacts occurs as the claimant contacts the solicitor on receipt of each communication from the Board. This, it was presumed, would result in higher solicitor fees.

The assumption underlying this argument is questionable, as is the conclusion inferred from the assumption. The assumption is that the ongoing correspondence will result in more solicitor/client contact than the solicitor acting alone. This may not be true if the PIAB, through its helpline and general assistance, effectively guides the claimant through the procedure, obviating the need for the claimant to discuss every issue with his solicitor.[109] Then, only in unusual cases where a solicitor's hand is needed to guide every step will the policy become uneconomical. Even accepting the argument's assumption, the inference that a set of contacts involving legal advice will result in higher legal fees than if the solicitor handles the entire claim may also be incorrect. In engaging in a series of distinct legal contacts seeking specific advice, the claimant is in a stronger position to understand exactly what services are being rendered by the solicitor. The degree of vagueness in solicitor's bills for legal services has been identified as problematic by the Competition Authority. In some cases amounts may be extremely detailed, but most are sparse, with most of the total amount falling under the heading of "professional fee." It is often difficult for clients to judge the quality of services received, and whether fees are appropriate.[110]

In a situation where the client retains control of his or her claim, and contacts his solicitor only for clarification of specific issues, he or she may only be billed for these specific services, and not for a general "professional fee." Hence, it is reasonable to assume that costs will be lower with direct claimant correspondence with the PIAB than if the client effectively relinquishes control of the claim to his or her solicitor, although ultimately this question can only be resolved by empirical data.

---

[108] *Ibid.*, p.20.

[109] The PIAB is under a duty to advise claimants to seek legal advice where it appears that the claimant is completing or may complete a step required by the PIAB procedure, where he or she does not have a sufficient appreciation of the consequences of the step.

[110] The Competition Authority, *Study of Competition in Legal Services: Preliminary Report* (Dublin, 2005), p.105.

Also, the conclusion that the PIAB policy lacked an economic foundation did not take into account the possibility of the PIAB award being rejected, and legal expenses being sought after an authorisation is issued. Based on past behaviour, and assuming economic rationality (decision making based on one's own best economic interest), such tactics seem inevitable. PIAB awards will be rejected, and claimant's solicitors and other legal professionals or experts will have their fees paid in full by the respondent. The PIAB policy of insisting on communicating directly with claimants was designed to prevent these costs from ever accumulating. Nonetheless, the court refused to find that this power was "necessary, expedient or incidental" to the PIAB function of reducing legal costs in personal injury claims.[111]

3.2 The legislative understanding

The legislature clearly intended the PIAB to have the power to communicate directly with claimants. In fact, an amendment that sought to insert a right to legal representation in the PIAB procedure was defeated by 31 votes to 11 in the *Seanad*.[112] The amendment was proposed by Senator Coughlan, who moved to insert the words "and legal representation" into section 7(1) of the Bill after the words "legal advice". Section 7, as enacted, reads:

> 7. (1) Nothing in this Act is to be read as affecting the right of any person to seek legal advice in respect of his or her relevant claim and no rule shall be made under *section 46* that affects that right.
>
> (2) *Subsection (1)* shall not be read as requiring any procedure to be followed by the Board or hearing to be conducted by it that would be required to be followed by a court were the claim concerned to be the subject of proceedings.

---

[111] *O'Brien v. Personal Injuries Assessment Board*, n.2, p.28, referring to the Personal Injuries Assessment Board Act 2003, s.52(2). "The Board shall have all such powers as are necessary or expedient for, or incidental to, the performance of its functions under the Act." How the general goal of reducing personal injuries costs can be considered a function of the Board is addressed below (*Section 3.3.3: A Broad Construction of the Act of 2003*).

[112] Seanad Debates, November 25, 2003.

The proposed amendment was intended to protect the right of persons to appoint a legal representative to complete the PIAB process on their behalf; in other words, the amendment would have had the same effect as the *O'Brien* judgment. The proposal was supported by some members of the *Seanad* as it would (i) prevent an imbalance of power between respondent and claimant,[113] (ii) afford protection to claimants in a sphere where determinations of legal issues will be made,[114] and (iii) protect what was described as the solicitor's right to earn a living.[115] Members of the Seanad opposing the amendment noted that the Board did not conduct oral hearings or make any determinations on liability.

> "There is no place to be represented in the operation of the PIAB. It is inquisitorial, not adversarial. It works on the basis of paper. Its *raison d'être* is to see if we can deal with cases without dealing with lawyers."[116]

Crucial to most of the speakers was the fact that the Bill did not interfere with the right to seek legal advice. Also, speakers opposing the amendment noted the economic rationale of attempting to minimize the involvement of the legal profession in the procedure.[117]

> "The purpose of this amendment is to state that nothing in the Act is to be read as affecting the right of any person to seek "legal advice and legal representation" in respect of a claim. The amendment seeks to add "legal representation" and we reject that because the PIAB would then be required to communicate directly with solicitors. The board will always communicate with the claimant so he or she is continually up to date with progress on a claim. If the claimant so requests, the PIAB will copy the correspondence to a solicitor but the board will not determine legal issues."[118]

---

[113] *Ibid., per* Senator Coughlan.
[114] *Ibid.*
[115] *Ibid., per* Senator Leyden.
[116] *Ibid., per* Senator O'Toole.
[117] *Ibid., per* Dr. Mansergh.
[118] *Ibid., per* the Minister of State at the Department of Enterprise, Trade and Employment, Mr. M. Ahern.

The reason for the political will to exclude legal representation was, as argued, to prevent the accrual of legal expenses.

> "If one brings lawyers into this, another layer is added to the structure and costs are increased. With lawyers involved, before one knows where one is, costs will rise not merely by 40% but by a lot more."[119]

The members of the Seanad discussing the proposed amendment were certain that the Act excluded the possibility of legal representation. This is clear not only from the fact that the amendment inserting a right to legal representation was proposed, but also from the basis on which it was ultimately rejected. However, the extent to which this fact should have been taken into account by the High Court is debatable; there are several concerns with the use of Oireachtas debates in the interpretation of statutes.[120] It is not proposed to enter that interpretative discussion by proposing that the debates should have been considered *in extenso* by McMenamin J. However, the right to legal representation was rejected by a strong majority, and the rationale for this opposition was to ensure that the PIAB could "deal with cases without dealing with lawyers."[121] This supports the argument that the power to deal directly with claimants is necessary, expedient, or incidental to the functions of the Personal Injuries Assessment Board.[122]

3.3 Constitutional and administrative law critique: Alternative construction

The decision of McMenamin J. was based on interpretation of the powers of the PIAB, and the finding that the policy of communicating directly with claimants was not necessary, expedient, or incidental to the functions of the Board.[123] The judge also based his decision on protection of the

---

[119] *Ibid., per* Senator Quinn.
[120] On these issues, see The Law Reform Commission, *Report on Statutory Drafting and Interpretation: Plain Language and the Law* (Law Reform Commission, Dublin, 2000), pp. 63–68.
[121] Seanad Debates, November, 25, 2003, *per* Senator O'Toole.
[122] Section 3.3.3: Alternative Interpretation.
[123] *O'Brien v. Personal Injuries Assessment Board*, n.2, p.24.

right to legal representation and the right of access to the courts,[124] and also discussed the nature of the right to legal representation in *obiter dicta* statements.[125]

It will in this section, be argued that, first, the PIAB does not interfere with any substantive rights in a fashion comparable with the circumstances in the authorities on which the *O'Brien* decision relies (3.3.1), and, second, that the interests that McMenamin J. described as the basis for the decision are sufficiently protected internally through the PIAB procedure (3.3.2). In conclusion, an alternative construction of the powers of the PIAB under the Act of 2003 is proposed (3.3.3).

3.3.1 Authorities cited in the decision

Regarding the right to legal representation, the principal authority cited by McMenamin J. is the decision of Kelly J. in *Re Commission to Inquire into Child Abuse*.[126] He quotes several sections of this judgment, which concerned the legality of a decision by the Commission to Inquire into Child Abuse. The Commission had "sought to impose a restriction upon the number of lawyers who might act by being present during a particularly important part of a case."[127] Kelly J. had found that this "novel and far reaching power" [128] restricted the client's ability to decide "how best to defend the case."[129]

McMenamin J. notes that Kelly J. was concerned with the protection of the right to a good name in the context of an adjudicative inquiry. It is true, as the court stated, that *Re Commission to Inquire into Child Abuse* emphasises the importance of legal representation even "outside the sphere of the administration of justice proper."[130] But, it does not create an absolute right to legal representation in all situations. There are clearly "distinguishing factors" between the facts of *O'Brien* and of *Re Commission to Inquire into Child Abuse*.[131]

---

[124] *O'Brien v. Personal Injuries Assessment Board*, p.28.
[125] *Ibid.*, pp.28–29.
[126] [2002] 3 I.R. 459.
[127] *O'Brien v. Personal Injuries Assessment Board*, p.25.
[128] *Re Commission to Inquire into Child Abuse* [2002] 3 I.R. 459 at 478.
[129] *Ibid.*, p.476.
[130] *O'Brien v. Personal Injuries Assessment Board*, n.2, p.26.
[131] *Ibid.*

The right to legal representation in certain situations outside the normal administration of justice is an undeniable, and important, feature of Irish constitutional and administrative law.[132] Where administrative tribunals will affect one's property rights, freedom, right to good name, or livelihood, the right to legal representation is often appropriate. However, an overview of the authorities indicates that the entitlement to legal representation, when found, tends to manifest itself in particular situations. Most Irish precedent on the subject stems from oral tribunals of inquiry, oral employment or disciplinary hearings, or other situations where lay tribunals act quasi-judicially.[133] In all cases where the right to representation is found, tangible rights (good name, employment or college status, freedom) are at stake. There is no general precedent for a right to legal representation in the context of tribunals, nor is the author aware of any precedent for such a right in written correspondence.

> "No precedent or authority has been produced for the general proposition that a lay tribunal exercising a quasi-judicial function must afford the parties appearing before it an opportunity to procure legal advice and be represented by lawyers."[134]

In situations where there is no adversarial process, there is little precedent to suggest a right to legal representation. In *Barry v. Sentence Review Group*, Butler J. declined to find an entitlement to legal representation before a body that advised the Minister for Justice on the administration of long-term prison sentences.[135] Stating that the applicant's right to legal advice and representation was satisfied in other contexts, Butler J. stated that an entitlement was not needed before the Sentence Review Group as the body was advisory, and came to recommendations in a "non-adversarial way."[136] In the *O'Brien* decision, neither applicant nor *amicus*

---

[132] See G. Hogan & G. Whyte (eds), *Kelly: The Irish Constitution* (4th ed., Lexis Nexis, Dublin, 2003), pp.644–647.

[133] *Haughey, re* [1971] I.R. 217, *Maguire v. Ardagh* [2002] 1 I.R. 385, *Gallagher v. Revenue Commissioners (No.2)* [1995] 1 I.R. 55 and *Flanagan v. University College, Dublin* [1988] I.R. 724.

[134] *Corcoran v. Minister for Social Welfare* [1991] 2 I.R. 175 at 183, *per* Murphy J.

[135] [2001] I.R. 167.

[136] *Ibid.*, p.169.

curiae submissions contained any reference to a right to legal representation in a procedure akin to that of the PIAB.[137]

3.3.2 Claimant protection in the PIAB procedure

In the *amicus curiae* submissions, and in the *O'Brien* judgment itself, little reference is made to the means by which the PIAB procedure protects the claimant. The assumption underlying the Law Society's submissions – and the reasoning of the court – seems to be that the PIAB procedure is adverse to the claimant's interests, and that the direct intervention of a legal representative is the sole means of protecting the claimant. This issue must be addressed. Also, the argument already made regarding the economic benefits of a lawyer-free PIAB process was conditional upon a contentious assumption: that the involvement of a legal representative (as opposed to legal advice) in the PIAB process will not change the quantum of the PIAB assessment or the degree of protection of the claimant's interests. Here, the reason for these assumptions will be established, and the protections inherent in the PIAB procedure considered. It will be argued that the PIAB procedure is designed to protect the rights and interests that the Law Society argued could only be protected through the intervention of a legal representative.

The first interest that the Law Society argued would be compromised by the PIAB policy of direct communication was the solicitor/client relationship. Submissions emphasized the undisputed importance of the legal professional privilege. It was argued that by refusing to communicate only with the solicitor, and by requiring the claimant to complete a specific piece of paperwork in order to have his solicitor copied on correspondence, the PIAB interfered with this relationship.

It is difficult to see how the PIAB interferes with the privacy of the solicitor-client relationship. The claimant may still engage completely with his or her solicitor, and may authorise his solicitor to complete all PIAB correspondence.[138] Certainly, the PIAB has no power to access confidential communications between the claimant and his or her solicitor.

---

[137] The cases cited that at least touched on the right to legal representation in non-judicial contexts are *R.B. v. A.S.* [2002] 2 I.R. 428, *Dunne v. Donohoe* [2002] 2 I.R. 533, *In Re Haughey* [1971] I.R. 217, *Howard v. Commissioner of Public Works* [1994] 1 I.R. 101 and *Kiely v. Minister for Social Welfare* [1977] 2 I.R. 267.

[138] Personal Injuries Assessment Board Act 2003, s.7(1).

If the claimant wishes his or her solicitor to deal with the PIAB, he need not complete the PIAB correspondence. The fact that a PIAB-issued form must be completed in order for the claimant's solicitor to receive copies of all correspondence from the PIAB is hardly a significant burden, and it presumably simplifies paperwork for the PIAB assessors, who would otherwise have to decipher the meaning of different solicitor-client contracts regarding representation.

The Law Society identified a situation where the PIAB insistence on communicating directly with claimants may be harmful: where the claimant has low educational attainment or poor literacy skills. This concern may be allayed quite simply. The PIAB procedure does not interfere with the right to legal advice. A vulnerable claimant can (i) insist his or her solicitor be copied on all correspondence, and (ii) allow his or her solicitor to complete, or approve, all communications sent to the PIAB. Presumably, someone who has low literacy skills will not attempt to navigate the PIAB process on their own, no more than they would start a personal injuries claim on their own. However, even if they do, the PIAB introduces a new layer of protection for vulnerable claimants. Should the Board infer from the "manner in which a claimant or respondent has completed, or is completing or attempting to complete," a step required under the Act, that he or she does not have a sufficient appreciation of the legal consequences of taking that step, or of following the Act's procedures generally, as his or her rights or obligations in relation to the claim are concerned, the Board is under a duty to advise the claimant to obtain legal advice, explain the legal consequences of each step of the procedure, and/or provide assistance in taking (or re-taking) steps in the PIAB procedure.[139] The consequences of the Board's breaching this duty are not specified in the Act, but presumably it might open itself to civil litigation for breach of a duty of care towards the claimant.[140] This duty is limited, however. A statement contained in the documents furnished to the assessors cannot, of itself, give rise to the duty to take one of the above steps.[141] Also, in its submissions, the Law Society noted that the PIAB may have no means of identifying vulnerable claimants.[142] This

[139] Personal Injuries Assessment Board Act 2003, s.29.
[140] See, however, *Glencar Exploration plc v. Mayo County Council* [2002] 1 I.R. 112 (SC); 1 I.L.R.M. 481.
[141] Personal Injuries Assessment Board Act 2003, s.29(5).
[142] *O'Brien v. Personal Injuries Assessment Board*, n.2, p.20.

criticism is legitimate, though it could be answered that at present, the courts system has no such means either; in that sense the PIAB procedure is an improvement on the status quo, and, when combined with legal advice, the procedure should prevent the vulnerable from making-missteps in their claim.

Importantly, the formalities of the PIAB procedure are fundamentally unlike those of a court. If the claimant makes a mistake in some step, there is no indication that the assessment will be thrown out, or prejudiced. In fact, throwing out or prejudicing the claim may open the PIAB to civil litigation and discourage other claimants from engaging directly in its procedure.[143] Hence, the PIAB should be fastidious in aiding claimants and ensuring that they maximise the value of their claims in their applications. Finally, vulnerable parties are further protected by section 45 of the Act of 2003, which recognises that where a claimant lacks full legal capacity (as a minor or person of unsound mind), court approval is required and the claimant's legal representation will be directed to be paid by the respondent.

The Law Society raised the issue of "equality of arms" in its submissions. It was argued that claimants are disadvantaged as defendants will have professional in-house legal advice.[144] The inference is that a policy of communicating directly with claimant and respondent converts, in practice, into a policy of communicating directly with claimant, but with respondent's in-house counsel. This imbalance appears stark when seen in an adversarial light. But it may be regarded as fictional in three important senses. First, the PIAB procedure is not comparable with that of a court. It involves a claimant submitting an application to the PIAB, which includes a medical report on which the PIAB bases an assessment of damages. The respondent's role is merely to accept or deny liability for the claim for the purposes of the assessment. It makes no submissions to the PIAB. Hence, even with an army of legal advisors, the respondent must still either accept liability for the claim or not.

The second reason why the "inequality of arms" argument is unconvincing is the fact that the claimant may seek as much legal advice as he or she wishes.[145] This is complemented by the PIAB policy that the claim-

---

[143] Personal Injuries Assessment Board Act 2003, s.29.
[144] *O'Brien v. Personal Injuries Assessment Board*, n.2, p.20.
[145] Personal Injuries Assessment Board Act 2003, s.7

ant's solicitor will be copied on correspondence if the claimant so wishes.[146] Admittedly, the PIAB maintained that this policy was within their discretion, thereby implying that they are not obliged to do so. Arguably, there are some situations where the PIAB should or must do so. But even if it was accepted that the PIAB has this discretion, if it refused to copy a solicitor in a situation where constitutional justice demanded it to do so, the PIAB would be acting *ultra vires* the discretion, and court intervention would be appropriate. The possibility of a discretion being misused does not mean that the discretion itself is unconstitutional.[147]

The third factor that undermines the relevance of "equality of arms" is that the PIAB assessment procedure has no negative consequences for the validity, or substance, of the underlying claim. As McMenamin J. states, "[t]he Assessment is not binding on either the claimant or on the respondent to a claim."[148] The assessment is not admissible in evidence in any proceedings in relation to the claim, unless the proceedings relate to enforcement of the assessment.[149] If the respondent declines to accept the PIAB assessment, the claimant may commence court proceedings, with no restrictions on his or her right to legal representation.[150] Also, nothing in the Act restricts the claimant's access to legal representation in order to seek an injunction to preserve evidence or prevent the transfer or dissipation of assets by the respondent.[151]

This discussion highlights the safeguards within the PIAB system. The existence of these safeguards undermines the contention that legal representation is specifically necessary to protect the claimant from pathologies or mistakes in the PIAB procedure, though the suspicion that legal representation is necessary to protect the claimant's interests will

---

[146] *O'Brien v. Personal Injuries Assessment Board*, n.2, p.16.

[147] There is a presumption that the Oireachtas intends that any proceedings, procedures, discretions or adjudications permitted, provided for, or prescribed by any enactment will be conducted in accordance with the principles of constitutional justice and that any departure from those principles will be restrained or corrected by the courts. *East Donegal Co-operative Livestock Mart Ltd. v. Attorney General* [1970] I.R. 317, applied by Keane C.J. in *DK v. Crowley* [2002] 2 I.R. 744. See Quigley, "The Constitutionality of the PIAB Act" in Quigley & Binchy (eds.), *The Personal Injuries Assessment Board: Implications for Legal Practice* (Firstlaw, Dublin, 2004), 60.

[148] *O'Brien v. Personal Injuries Assessment Board*, n.2, p.9.

[149] Personal Injuries Assessment Board Act 2003, s.51.

[150] *Ibid.*, s.31.

[151] *Ibid.,*, s.12(2).

probably remain in the mind of an adversarial lawyer. The reason for this suspicion is illustrated by the two authorities cited by McMenamin J. in an *obiter* discussion on the importance of the right to legal representation.

The first of these, *Powell v. Alabama*,[152] is cited to support the proposition that the right to legal representation "inheres in each of the steps which are necessary, ancillary and preliminary to the bringing of court proceedings."[153] *Powell* concerned a death row appeal by a man who was convicted of murder in audacious circumstances. His defence counsel was not actually appointed until the opening day of his trial.[154] The due process clause of the U.S. Constitution was found to have been violated. The second case, *Mosley et al v. St. Louis South Western Railway*,[155] concerned a racial discrimination action by plaintiffs who claimed that their dismissal was racially motivated. At an Equal Employment Opportunity Commission (EEOC) mediation, the EEOC officer compelled the plaintiffs to sign a waiver of their claim after their attorney had left. They initially refused to sign the waiver, but eventually did after the employment officer "told plaintiffs that the terms offered by defendant were the best she could obtain, and intimated that if plaintiffs elected to sue, they might be held liable for attorney's fees."[156]

As McMenamin J. states, these cases illustrate the importance of "equality of arms in litigation and various types of litigation processes."[157] The right to legal representation "inheres in the very notion of an adversarial system of justice."[158] However, the cases are scarcely comparable with the issue at hand. The PIAB procedure is not an adversarial process. The PIAB is not a state seeking to execute the claimant. Nor does it force the claimant to waive his legal rights when his or her legal advisor is not present. It is an administrative procedure that delivers a voluntary assessment to the claimant, to be accepted at his or her discretion (with the assistance, if wished for, of legal advice).

The PIAB exists outside of the adversarial legal system. The effects of its determinations are carefully circumscribed, to avoid prejudicing

---

152 *Powell v. Alabama* 287 U.S. 45 (1932).
153 *O'Brien v. Personal Injuries Assessment Board*, n.2, p.29.
154 287 U.S. 45, p.53.
155 634 F.2d 942 (1981) (Fifth Circuit Court of Appeals).
156 *Ibid.*, p.945.
157 *O'Brien v. Personal Injuries Assessment Board*, n.2, p.30.
158 634 F.2d 942 at 945.

the rights of the claimant in the adversarial system. The PIAB procedure contains numerous safeguards, and its success as an institution is conditional upon its giving fair awards to claimants. Hence, the usual rationales underlying the demand for legal representation do not apply. Fundamentally, the claimant's property and other interests are protected in a different way than in normal adversarial proceedings.

In an adversarial legal culture, the right to legal representation is one of the fundamental means of protecting the interests of a litigant. But the right is unnecessary if the PIAB functions as it should. When it struck down the policy of direct claimant communication, the High Court arguably viewed the new procedure through the wrong lens. In adversarial procedures, the right to legal representation is often vital. But this is not an adversarial procedure; it is one of assessment.

3.3.3 A broad construction of the Act of 2003

An alternative construction of the Act of 2003 is proposed. First, it has been argued that the policy of direct communication had direct economic benefits in reducing legal expenses. Assuming this, is the policy then "necessary or expedient for, or incidental to" to the performance of the functions of the PIAB?[159] The question becomes whether the functions of the PIAB include reducing the legal fees associated with personal injuries claims. Arguably they do. The long title of the Act states that that its purpose is to "enable, in certain situations, the making of assessments without the need for legal proceedings." If substantial legal costs are incurred by the claimant, then the claimant will have reason to reject the PIAB assessment, and bring legal proceedings to seek legal costs from the respondent, contrary to the purpose of the Act.[160] Also, as noted, the legislative intent was that the Board have this power.[161] This intent is reflected in the structure of the Act, which makes no reference to legal representation for normal applications, and specifically states that the section 7(1) right to legal advice should not be read as requiring the Board to follow any specific procedures akin to those required by court proceedings.[162] Legal representation is one such procedure. This

---

[159] This brings the policy within the PIAB's powers under s.54 of the Act of 2003.
[160] See *Section 3.1: The economic rationale for the policy of direct communication.*
[161] See *Section 3.2: The Legislative Understanding.*
[162] Personal Injuries Assessment Board Act 2003, s.7(2).

conclusion is particularly reasonable when one considers that the principal purpose for creating the PIAB was to reduce legal expenses. The Act of 2003 should be purposively interpreted in this light.

Even with this construction, the courts could still review the exercise of the power of direct communication, to ensure that it is pursued in accordance with the principles of constitutional justice. If the Board unjustly refused to communicate with a claimant's solicitor in a deserving situation (where, for instance, the claimant was of no fixed abode, or was vulnerable for other reasons), a court might find the Board to have exercised its discretion unreasonably, amounting to a breach of fair procedures.[163] In this fashion, the property interests of the claimant would be protected. But there is no reason at present to suspect that the Board may unreasonably refuse to recognize legal representation when demanded to do so by constitutional justice, so the presumption of constitutionality should apply to the exercise of the discretion.[164]

4. Implications for Future Compensation Frameworks

Rather than impose an obligation to effect the policy of direct communication in a constitutional fashion, the High Court found that the PIAB simply lacked the power to adopt the policy at all. The success of this action may mean that other challenges to the PIAB will follow on its heels.

> "'There will be so many challenges to the board and I have a few more lined up', said Denis Boland, Mr O'Brien's solicitor.[165]

It is likely that the future challenges to which Mr Boland refers will also

---

163 See the decision of Barron J in *O'Sullivan v. Minister for Social Welfare* [1997] 1 I.R. 464. There, the power of a social welfare appeals officer to decide whether to award an appellant the expenses associated with her appeal was upheld, but the decision to refuse to award them in that particular case was a breach of fair procedures.

164 There is a presumption that statutory-derived executive powers are to be exercised in a constitutional manner. *East Donegal Co-operative Ltd v. Attorney General* [1970] I.R. 317. See, also: *McDonald v. Board nag Con (No.2)* 1965 I.R. 217, *The State (Quinn) v. Ryan* [1965] I.R. 70, See G. Hogan & G. Whyte (eds), *Kelly: The Irish Constitution* (4th ed., Lesix Nexis, Dublin, 2003), pp.853–867.

165 News Item from the Claims Standards Council, December 15, 2004. http://www.claimscouncil.org/newsitem.html?itemno=82 (last visited, March 7, 2005).

involve rights derived from the Constitution and from principles of natural justice.[166] This, the final section of this chapter, argues that the courts, in adjudicating future challenges to the PIAB procedure, the Civil Liability and Courts Act 2004, or to other reforms of tort compensation, should protect the substance, not the forms, of claimants' property rights. Administrative law rights, when used to formalise court-oriented procedures, undemocratically institutionalise the status quo. This may prove a problematic issue for the courts when faced with upcoming mass compensation actions of unprecedented scale.

While the *O'Brien* decision turned on the question of *vires* and the powers of the Board, most of the substance of the judgment revolved around the right to legal representation. The decision is replete with lyrical and forceful quotes about the importance of legal representation in the vindication of rights.[167] However, there are few links between the factual interferences that inspired these quotes (which were often significant and draconian) and the substance of the actual PIAB interference with the right to legal representation.[168] Instead, the importance of the right was stated and restated, and the mere fact of any interference was deemed sufficient to condemn the policy of direct communication.[169]

The right to legal representation cannot be divorced from its context, and this context is best understood in terms of the interests this right is supposed to protect. In the Irish legal order, the right to legal representation historically stems from the "natural justice" principle of *audi alteram partem* – the requirement to hear the other side.[170] Hence, as noted, most examples of its use in Irish constitutional law involve adversarial proceedings; particularly oral hearings where significant constitutionally

---

[166] Perhaps the next challenge might be a curtailment of the PIAB policy of refusing to award legal expenses incurred in the procedure. The PIAB may award expenses that have been "reasonably and necessarily" incurred by claimants (s.44(2) of the 2003 Act), but has indicated that such expenses will not include legal fees in most cases. This refusal to award legal fees may also be interpreted as interference with the right to legal representation or legal advice, and found to be *ultra vires*. But, to follow the argument outlined above, such a finding would misunderstand the non-adversarial, claimant-oriented PIAB process.

[167] *O'Brien v. Personal Injuries Assessment Board*, *op. cit.*, n.2, pp.14, 22, 23, 25, 26, 29 and 30 of the unreported judgment.

[168] *Ibid.* at pp.29–30.

[169] *Ibid.*, at pp.19, 23, 27 and 28.

[170] See G. Hogan & G. Whyte (eds), *Kelly: The Irish Constitution* (4th ed., Lexis Nexis, Dublin, 2003), pp.640–647.

protected interests are at stake.[171] A criminal cannot rely on this right of legal representation to send his lawyer to prison in his place, and a newlywed cannot expect his legal representative to consummate his marriage on his behalf. The right to legal representation is designed for situations with certain features. It is not a free-floating norm.

The PIAB is not an institution that gives rise to any substantive justification for the invocation of a right to legal representation. There are no oral hearings, no adversarial submissions, and, above all, no threats to property rights or other interests.[172] The assessment may always be rejected later on. Furthermore, the PIAB's institutional interests are aligned with those of claimants: the PIAB will only succeed as an institution if it wins the trust of claimants.[173] Hence, there is no rationale to justify the imposition of a right to legal representation into the procedure.

Determining that protection of the right to legal representation is essential to vindication of property rights in non-adversarial administrative procedures is not only unnecessary, it also institutionalises the status quo. A property right is a legal construct. In a situation where courts are the only means of vindicating property rights, the right to legal representation becomes linked to effective vindication of one's property rights. The PIAB procedure is different; it protects the property rights through a different method.[174]

If even the small, circumscribed change made by the PIAB procedure could be unconstitutional, perhaps constitutional amendments are the only means of tweaking with the court-based system of personal injuries, even slightly.[175] The judiciary – in a constitutional democracy – interpret the

---

[171] See, generally; *Re Haughey* [1971] I.R. 217, *Maguire v. Ardagh* [2002] 1 I.R. 385, *Gallagher v. Revenue Commissioners (No.2)* [1995] 1 I.R 55 and *Flanagan v. University College Dublin* [1988] I.R. 724.

[172] See, above, *section 3.3.2: Claimant protection in the PIAB procedure.*

[173] See, above, *sections 3.1.3: Potential economic effects of the* O'Brien *decision.*

[174] See, above, *section 3.3.2: Claimant protection in the PIAB procedure.*

[175] Quigley, "The Constitutionality of the PIAB Act", in Quigley & Binchy (eds.), *The Personal Injuries Assessment Board: Implications for Legal Practice* (First Law, Dublin, 2004), p.60. On the other types of reforms considered by the government, see: Sutherland, *Alternative Approaches to Personal Injuries Compensation – A Survey of Selected Foreign Systems*, Appendix 2 of the Second Report of the Special Working Group on Personal Injury Compensation (The McAuley Report) (Department of Enterprise, Trade and Employment, Dublin, 2001).

Constitution in a way that keeps open the channels of public change.[176] The Seanad rejected the idea of a right to legal representation in private dealings with the PIAB by almost a 3:1 majority.[177] This determination was effectively overridden by the High Court. Prescribing the types of procedures that the Oireachtas may legitimately create is a power of the courts in the Irish constitutional order. These prescriptions arguably should be guided by the protection of substantive interests rather than the constitutional institutionalisation of the present system.

With the emerging possibility of another major compensation action of a hitherto unprecedented scale, the courts may again be presented with challenges to the constitutionality or *vires* of statutory bodies designed to cut down the delivery costs and delays in arranging compensation.[178] Because of the scale of the illegal nursing home charges and institutional abuse actions (RIRB) (each of which may run to billions of euros), the government may find it undesirable to deliver this compensation through a method with expenses that amount to a third, or more, of the quantum of awards.

The sole previous litigation on a scale comparable with actions of this nature is the army deafness claims. Lawyer's fees accounted for one third of the €276.8m that was paid out in army deafness claims by August 20, 2004.[179] Members of the government may argue that, when claims are similar in nature or in scale, there should be ways to administer compensation that will cost substantially less than the €9,000 per claim reported in some army deafness cases.

If new procedures are created to administer these large-scale compensation claims, administrative law challenges will quickly follow. There will undoubtedly be interests who would prefer to see these claims

---

[176] John Hart Ely, *Democracy and Distrust: A Theory of Judicial Review*, pp.73–104 (1980).

[177] Seanad Debates, November 25, 2003. The tally was 31 against the insertion of a right to legal representation, 11 for.

[178] "316,000 could be eligible for payments" *The Irish Times*, March 4, 2005. The two major potential sources of litigation in 2005 are persons who seek redress for sexual and physical abuse in state institutions (and litigation arising from illegal charges on elderly hospital patients (see *In the Matter of Article 26 of the Constitution and In the Matter of the Health (Amendment) (No.2) Bill 2004* [2005] I.E.S.C. 7).

[179] "Deafness claims outnumber soldiers two to one", *Irish Independent*, August 20, 2004.

administered through courts, or court-like tribunals. Of course, the courts must ensure that any new administrative bodies protect the substance of underlying claims. However, given the scale of these claims, and the costs of litigation and court-like proceedings, it may be desirable to recognise that these interests can be protected through means other than recourse to courts, and court-oriented administrative law rights. In constitutionally cementing legal professionals and procedures into the very idea of compensation for personal injuries, the only interest that is vindicated is counsel's fundamental right to client.[180]

[180] Interestingly, the lawyer's right to make a living was one of the issues discussed in the debate concerning the amendment to insert a right to legal representation into the Act of 2003. Refusing to insert a right of legal representation into the Act of 2003 undermined, according to one deputy, the solicitor's right to earn a living. See, *O'Brien v. Personal Injuries Assessment Board & ors* [2005] I.E.H.C. 101 (March 11 2005) where McMenamin J., in determining the form of the order to be made, made it clear that what was involved was not just the question of *vires* under section 7 of the Act of 2003 but that of *vires* in the context of the entire Act.

The Rise and Rise of Personal Injury Liability – A Temporary Difficulty or a Permanent Crisis?

STEVE HEDLEY*

This evening I consider the way legal systems respond to accidental injury, and in particular, claims for damages. The basic idea is a simple one. If someone is injured in an accident, then they will almost certainly ask themselves how it happened. And sometimes when they do so, they realise that the accident was the fault of someone else. Many injuries on the road can be traced to poor driving by some party or other, for example. What the action for damages does is to let the victim sue whoever was at fault. The emotional pain of the injury must stay with the victim who suffered it, but the financial pain at least can be moved to the wrongdoer, who was truly responsible for it.

This is a very basic legal idea, which (so far as is known) crops up in just about every legal system there is, to some degree at least. The very words used today are ancient ones. The wrongful injury is called in law a tort – *tort* being an old word for *wrong* – and the wrongdoer (who caused the injury) is usually said to be *negligent*, that is, neglectful of the care they should show to others.

Most societies seem to have hit on the notion of (what we now call) tort liability. Tort appears under different names in all the ancient legal systems. There are many variants, in Brehon law, in Roman law, in mediaeval common law. The core idea is always the same. If an accident

---

*Steve Hedley is Professor of Law at University College, Cork. This paper is the text of his Inaugural Lecture delivered to a University audience at University College Cork, on January 22, 2004.

occurs due to fault or negligence, then the person at fault should do something to compensate the victim and the victim's family. The ancient codes of laws tended to have lists of injuries, each with its own price tag for the compensation appropriate. Brehon law, for example, listed a variety of injuries that would attract a money payment – the precise amount varied with the severity of the injury, how quickly the victim recovered, and whether a permanent mark would be left. And of course it varied with the social rank of the victim – injuring some royal was much more serious than injuring a servant. If long-term medical care was needed, the wrongdoer had to provide it, though in certain specified cases a money payment could be substituted. And so on.[1]

All very sensible, indeed inevitable where there is no public health care, and little by way of law enforcement machinery. Putting it in modern terms, I suppose you could say that this ancient law had three main functions.

Firstly, the function of finding out what happened, of establishing the truth. Sometimes the truth will be obvious but often it will not, and some legal official is needed to make findings of fact. It would be useless for the law to say only that "whoever was at fault must pay": there must also be a judge or tribunal who can say, authoritatively, whose fault it was and how much money is appropriate.

The second function is to see to the needs of the victim and the victim's family. Any serious injury will have painful consequences, painful both physically and economically. Even societies that largely leave their members to look after themselves can see that something needs to be done to help the victim of wrongdoing. And of course a serious injury never affects the victim *alone*: the victim's nearest and dearest are also injured, emotionally or in their pockets or both. Something has to be done.

And the third function is that of punishment. Injuring other people *has* to have consequences, of an unpleasant kind, for whoever did it. Conceivably it will make the victim feel better about it; equally importantly, it will deter both this wrongdoer and others from repeating dangerous behaviour in the future.

See how conveniently, how neatly, for relatively poor societies, tort

---

1 See especially F. Kelly, *A Guide to Early Irish Law* (Dublin, 1988), 129–134, 149–151.

liability fulfils all three functions, all at once. When a claim for damages is made, the court will step in and firstly, determine what happened – the first function. If compensation is awarded, it will go some way towards satisfying the victim's needs, satisfying the second. And having to pay the compensation will certainly feel like a punishment to the defendant; a strong deterrent against repeating that sort of conduct. So, with these three useful functions combined in one, it is not surprising that so many societies hit on this solution. It is not perfect, but it satisfies quite a lot of the demands that will be made after any significant accident: to find out what happened; to compensate those who have unfairly lost out; and to punish those responsible.

What *is* surprising is that we have stuck with this solution right up to the present day.[2] Today, the political and legal systems have become much more complicated and sophisticated. There is much better provision for all of the three functions I mentioned: better ways of enquiring into the truth, an elaborate medical and social security system to see to the needs of the sick, and detailed safety regulations to minimise risks and punish those who unnecessarily add to them. Yet still we have this mediaeval response to accidents built into the legal system; it has not been allowed to fade away, but has been tolerated, and in some ways deliberately encouraged to grow.

So we have not abolished the old idea of liability for fault; very much the contrary. And the amount of claims is large: so in 2002 about two-thirds of all High Court plenary summonses were for personal injury claims.[3] The idea has been broadened, applied more broadly, made more and more abstract so that it can be applied in almost any situation. The guiding principle (which all new lawyers learn) was laid down over 70 years ago, in a judgment in a Scottish case, which has rightly been repeated and copied across the common law world. In the case, Lord Atkin observed that:

> "You must take reasonable care to avoid acts or omissions which

---

[2] On the growth of the system historically see Gearoid Carey, "A Critique of the Development of Occupational Injuries Liability in Irish Torts Law" [2001] *Irish Law Times* (8) 130.

[3] *Court Service Annual Report 2003* (10,600 out of 16,400 summonses). The initial signs are that the number is now falling: 'Fall off in court proceedings confirmed' [2003] *Health and Safety Review* (October) 1.

> you can reasonably foresee would be likely to injure your neighbour. Who, then, in law is my neighbour? The answer seems to be – persons who are so closely and directly affected by my act that I ought reasonably to have them in contemplation as being so affected when I am directing my mind to the acts or omissions which are called in question."[4]

So the idea of fault, of negligence, is at its most general. Atkin deliberately used the most abstract language he could, so that tort liability could extend to almost any context. *Whenever* an accident happens, the victim can ask – Who should have foreseen this? Who is my "neighbour in law" (as Atkin put it) and so should have prevented this from happening to me? It is this abstract character that is one of the leading characteristics of the modern law. Now the actual facts before that Scottish court were most specific, not to say bizarre – a plaintiff who suffered an unhealthy encounter with a decomposing snail in the carbonated beverage she was consuming. But the beauty of the Atkin formula is that it avoids these petty details. Its generality enables liability to be extended to new situations which bear little resemblance to the old. The law can always respond to new situations even if they are very different from the old. It allows it to be driven by plaintiffs, often plaintiffs who can show no similarity between their case and any previous one, but who nonetheless say, the defendant in this case is, in law, my neighbour – he ought reasonably to have had me in his thoughts when carrying out this dangerous activities, he should have directed his mind to my situation. This makes the law of tort a very flexible solution to the problem of personal injuries. For the government to issue safety regulations is always complex, controversial and needing long consultations. For the tort lawyers, it is simpler. Their main command to everyone who could harm others is: act in a reasonable fashion, or we may make you compensate those who get hurt.

So this general liability, this abstract idea that everyone must act reasonably in relation to everyone else, is obviously going to be very popular with plaintiffs. Whenever someone is injured, they can cast around

---

[4] *M'Alister (or Donoghue) v. Stevenson* [1932] A.C. 562 at 580. For the background to the case see S. Hedley, "*M'Alister (or Donoghue) v. Stevenson*" in E. O'Dell (ed.), *Leading cases of the 20th century* (Round Hall, Dublin, 2000) 64.

for someone else who might have prevented it, someone who can be said to have been unreasonably caring of the plaintiff's interests; and if they can find such a person, as they often can, then they can sue.

Now how much is this like the traditional approach, like the Brehon law or the old common law of centuries ago? The words used are often the same, but the reality is different. Recall the three functions of the traditional law: establishing the truth, providing compensation, and punishing dangerous conduct. What we see today is that one of these functions – that of providing compensation – is swallowing up the others. The system of today is not serious about really finding out what happened, nor does it do a very good job of deterring anyone. A few points to illustrate this.

To say that the modern system is not really about establishing the truth sounds like a serious criticism. In fact, it's inevitable if the modern system is to work at all. We don't *want* every case to go to trial, to hear all witnesses with something to say, to look at every relevant document. It all costs too much. The modern pressure is for the parties *not* to go to court but to settle as soon as possible. Getting a quick settlement should usually be in the interests of all concerned. And of course when a claim is settled, the defendant does not usually admit anything; part of what they are paying their money for is to *avoid* any admission, to settle the matter without an admission, without prejudice, and largely without publicity. Truth is not what it is mainly about. Truth costs too much.

We see this most clearly, by comparing ordinary tort cases with the very few cases where it *is* thought that truth is important, and so a tribunal is established to get at that truth. When a judge goes all out for the truth and nothing but, then an expensive time is had by all. Many examples could be given, which I'm sure you are familiar with. The victims of whatever disaster is being looked at have no incentive to keep matters short. This is their opportunity to tell the world what happened to them, and to claim justice – very probably they will have no other opportunity – and they will not want to be curtailed or told to be brief. Also, whoever is said to be at fault very probably has no reason to deal with the matter quickly. Their reputation will be greatly at stake, and it would be a terrible blow to them if the tribunal were to find them responsible. So they too will argue mightily, and spend much on lawyers; and whoever is chairing the tribunal may find (as Miss Justice Laffoy recently did) that some of the parties are not being as cooperative as they might. Now, this approach can be right for cases of outstanding public importance, but it cannot be the norm. Enquiring deeply into the truth is just too expensive for ordinary cases. It cannot be afforded.

Equally, any idea that modern tort law punishes the person truly responsible for the harm has largely gone by the wayside. It is only rarely the person actually at fault who pays – the actual person whose fault the accident was hardly ever has to put their hand in their pocket. Usually the claim is within an insurance policy: the driver sued for injuries caused by bad driving, or the doctor sued for poor medical technique do not pay personally. And where injury is caused by someone working for an organisation – an employee of a private firm, or a civil servant or whatever – it is usually the organisation that is made to pay. The blame is borne not by any real person but by more diffuse entities – "the company", "the local authority", even "the Republic of Ireland". The idea that tort law makes wrongdoers pay has gone.

Of course, it is still true that individuals are affected by the cost of the system – there are always quarrels over precisely how insurance cover is paid for. But the point is that *everyone* pays. All doctors must be insured, including the ones with excellent or perfect safety records; ditto drivers and employers. No-one is allowed to say, "I am a safe driver, no-one will get hurt because of me, so I needn't contribute". The system doesn't work that way. Individually negligent people do not pay tort damages. Rather, the cost is diffused and spread across the community through insurance and tax; ultimately, the bill for the tort of negligence is met by the entire community. The idea that tort law makes wrongdoers pay has gone.

This does not mean, I think, that the law has given up on ideas of personal responsibility in safety law. On the contrary, it insists on it in many ways, but it does so largely though the criminal law. For poor driving there is a whole range of penalties, from the sledgehammer of manslaughter prosecutions right down to slap-on-the-wrist methods such as penalty points.[5] Again, in cases of medical negligence, the criminal law is beginning to intervene in more serious cases,[6] and there are calls to

---

5 See "Editorial: What's the Point of Road Deaths?" (2003) 9 *Medico-Legal Journal of Ireland* (1) 2.

6 See "Editorial: The Criminalisation of Fatal Medical Mistakes" (2003) 327 *British Medical Journal* 1118 (15 November).

make poor treatment a disciplinary matter. The legal system has not, then, given up on the idea of personal responsibility for fault. But the link with damages has effectively been severed. To be found guilty of negligence may be embarrassing or even professionally damaging, but we no longer punish individuals by making them pay.

So that is the modern system, which as I say today emphasises compensation above all else. And all the signs are that the system will continue to grow, if left to its own devices; that is certainly what it has done in the past. What, then can be done? It is not hard to criticise the system, on many grounds: waste, sloth, the prevalence of fraud, and that too much of the money circulating in the system ends up with the lawyers and insurers. The difficulty is not that the criticisms are wrong – on the contrary, they are usually fair points. But what is not clear is what would be a better system. Everyone can agree that it would be much better if we arranged matters so that there were fewer accidents in the first place – *any* system for sweeping up after accidents have happened is bound to be gruesome and unsatisfactory to some degree. But how could we do this? And if the current system is in some way unfair, what would a fairer system look like?

There is an extensive international literature on possible solutions, for the problem is a world-wide one. This is not just a local problem. Ireland is particularly worried about the "compo culture" at the moment, but most of the developed world has the same problem to some degree: as the Irish worry about their road traffic premiums, the Australians worry about medical liability and the British worry about the cost of employers' insurance. And the Americans' disdain for their personal injury lawyers is practically part of the landscape. How many personal injury attorneys, they would ask, does it take to change a light bulb? Three – one to turn the bulb, a second to shake him off the ladder, and the third to sue the ladder company. The law of tort has few friends and many enemies. Lots of people across the world are looking for a better solution. Yet there is actually very little that can be done; the menu of choices is restricted.

The first choice is to abolish tort entirely – to say that as from a certain date, no-one should be allowed to sue anyone else for inflicting personal injuries on them. This proposal has been made relatively recently, by a leading scholar in the field, Professor Patrick Atiyah of Oxford.[7] And it

---

7 See especially P.S. Atiyah, *The Damages Lottery* (Oxford, 1997).

has a surprising amount to be said for it. It would certainly mean that less money would go to the lawyers and other intermediaries, which many would regard as a good thing. It also appeals strongly to a certain type of economist, who would say that people should be encouraged to provide for their own future by saving and buying insurance, rather than relying on others to compensate them. *Nonetheless*, there seems to be no country or legal system anywhere that has actually done this, and you can understand why. It seems heartless to deprive the victim of serious negligence of any right of compensation, indeed I doubt if it is constitutional. Of course there will be support for doing away with the possibility of false or fraudulent claims, but not at the cost of taking away all the good and honest ones too. Any proposed abolition would be certain to meet concerted opposition from the main professional groups involved – lawyers, insurers, and unions. All in all, I don't think it is a real political possibility.

The second approach certainly *is* possible – this is to replace tort liability with a state injury fund. Those who now pay for the tort system through their insurance premiums – drivers, employers, any major institution – will rather pay to a state-run agency. That agency will then pay sums in benefits to *anyone* accidentally injured, regardless of whose fault the injury was. We would no longer ask whose fault an accident was, or refuse payment if no-one was at fault. The victim would be entitled to benefits simply on proof of injury.

Would this work, and if it did would it be better? Well, we know that a system like that *can* work, because it does. Until 1974, New Zealand had a common law system of liability much like Ireland does now, but was abolished in favour of a state fund much as I have described.[8]

Is this New Zealand system better than what Ireland has now? The New Zealand system has not been trouble-free – there have been crises from time to time over funding, just as under the tort system. But overall, it stands up well when compared with tort. The scheme works with reasonable efficiency. There is far less resort to the law courts. And a far

---

8 On the system generally see S. Todd (ed.), *The Law of Torts in New Zealand* (3rd ed., Wellington, 2001) chaps 1 and 2; see also the Accident Compensation Corporation's own website (http://www.acc.co.nz/). For assessment and discussion see Symposium proceedings, "Looking back at accident compensation" (2003) 34 *Victoria University of Wellington Law Review* (2, June).

higher proportion of the money circulating within the system actually ends up with the injured people the system is meant to protect: for every dollar paid into the New Zealand fund, about 80c or 90c will end up being awarded to a claimant, whereas for every € paid in liability insurance premiums in Ireland only perhaps 55c or 65c will end up with the victims.[9] And while the New Zealand system is not entirely free of fraud – no system is – it seems to be much less of a problem than in more traditional systems. So in some respects at least the New Zealand system is clearly better.

But in other respects it is simply different. It makes no sense to say that it is better or worse, it is just not trying to achieve the same thing. Traditional common law systems award a relatively high level of benefits. Everything that the victim of wrongdoing has lost is potentially recoverable – earnings lost in the past and future, costs of medical care, a figure for emotional distress, and something towards their legal costs. But if we go down the New Zealand route and allow *everyone* to claim, even if they cannot establish wrongdoing on anyone else's part, then obviously the remedy cannot be so generous. Many more people will claim, and so unless the cost of the scheme is allowed to let rip, the benefits to each individual claimant must be much, much lower than under common law rules. The New Zealand system spreads the money more widely, and so cannot be so generous in individual cases.

The New Zealand scheme has always been a focus of controversy, just like the system in Ireland has. The scheme has not been extended to cover every accident that the common law dealt with – lawyers there are always on the lookout for gaps in the scheme, so that it may be evaded and resort be had to common law damages. Claims grow from year to year, as they seem to under any system. This means that either there must be must be more generous funding, or benefits must somehow be cut. Neither will be popular. It seems, on the experience so far, that the New Zealand scheme is not quite as resilient as common law schemes. During

---

9 It is difficult to obtain reliable estimates for either system; it seems to be the case that the higher the award of damages, the lower the proportion which goes in costs. The most comprehensive study of the Irish system in the last 10 years is a 1996 report by Deloitte and Touche, commissioned by the Ministry for Commerce Science and Technology. The main findings are summarised in B. McMahon and W. Binchy, *Law of Torts* (3rd ed., Butterworths, Dublin, 2000), 1.168–1.174.

economic downturns, the easiest solution politically is to cut the benefits. The accident compensation scheme is seen as a part of the social security system, and reducing benefits to make the books balance is often far more politically acceptable than taking away people's legal rights can ever be. It is therefore much easier to assert downward pressure on benefits under a New Zealand-type system than under an Irish system. New Zealand doesn't have debates over the compo culture. If the system costs too much, victims of accidents just get paid less.

Whether this is good or bad depends on what you think the system should be for. The benefits under a New Zealand-type system are low, and the victim of harm will never recoup the whole of the loss they suffer. Yet what that system does, it does fairly, giving equal benefits to all the victims of accidents, and spending only the bare minimum on lawyers and administrators. You pays your money and you takes your choice.

The current choice in Ireland is to stick with a common law system, but with rather vigorous attempts to cut out wastage and fraud. Many individuals and public bodies have been at work here, driven by anxieties about increases in insurance premiums.[10] In the last few years, the Supreme Court especially have been very unwilling to extend the law, deciding any dubious case against the plaintiff, and emphasising that they will not tolerate exaggeration or fabrication of claims.[11] Bodies that are sued on a regular basis, particularly governmental bodies, are adopting an increasingly well-organised and professional attitude to claims.[12] And defendants generally have become more aggressive in attempts to identify fraud. A personal injury claimant today may very probably find themselves being followed or spied on by a private investigator, testing the possibility that they have lied on important matters; and the Irish Insurance Federation have opened a confidential call line for those who wish to shop friends or colleagues who appear to be making fraudulent claims.[13] The Government also have responded to the problem. A new Personal Injuries Assessment

---

[10] For figures see e.g. *IIF Factfile 2002* (available as a PDF document on the Irish Insurance Federation's website, http://www.iif.ie/statistics.htm).

[11] See especially *O'Connor v. Bus Átha Cliath/Dublin Bus* [2003] 4 I.R. 459 (SC); [2003] I.E.S.C. 59.

[12] See e.g. "Claims: the Era of Systematic Management" [2002] *Health and Safety Review* (May) 21.

[13] See "Suspected cases of insurance fraud are reported", *Irish Times*, October 13, 2003. The number is 1890–333333.

Board has been established, to standardise and speed up the calculation of the right sum in damages, without needing a court hearing.[14] Modifications are also planned to legal procedures, to shorten the period within which claims can be brought at all, to streamline the procedures for legal action, to provide for mediation, and to combat fraudulent claims.[15]

Can all these moves be regarded as improvements to the system? I think that they can, but they should properly be regarded as the beginning of the fight, not the end. They seem like the right moves to make, but whether they will work is anyone's guess. In the case of the new legislation especially, it is not obvious that any of it will have the intended effect. *Perhaps* reducing the limitation period will reduce the number of claims, but equally it may have the reverse effect: lawyers will know that if they do not sue quickly they will not be able to sue at all, and so perhaps they will issue a summons where they might earlier have let matters ride. *Perhaps* standardising and policing these claims within the court system will mean that they will be dealt with more efficiently, though it has to be said that similar reforms in England have not had that effect.[16] *Perhaps* the new provisions on fraud will deter some of the more outrageous lies and fabrications. But while everyone knows that there is fraud, nobody really knows how much there is, or how easy it will be to detect; it is not obvious, therefore, how great a reduction in claims can be achieved by this method. And if the effect of all these changes together is to place insurmountable obstacles in the path of genuine plaintiffs, it is by no means impossible that some of the obstacles may be declared contrary to the constitution.

The greatest experiment of all is the Personal Injuries Assessment Board, to which uncontested claims are to go for assessment of damages before the plaintiff can go to a court. This might achieve a great deal. The Board is certainly in a position to promote a high degree of consistency, avoiding the much-repeated criticism that the amount of compensation varies from judge to judge. But the Board will only play a

---

[14] Personal Injuries Assessment Board Act 2003, which became law on December 28, 2003.

[15] Civil Liability and Courts Bill, so far not yet debated in the Oireachtas; see draft at http://www.feargalquinn.ie/bills/2003/liab(h).htm.

[16] For comment see "The Courts Bill 2003: Beware of Hidden Dangers" [2003] *Health and Safety Review* (September) 11.

limited role in the legal system at first. In its initial phase it will apply only to workplace injury claims. The case can only go to the Board if the defendant is prepared to admit that they are legally liable, and is only disputing the amount. And neither party to the dispute can be forced to accept whatever sum the Board proposes; when the Board names the sum they feel is appropriate, either party will be free to go to court to see if they can get a better deal. The hope is, of course, that they will not; but we will have to see. At least one prominent judge thinks that it will not work: Mr Justice Joseph Finnegan, President of the High Court, guesses that the 4,000 or so cases per year which do not settle under the current system will not under the new system either – so the cases that are actually generating the main expense of the system will not be affected.[17] Perhaps he is wrong; the Tánaiste thinks so.[18] But there is an unfortunate history here, of reforms to the tort system which do not have their intended effect. So when civil juries were abolished in personal injuries in the late 1980s,[19] it was widely assumed that this would reduce the overall bill for liability; but that did not happen. We must wait and see whether the new reforms fair any better.

The next phase of the struggle is therefore to see how this works out. But while it is not unreasonable to hope for a reduction in insurance premiums as a result, the system is complicated, and reforms can have perverse effects. It is far from obvious that the proposed reforms will lead to lower legal bills. Even if they do, it does not follow that awards of damages will be lower. It is important to realise that while the Board may well make damages awards more consistent, they have no mandate to *reduce* the level payable. On the contrary, they are supposed to codify current practice and leave the level of awards where it is. So the most that can be expected is that a slightly lower proportion of the sums involved will go the lawyers – there is no reason to suppose that damage awards themselves will go down. And what if they did? Reducing damages awards does not necessarily lead to lower insurance premiums, because premiums depend on other factors as well. The level of damages awards are one major factor affecting insurance company balance sheets, but only one.

---

[17] "Injuries board won't cut cases, says top judge", *Sunday Business Post,* January 18, 2004.

[18] "PIAB 'will cut level of injury cases'", *Irish Examiner,* January 19, 2004.

[19] Courts Act 1988, in force August 1, 1988.

No insurance company has promised to reduce their premiums when the Board is fully on stream – nor is it reasonable to expect that they should.

But the final point is that there will always be a next question of this sort. People are always getting injured; if the most generous system of compensation on offer is the common law tort system, then there are always plenty who will make a case under it. The effects of the recent reforms, which may reduce the total bill, should soon be felt; but equally there are other matters just on the horizon which may increase the bill – such as the rise of the asbestos safety cases,[20] and the possible new EU directive on cyclists, making car drivers liable in accidents with cyclists whether or not fault can be proved.[21]

The problem of too many tort claims is therefore not a temporary little difficulty which can simply be removed by some legislation. Whatever we do to patch it up for now will only take the pressure off for a short while. The law's expansionist tendencies mean that there is a permanent crisis, which we will always need to keep an eye on.

---

[20] "Asbestos: the new army deafness claims?" [2003] *Health and Safety Review* (October) S2.

[21] Proposed 5th Motor Insurance Directive.

Appendix 1

CIVIL LIABILITY AND COURTS ACT 2004

(2004 No. 31)

ARRANGEMENT OF SECTIONS

PART 1

PRELIMINARY AND GENERAL

SECT.

1. Short title and commencement.
2. Interpretation.
3. Orders and regulations.
4. Service of notices.
5. Expenses.

PART 2

CIVIL LIABILITY

6. Application of Part.
7. Amendments of Statute of Limitations (Amendment) Act 1991.
8. Letter of claim.
9. Rules of court.
10. Bringing of proceedings.
11. Request for further information.
12. Defence and counterclaim.
13. Pleadings generally.
14. Verifying affidavit.
15. Mediation conference.
16. Report of chairperson of mediation conference.
17. Formal offers.
18. Pre-trial hearings.
19. Evidence.
20. Expert evidence.
21. Intervention in a personal injuries action.
22. Matter to be taken into account by the court when assessing damages.
23. Actuarial tables.
24. Discount rate.
25. False evidence, etc.
26. Fraudulent actions.
27. Collateral benefits.

PART 3

COURTS

Chapter 1

Funds of Suitors

Chapter 2

Miscellaneous Provisions

An Act to provide for certain procedural and other changes in actions to recover damages for personal injuries; to provide that an action for personal injuries shall not be brought after the expiration of 2 years from the date of accrual of the cause of action or the date of knowledge of the cause of action whichever occurs later; to provide that where a plaintiff in a personal injuries action gives false evidence, the court may dismiss the plaintiff's action; to make provision in relation to the assessment of damages in a personal injuries action; to make provision in relation to the jurisdiction of the Circuit Court in proceedings relating to land; to provide for the disposal of part of the funds of suitors vested in the Accountant of the Courts of Justice; to make provision in relation to the publication of reports, and production of documents prepared for the purposes, of proceedings to be heard otherwise than in public; and, for those and other purposes, to amend the Statute of Limitations (Amendment) Act 1991, the Civil Liability Act 1961 and certain other enactments; and to provide for related matters. [21*st July* 2004]

Acts Referred to

Building Societies Act 1989	1989, No. 17
Central Bank Act 1971	1971, No. 24
Civil Liability Act 1961	1961, No. 41
Civil Liability (Amendment) Act 1964	1964, No. 17
Companies Acts 1963 to 2003	
Court Officers Act 1926	1926, No. 27
Courts Act 1971	1971, No. 36
Courts Act 1981	1981, No. 11
Courts Act 1991	1991, No. 20
Courts and Court Officers Act 1995	1995, No. 31
Courts and Court Officers Act 2002	2002, No. 15
Courts (No. 3) Act 1986	1986, No. 33
Courts (No. 2) Act 1997	1997, No. 43
Courts Service Act 1998	1998, No. 8
Courts (Supplemental Provisions) Act 1961	1961, No. 39
Criminal Procedure Act 1967	1967, No. 12
Debtors (Ireland) Act 1840	3 & 4 Vict., c. 105
Domestic Violence Act 1996	1996, No. 1
Family Home Protection Act 1976	1976, No. 27
Family Law Act 1995	1995, No. 26
Family Law (Divorce) Act 1996	1996, No. 33
Family Law (Maintenance of Spouses and Children) Act 1976	1976, No. 11
Garda Síochána (Compensation) Acts 1941 and 1945	
Judicial Separation and Family Law Reform Act 1989	1989, No. 6
Legitimacy Act 1931	1931, No. 13
Maintenance Act 1994	1994, No. 28
Personal Injuries Assessment Board Act 2003	2003, No. 46
Planning and Development Act 2000	2000, No. 30
Registration of Title Act 1964	1964, No. 16
Social Welfare Act 1998	1998, No. 6
Social Welfare (Consolidation) Act 1993	1993, No. 27

Status of Children Act 1987	1987, No. 26
Statute of Limitations (Amendment) Act 1991	1991, No. 18
Succession Act 1965	1965, No. 27
Taxes Consolidation Act 1997	1997, No. 39
The Courts of Justice Act 1924	1924, No. 10

Be it enacted by the Oireachtas as follows:

PART 1

PRELIMINARY AND GENERAL

Short title and commencement

1.—(1) This Act may be cited as the Civil Liability and Courts Act 2004.

(2) This Act, other than the provisions specified in *subsection (3)*, shall come into operation on such day or days as the Minister may appoint by order or orders either generally or with reference to any particular purpose or provision and different days may be so appointed for different purposes or provisions.

(3) *Sections 2* to *4, 31* and *32, Chapter 1* of *Part 3* and *sections 49* and *56* shall come into operation upon the passing of this Act.

Interpretation

2.—(1) In this Act, except where the context otherwise requires—
"act" has the same meaning as it has in the Act of 1961;
"Act of 1961" means the Civil Liability Act 1961;
"Act of 1993" means the Social Welfare (Consolidation) Act 1993;
"Act of 1998" means the Social Welfare Act 1998;
"Act of 2002" means the Courts and Court Officers Act 2002;
"Act of 2003" means the Personal Injuries Assessment Board Act 2003;
"court" means, in relation to a personal injuries action, the court in which that action has been brought, being the High Court, Circuit Court or District Court, as the case may be;
"date of knowledge" shall be construed in accordance with the Statute of Limitations (Amendment) Act 1991;
"defendant" has the same meaning as it has in the Act of 1961;
"expert evidence" means evidence of fact or opinion given by a person who would not be competent to give such evidence unless he or she had a special skill or expertise;
"further information" has the meaning assigned to it by *section 11*;

"mediation conference" has the meaning assigned to it by *section 15*;
"Minister" means the Minister for Justice, Equality and Law Reform;
"negligence" includes nuisance and breach of duty (whether the duty exists by virtue of a contract, a provision of a statute, an instrument under a statute, or otherwise);
"personal injuries action" means an action for the recovery of damages, in respect of a wrong—

(*a*) for personal injuries,

(*b*) for both such injuries and damage to property (but only if both have been caused by the same wrong), or

(*c*) under section 48 of the Act of 1961,

but shall not include an application for compensation under the Garda Síochána (Compensation) Acts 1941 and 1945, or an action where the damages claimed include damages for false imprisonment or trespass to the person;
"personal injuries summons" has the meaning assigned to it by *section 10*;
"personal injury" has the same meaning as it has in the Act of 1961;
"plaintiff" has the same meaning as it has in the Act of 1961;
"pleading" means, in relation to a personal injuries action, a personal injuries summons, a defence, a defence and counterclaim or any other document (other than an affidavit or a report prepared by a person who is not a party to that action) that, under rules of court, is required to be, or may be, served (within such period as is prescribed by those rules) by a party to the action on another party to that action;
"settlement" includes, in relation to a personal injuries action, a settlement of the action in part only, and cognate words shall be construed accordingly;
"third party" has the same meaning as it has in the Act of 1961;
"wrong" has the same meaning as it has in the Act of 1961;
"wrongdoer" has the same meaning as it has in the Act of 1961.

(2) In this Act—

(*a*) a reference to a section or Part is a reference to a section or Part of this Act, unless it is indicated that a reference to some other enactment is intended,

(*b*) a reference to a subsection, paragraph or subparagraph is a reference to a subsection, paragraph or subparagraph of the provision in which the reference occurs, unless it is indicated that a reference to some other provision is intended, and

(*c*) a reference to any enactment is a reference to that enactment as amended, extended or adapted whether before or after the coming into operation of this Act, by or under any subsequent enactment.

Orders and regulations

3.—Every order (other than an order under *section 1*(*2*)) and regulation under this Act shall be laid by the Minister before both Houses of the Oireachtas as soon as may be after it is made and, if a resolution annulling the order is passed by either such House within the next 21 days on which that House sits after the order or regulation is laid before it, the order or regulation shall be annulled accordingly but without prejudice to the validity of anything previously done thereunder.

Service of notices

4.—(1) A notice under *section 8* or *section 17* shall be addressed to the person concerned by name, and may be served on or given to the person in one of the following ways:

(*a*) by delivering it to the person;

(*b*) by leaving it at the address at which the person ordinarily resides or, in a case in which an address for service has been furnished, at that address; or

(*c*) by sending it by post in a prepaid registered letter to the address at which the person ordinarily resides or, in a case in which an address for service has been furnished, to that address.

(2) For the purposes of this section, a company within the meaning of the Companies Acts 1963 to 2003 shall be deemed to be ordinarily resident at its registered office, and every other body corporate and every unincorporated body shall be deemed to be ordinarily resident at its principal office or place of business.

Expenses

5.—The expenses incurred by the Minister in the administration of this Act shall, to such extent as may be sanctioned by the Minister for Finance, be paid out of moneys provided by the Oireachtas.

PART 2

CIVIL LIABILITY

Application of Part

6.—Subject to *sections 14*(*8*), *25*(*4*), *26*(*4*), *27*(*3*) and *28*(*2*), a provision of this Part applies only to personal injuries actions brought after the date of the commencement of that provision.

Amendments of Statute of Limitations (Amendment) Act 1991

7.—The Statute of Limitations (Amendment) Act 1991 is amended by—

(*a*) the substitution in subsection (1) of section 3 of "2 years" for "three years",

(*b*) the substitution in subsection (1) of section 4 of "2 years" for "three years",

(*c*) the substitution in subsection (1) of section 5 of "2 years" for "three years",

(*d*) the insertion of the following section:

"5A.—(1) Where the relevant date in respect of a cause of action falls before the commencement of *section 7* of the *Civil Liability and Courts Act 2004*, an action (being an action to which section 3(1), 4(1), 5(1) or 6(1) of this Act applies) in respect of that cause of action shall not be brought after the expiration of—

(*a*) 2 years from the said commencement, or

(*b*) 3 years from the relevant date, whichever occurs first.

(2) In this section 'relevant date' means the date of accrual of the cause of action or the date of knowledge of the person concerned as respects that cause of action whichever occurs later.",

and

(*e*) the substitution in subsection (1) of section 6 of "2 years" for "three years".

Letter of claim

8.—(1) Where a plaintiff in a personal injuries action fails, without reasonable cause, to serve a notice in writing, before the expiration of 2 months from the date of the cause of action, or as soon as practicable thereafter, on the wrongdoer or alleged wrongdoer stating the nature of the wrong alleged to have been committed by him or her, the court hearing the action may—

(*a*) draw such inferences from the failure as appear proper, and

(*b*) where the interests of justice so require—

(i) make no order as to the payment of costs to the plaintiff, or

(ii) deduct such amount from the costs that would, but for this section, be payable to the plaintiff as it considers appropriate.

(2) In this section "date of the cause of action" means—

(*a*) the date of accrual of the cause of action, or

(*b*) the date of knowledge, as respects the cause of action concerned, of the person against whom the wrong was committed or alleged to have been committed,

whichever occurs later.

Rules of court

9.—(1) It shall be a function of the courts in personal injuries actions to ensure that parties to such actions comply with such rules of court as apply in relation to personal injuries actions so that the trial of personal injuries actions within a reasonable period of their having been commenced is secured.

(2) Where rules of court prescribe a period of time for the service of a document, or the doing of any other thing, in relation to a personal injuries action, the period within which that document may be served or thing may be done shall not be extended beyond the period so prescribed unless—

(*a*) the parties to the action agree to the period being extended, or

(*b*) the court considers that—

(i) in all the circumstances the extension of the period by such further period as it may direct is necessary or expedient to enable the action to be properly prosecuted or defended, and

(ii) the interests of justice require the extension of the period by that further period.

(3) For the purposes of ensuring compliance by a party to a personal injuries action with rules of court, a court may make such orders as to the payment of costs as it considers appropriate.

(4) Nothing in this Act shall be construed as limiting or reducing the power of an authority, having (for the time being) power to make rules regulating the practice and procedure of a court, to—

(*a*) make such rules in relation to personal injuries actions provided such rules do not derogate from, and are not inconsistent with, any provision of this Act, or

(*b*) make such rules in relation to proceedings or actions other than personal injuries actions.

(5) In *subsections* (*1*) and (*2*) a reference to the courts or the court includes a reference to the Master of the High Court and a county registrar.

Bringing of proceedings

10.—(1) Proceedings in the High Court, Circuit Court or District Court, in respect of a personal injuries action, shall be commenced by a summons to be known as and referred to in this Act as a "personal injuries summons".

(2) A personal injuries summons shall specify—

(*a*) the plaintiff's name, the address at which he or she ordinarily resides and his or her occupation,

(*b*) the personal public service number allocated and issued to the plaintiff under section 223 (inserted by section 14 of the Act of 1998) of the Act of 1993,

(*c*) the defendant's name, the address at which he or she ordinarily resides (if known to the plaintiff) and his or her occupation (if known to the plaintiff),

(*d*) the injuries to the plaintiff alleged to have been occasioned by the wrong of the defendant,

(*e*) full particulars of all items of special damage in respect of which the plaintiff is making a claim,

(*f*) full particulars of the acts of the defendant constituting the said wrong and the circumstances relating to the commission of the said wrong,

(*g*) full particulars of each instance of negligence by the defendant.

(3) Where a plaintiff fails to comply with this section—

(*a*) the court may—

(i) direct that the action shall not proceed any further until the plaintiff complies with such conditions as the court may specify, or

(ii) where it considers that the interests of justice so require, dismiss the plaintiff's action,

and

(*b*) the court shall take such failure into account when deciding whether to make an order as to the payment of the costs of the personal injuries action concerned, or the amount of such costs.

(4) Where a plaintiff fails to comply with this section, the court hearing the personal injuries action concerned may draw such inferences from the failure as appear proper.

Request for further information

11.—(1) Upon the request of a defendant in a personal injuries action, the plaintiff shall provide the defendant with—

(*a*) particulars of any personal injuries action brought by the plaintiff in which a court made an award of damages,

(*b*) particulars of any personal injuries action brought by the plaintiff which was withdrawn or settled,

(*c*) particulars of any injuries sustained or treatment administered to the plaintiff that would have a bearing on the personal injuries to which the personal injuries action relates, and

(*d*) the name of any persons from whom the plaintiff received such medical treatment,

in this Act referred to as "further information".

(2) Upon the request of a defendant in a personal injuries action, the plaintiff shall provide the defendant with documents, of such a class as may be prescribed from time to time by the Minister, from the Revenue Commissioners or the Minister for Social and Family Affairs, as may be appropriate, relating to any earnings or other income in respect of which the plaintiff is making a claim.

(3) Where a plaintiff fails to comply with a request under *subsection* (*1*) or (*2*)—

(*a*) the court may—

(i) direct that the personal injuries action concerned shall not proceed any further until the plaintiff complies with such conditions as the court may specify, or

(ii) where it considers that the interests of justice so require, dismiss the plaintiff's action,

and

(*b*) the court shall, at the hearing of the action, take such failure into account when deciding whether to make any order as to the payment of the costs of the action, or the amount of such costs.

(4) Where, upon a request referred to in *subsection* (*1*), a plaintiff fails to comply with that subsection, the court hearing the personal injuries action concerned may draw such inferences from the failure as appear proper.

(5) Where, for the purposes of complying with *subsection* (*2*), a plaintiff requests the Revenue Commissioners or the Minister for Social and Family Affairs to furnish him or her with documents referred to in that paragraph, the Revenue Commissioners or the said Minister shall furnish him or her with such documents as are in their, or his or her, possession or procurement.

Defence and counterclaim

12.—(1) A defence to a personal injuries action shall specify—

(*a*) the allegations specified, or matters pleaded, in the personal injuries summons of which the defendant does not require proof,

(*b*) the allegations specified, or matters pleaded in the personal injuries summons of which he or she requires proof,

(*c*) the grounds upon which the defendant claims that he or she is not liable for any injuries suffered by the plaintiff, and

(*d*) where the defendant alleges that some or all of the personal injuries suffered by the plaintiff were occasioned in whole or in part by the plaintiff's own acts, the grounds upon which he or she so alleges.

(2) A counterclaim in a personal injuries action shall specify—

(*a*) the personal public service number allocated and issued to the defendant under section 223 (inserted by section 14 of the Act of 1998) of the Act of 1993,

(*b*) the injuries to the defendant alleged to have been occasioned by the wrong of the plaintiff,

(*c*) full particulars of all items of special damage in respect of which the defendant is making a claim,

(*d*) full particulars of the acts of the plaintiff constituting the said wrong and the circumstances relating to the commission of the said wrong,

(*e*) full particulars of each instance of negligence by the plaintiff.

(3) Where a defendant fails to comply with this section—

(*a*) the court may—

(i) direct that the action shall not proceed further until the defendant complies with such conditions as the court may specify, or

(ii) where it considers that the interests of justice so require, give judgment in favour of the plaintiff,

and

(*b*) the court shall take such failure or refusal into account when deciding whether to make any order as to the payment of the costs of the personal injuries action concerned, or the amount of such costs.

(4) Where a defendant fails to comply with this section, the court hearing the personal injuries action concerned may draw such inferences from the failure as appear proper.

Pleadings generally

13.—(1) All pleadings in a personal injuries action shall—

(*a*) in the case of a pleading served by the plaintiff, contain full and detailed particulars of the claim of which the action consists and of each allegation, assertion or plea comprising that claim, or

(*b*) in the case of a pleading served by the defendant or a third party contain full and detailed particulars of each denial or traverse, and of each allegation, assertion or plea, comprising his or her defence.

(2) Subject to this Act, pleadings in a personal injuries action shall be in such form as are prescribed by rules of court.

Verifying affidavit

14.—(1) Where the plaintiff in a personal injuries action—

(*a*) serves on the defendant any pleading containing assertions or allegations, or

(*b*) provides further information to the defendant,

the plaintiff (or in the case of a personal injuries action brought on behalf of an infant or person of unsound mind by a next friend or a committee of the infant or person, the next friend or committee) shall swear an affidavit verifying those assertions or allegations, or that further information.

(2) Where the defendant or a third party in a personal injuries action serves on another party to the action any pleading containing assertions or allegations, the defendant or third party, as the case may be, shall swear an affidavit verifying those assertions or allegations.

(3) Where a personal injuries action is brought on behalf of an infant or a person of unsound mind by a next friend or a committee of the infant or person, an affidavit to which *subsection* (*1*) applies sworn by the next friend or committee concerned shall, in respect of assertions, allegations or further information, of which he or she does not have personal knowledge, state that he or she honestly believes the assertions, allegations or further information, to be true.

(4) An affidavit under this section shall be lodged in court not later than—

(*a*) 21 days after the service of the pleading concerned or such longer period as the court may direct or the parties may agree, or

(*b*) in the case of a requirement to which *subsection* (*8*)(*b*) applies, 7 days before the date fixed for the trial of the personal injuries action concerned.

(5) If a person makes a statement in an affidavit under this section—

(*a*) that is false or misleading in any material respect, and

(*b*) that he or she knows to be false or misleading,

he or she shall be guilty of an offence.

(6) The reference to court in *subsection* (*4*) shall—

(*a*) in the case of a personal injuries action brought in the High Court, include a reference to the Master of the High Court, and

(*b*) in the case of a personal injuries action brought in the Circuit Court, include a reference to the county registrar for the county in which the proceedings concerned were issued.

(7) An affidavit sworn under this section shall include a statement by the deponent that he or she is aware that the making of a statement by him or her in the affidavit that is false or misleading in any material respect and that he or she knows to be false or misleading is an offence.

(8) This section applies to personal injuries actions brought—

(*a*) on or after the commencement of this section, and
(*b*) before such commencement, where a party to the action requires (not later than 21 days before the date fixed for the trial of the action) another party to the action to swear an affidavit in accordance with this section.

Mediation conference

15.—(1) Upon the request of any party to a personal injuries action, the court may—

(*a*) at any time before the trial of such action, and
(*b*) if it considers that the holding of a meeting pursuant to a direction under this subsection would assist in reaching a settlement in the action,

direct that the parties to the action meet to discuss and attempt to settle the action, and a meeting held pursuant to a direction under this subsection is in this Act referred to as a "mediation conference".

(2) Where the court gives a direction under *subsection (1)*, each party to the personal injuries action concerned shall comply with that direction.

(3) A mediation conference shall take place—

(*a*) at a time and place agreed by the parties to the personal injuries action concerned, or
(*b*) where the parties do not agree a time and place, at a time and place specified by the court.

(4) There shall be a chairperson of a mediation conference who shall—

(*a*) be a person appointed by agreement of all the parties to the personal injuries action concerned, or
(*b*) where no such agreement is reached—
(i) be a person appointed by the court, and
(ii) (I) be a practising barrister or practising solicitor of not less than 5 years standing, or
(II) a person nominated by a body prescribed, for the purpose of this section, by order of the Minister.

(5) The notes of the chairperson of a mediation conference and all communications during a mediation conference or any records or other evidence thereof shall be confidential and shall not be used in evidence in any proceedings whether civil or criminal.

(6) The costs incurred in the holding and conducting of a mediation conference shall be paid by such party to the personal injuries action concerned as the court hearing the action shall direct.

Report of chairperson of mediation conference

16.—(1) A person appointed under *section 15(4)* to be the chairperson of a mediation conference shall prepare and submit to the court hearing the personal injuries action concerned a report, which shall set out—

(*a*) where the mediation conference did not take place, a statement of the reasons as to why it did not take place, or

(*b*) where the mediation conference did take place—

(i) a statement as to whether or not a settlement has been reached in the personal injuries action concerned, and

(ii) where a settlement has been entered into, a statement of the terms of the settlement signed by the parties thereto.

(2) A copy of a report prepared under *subsection (1)* shall be given to each party to the personal injuries action at the same time as it is submitted to the court under that subsection.

(3) At the conclusion of a personal injuries action, the court may—

(*a*) after hearing submissions by or on behalf of the parties to the action, and

(*b*) if satisfied that a party to the action failed to comply with a direction under *section 15(1)*,

make an order directing that party to pay the costs of the action, or such part of the costs of the action as the court directs, incurred after the giving of the direction under *section 15(1)*.

Formal offers

17.—(1) The plaintiff in a personal injuries action shall, after the prescribed date, serve a notice in writing of an offer of terms of settlement on the defendant.

(2) The defendant in a personal injuries action shall, after the prescribed date, serve a notice in writing on the plaintiff—

(*a*) of an offer of terms of settlement, or

(*b*) stating that he or she is not prepared to pay any sum of money to the plaintiff in settlement of the action.

(3) A copy of a formal offer shall, after the expiration of the prescribed period be lodged in court by, or on behalf of, the plaintiff or defendant, as the case may be.

(4) The terms of a formal offer shall not be communicated to the judge in the trial of a personal injuries action until after he or she has delivered judgment in the action.

(5) The court shall, when considering the making of an order as to the payment of the costs in a personal injuries action have regard to—

(*a*) the terms of a formal offer, and
(*b*) the reasonableness of the conduct of the parties in making their formal offers.

(6) This section is in addition to and not in substitution for any rule of court providing for the payment into court of a sum of money in satisfaction of a cause of action or the making of an offer of tender of payment to the other party or parties to an action.

(7) In this section—

"formal offer" means an offer under *subsection* (*1*) or (*2*)(*a*), or a statement under *subsection* (*2*)(*b*);

"prescribed date" means such date before the date of the commencement of the trial of the personal injuries action concerned as is prescribed by order of the Minister;

"prescribed period" means such period commencing on the prescribed date as is prescribed by order of the Minister.

Pre-trial hearings

18.—(1) Where, in a personal injuries action, the court considers it appropriate, it shall direct that a hearing be held before the trial of the action for the purposes of determining what matters relating to the action are in dispute.

(2) All parties to a personal injuries action shall be entitled to be heard at a hearing held pursuant to a direction under *subsection* (*1*).

(3) A hearing held pursuant to a direction under *subsection* (*1*) shall be presided over by—

(*a*) in the case of a personal injuries action brought in the High Court, a judge of the High Court, the Master of the High Court, a Deputy Master of the High Court or an officer nominated under paragraph 6(1) of the Eighth Schedule to the Courts (Supplemental Provisions) Act 1961, as the President of the High Court may direct,
(*b*) in the case of a personal injuries action brought in the Circuit Court, a judge of the Circuit Court, the county registrar for the county in which the action was brought or a member of the staff of the Circuit Court Office in the county in which the action was brought, as the President of the Circuit Court may direct,
(*c*) in the case of a personal injuries action brought in the District Court, a judge of the District Court.

(4) This section is in addition to and not in substitution for any power of a court to give directions in relation to any matter in a personal injuries action.

Evidence

19.—(1) In a personal injuries action evidence as to any matter shall, where the court so directs, be given by affidavit.

(2) This section shall not operate to deny a party in a personal injuries action the right to cross-examine a witness who has given evidence by affidavit in accordance with a direction under *subsection (1)*.

Expert evidence

20.—(1) In a personal injuries action, the court may appoint such approved persons as it considers appropriate to carry out investigations into, and give expert evidence in relation to, such matters as the court directs.

(2) A party in a personal injuries action shall co-operate with a person appointed under this section and shall, in particular, provide the person with—

(*a*) (i) any report or other document prepared by the party, or

(ii) any report or other document prepared on behalf of the party concerned, for the purposes of or in contemplation of the personal injuries action,

and

(*b*) any document or information used or referred to for the purpose of preparing the report.

(3) The costs incurred in the appointment of, and carrying out of an investigation by, a person appointed under this section shall be paid by such party to the personal injuries action concerned as the court hearing the action shall direct.

(4) A party in a personal injuries action shall be entitled to cross-examine a person appointed under this section in relation to any matter that he or she was appointed to investigate and give expert evidence on.

(5) The President of the High Court in consultation with the President of the Circuit Court and the President of the District Court shall approve such persons as he or she considers appropriate for the purposes of this section, and a person so approved is in this section referred to as an "approved person".

Intervention in a personal injuries action

21.—(1) The Supreme Court may, upon an appeal to it in a personal injuries action, invite such persons as it considers appropriate to make submissions to the court—

(*a*) in relation to any matter concerning either liability or damages that it considers to be of exceptional public importance, and

(*b*) if the action belongs to a class of causes of action in which the same or a similar matter arises.

(2) The Supreme Court may perform functions under *subsection (1)*, either—

(*a*) upon receiving a request in that behalf from a party to the personal injuries action concerned, or from a person who is not such a party, or

(*b*) where no such request is made.

(3) Where a person declines an invitation to make submissions under this section he or she shall inform the court in writing stating his or her reason for so declining.

Matter to be taken into account by the court when assessing damages

22.—(1) The court shall, in assessing damages in a personal injuries action, have regard to the Book of Quantum.

(2) *Subsection (1)* shall not operate to prohibit a court from having regard to matters other than the Book of Quantum when assessing damages in a personal injuries action.

(3) In this section "Book of Quantum" means the Book of Quantum required to be prepared and published by the Personal Injuries Assessment Board under the Act of 2003.

Actuarial tables

23.—(1) The Minister may, by regulations, prescribe actuarial tables for the purpose of their being referred to by the courts when assessing damages in personal injuries actions in respect of future financial loss.

(2) A court in a personal injuries action shall, in assessing damages in respect of future financial loss, refer to such actuarial tables (if any) as are prescribed under *subsection (1)*.

(3) In this section "actuarial tables" means actuarial tables prepared by a person designated for that purpose by a body prescribed by regulations made by the Minister.

Discount rate

24.—(1) The Minister may, by regulations, prescribe the discount rate that shall apply for the purposes of the assessment of damages in respect of future financial loss.

(2) Regulations under *subsection (1)* may prescribe different rates in respect of different classes of financial loss or different periods of time.

(3) The court may apply a discount rate other than the rate prescribed under *subsection (1)* if it considers that the application of the rate prescribed would result in injustice being done.

(4) In this section "discount rate" means, in relation to the assessment of damages by a court, the rate commonly referred to by that name that is applied by the court for the purpose of determining the current value of any future financial loss.

False evidence, etc.

25.—(1) If, after the commencement of this section, a person gives or dishonestly causes to be given, or adduces or dishonestly causes to be adduced, evidence in a personal injuries action that—

(*a*) is false or misleading in any material respect, and

(*b*) he or she knows to be false or misleading, he or she shall be guilty of an offence.

(2) If, after the commencement of this section, a person gives, or dishonestly causes to be given, an instruction or information, in relation to a personal injuries action, to a solicitor, or person acting on behalf of a solicitor, or an expert, that—

(*a*) is false or misleading in any material respect, and

(*b*) he or she knows to be false or misleading,

he or she shall be guilty of an offence.

(3) For the purposes of this section, an act is done dishonestly by a person if he or she does the act with the intention of misleading the court.

(4) This section applies to personal injuries actions—

(*a*) brought on or after the commencement of this section, and

(*b*) pending on the date of such commencement.

(5) In this section "expert" means a person who has a special skill or expertise and who—

(*a*) has been engaged by or on behalf of a plaintiff or defendant in a personal injuries action to give expert evidence in that action, or

(*b*) for the purposes of or in contemplation of a personal injuries action has been requested to carry out an examination or investigation in relation to any matter for which such special skill or expertise is necessary.

Fraudulent actions

26.—(1) If, after the commencement of this section, a plaintiff in a personal injuries action gives or adduces, or dishonestly causes to be given or adduced, evidence that—

(*a*) is false or misleading, in any material respect, and

(*b*) he or she knows to be false or misleading,

the court shall dismiss the plaintiff's action unless, for reasons that the court shall state in its decision, the dismissal of the action would result in injustice being done.

(2) The court in a personal injuries action shall, if satisfied that a person has sworn an affidavit under *section 14* that—

(*a*) is false or misleading in any material respect, and

(*b*) that he or she knew to be false or misleading when swearing the affidavit,

dismiss the plaintiff's action unless, for reasons that the court shall state in its decision, the dismissal of the action would result in injustice being done.

(3) For the purposes of this section, an act is done dishonestly by a person if he or she does the act with the intention of misleading the court.

(4) This section applies to personal injuries actions—

(*a*) brought on or after the commencement of this section, and

(*b*) pending on the date of such commencement.

Collateral benefits

27.—(1) The Act of 1961 is amended by the insertion, in section 50, of the following subsection:

"(2) In assessing damages under this Part, account shall not be taken of any charitable gift (whether in the form of money or other property) made to the plaintiff in consequence of the death of the deceased unless—

(*a*) the defendant is the donor of the gift, and

(*b*) at the time of the making of the gift he or she informs the plaintiff in writing that, should the plaintiff recover damages in an action under this Part, the defendant will apply to the court for the damages to be reduced by an amount equal to the amount of the gift or the value of the gift, as may be appropriate.",

and the said section 50 as it stood immediately before the commencement of this subsection shall be referred to as subsection (1) of section 50.

(2) The Civil Liability (Amendment) Act 1964 is amended by the insertion, in section 2, of the following subsection:

"(2) In assessing damages in an action to recover damages in respect of a wrong resulting in personal injury not causing death, account shall not be taken of any charitable gift (whether in the form of money or other property) made to the plaintiff in respect of those injuries unless—

(*a*) the defendant is the donor of the gift, and

(*b*) (i) at the time of the making of the gift he or she informs the plaintiff in writing that, should the plaintiff recover damages in such an action, the defendant will apply to the court for the damages to be reduced by an amount equal to the amount of the gift or the value of the gift, as may be appropriate, or

(ii) in the case of a plaintiff who is employed by the defendant, the gift consists of a series of payments that resemble, in amount and frequency, the normal remuneration that the plaintiff would be entitled to receive from the defendant in the course of his or her employment.",

and the said section 2 as it stood immediately before the commencement of this subsection shall be referred to as subsection (1) of section 2.

(3) The amendments to—

(*a*) section 50 of the Act of 1961, and

(*b*) section 2 of the Civil Liability (Amendment) Act 1964,

effected by this section do not apply to causes of action accruing before the commencement of this section.

Income undeclared for tax purposes

28.—(1) In a personal injuries action (other than an action under section 48 of the Act of 1961), any income, profit or gain in respect of which—

(*a*) the plaintiff is making a claim, and

(*b*) (i) a return has not been made before the hearing of the action in accordance with the Taxes Consolidation Act 1997, or

(ii) the plaintiff has not otherwise notified the Revenue Commissioners,

shall, for the purposes of assessing damages, be disregarded by the court, unless the court considers that in all the circumstances it would be unjust to disregard such income, profit or gain.

(2) This section does not apply to causes of action accruing before the commencement of this section.

Offences

29.—(1) A person guilty of an offence under this Part shall be liable, upon conviction on indictment, to a fine not exceeding €100,000, or imprisonment for a term not exceeding 10 years, or to both.

(2) The District Court may try summarily a person charged with an offence under this Part if—

(*a*) the court is of the opinion that the facts proved or alleged constitute a minor offence fit to be tried summarily,

(*b*) the person, upon being informed by the court of his or her right to be tried with a jury, does not object to being tried summarily, and

(*c*) the Director of Public Prosecutions consents to the person being tried summarily for the offence.

(3) A person who is tried under and in accordance with *subsection* (*2*) shall be liable, upon conviction, to a fine not exceeding €3,000, or imprisonment for a term not exceeding 12 months, or to both.

(4) Section 13 of the Criminal Procedure Act 1967 shall apply in relation to an offence under this Part as if, in lieu of the penalties specified in subsection (3)(*a*) of that section, there were specified therein the penalties provided for in *subsection* (*3*), and the reference in subsection (2)(*a*) of the said section 13 to the penalties provided for by subsection (3) shall be construed and have effect accordingly.

Register of personal injuries actions

30.—(1) The Courts Service shall, on the commencement of this section, establish and maintain a register of personal injuries actions (in this section referred to as the "register").

(2) The Courts Service shall enter in the register—

(*a*) the name and address of the solicitor for each party to a personal injuries action,

(*b*) the name and occupation of each party to a personal injuries action, and

(*c*) the address at which he or she ordinarily resides,

as specified in the pleadings relating to the action.

(3) The register shall be made available to such persons as establish to the satisfaction of the Courts Service a sufficient interest in seeking access to it.

Amendment of Act of 2003

31.—The Act of 2003 is amended by the insertion of the following section:

> **"Requiring certain persons to provide information**
>
> 54A.—(1) The Board may require any person (including a Minister of the Government or a body established by or under any enactment) to provide it with such records, documents or information as it may reasonably require for the purposes of the performance of its functions under section 54(1)(*c*).
>
> (2) A person of whom a requirement is made under subsection (1) shall comply with that requirement.".

Other amendments of Act of 2003

32.—(1) For the avoidance of doubt, the reference in the definition of "proceedings" in section 4(1) of the Act of 2003 to "proceedings in court" includes, and shall be deemed to have always included, a reference to—

(*a*) proceedings by way of a counterclaim, and

(*b*) proceedings by way of the service of a third party notice (other than a third party notice claiming only an indemnity or a contribution).

(2) Section 30(4) of the Act of 2003 is amended by the insertion after "subsection (3)" of "or is one relating to a proposed action for damages under section 48 of the Act of 1961".

PART 3

COURTS

Chapter 1

Funds of Suitors

Definitions

33.—In this Chapter—

"accounts" means—

(*a*) the general cash account,

(*b*) the dormant account of the funds of suitors of the High Court,

(*c*) the ledger account, and

(*d*) the special account for small balances;

"Accountant" means the Accountant of the Courts of Justice as provided for in section 16 of the Court Officers Act 1926;

"dormant account of the funds of suitors of the High Court" means the general ledger account for dormant balance maintained in accordance with Order 77 of the Rules of the Superior Courts, containing the balances of funds standing to the credit of ledger accounts carried over to the said ledger account by the Accountant together with the interest and dividends accruing thereon;

"financial institution" means the person with which the accounts are maintained, being—

(*a*) a person in respect of whom a licence under section 9 of the Central Bank Act 1971 is in force, or

(*b*) a building society within the meaning of the Building Societies Act 1989;

"fully indemnified" means, in relation to a person—

(*a*) that, in the case of funds in the form of money, the person has been paid the amount standing to his or her credit on the date that the funds were paid into the dormant account of the funds of suitors of the High Court and any interest accruing from that date, and

(*b*) that, in the case of funds other than in the form of money, the person has been paid the amount standing to his or her credit on the date of their realisation and any interest accruing thereon from that date;

"general cash account" means the general cash account of the funds of suitors held with the financial institution in the name of the Accountant;

"ledger account" means an account opened in the name of the Accountant under—

(*a*) an order of the High Court or Supreme Court, or

(*b*) an Act of the Oireachtas,

into which any funds of suitors have been paid;

"small balances" means such moneys as, in accordance with rule 88 of Order 77 of the Rules of the Superior Courts, are carried over to the special account for small balances;

"special account for small balances" means the special account for small balances maintained for the purposes of the said rule 88.

Realisation of investment of dormant accounts of funds of suitors

34.—(1) The Chief Justice shall, as soon as may be after the commencement of this Chapter, order the Accountant to realise all of the investments of the dormant account of the funds of suitors of the High Court.

(2) The Chief Justice shall, not later than 3 months after—

(*a*) the expiration of 5 years from the making of an order under *subsection (1)*, and

(*b*) the expiration of each subsequent period of 5 years from the date on which an order under this section is made,

order the Accountant to realise all of the investments of the dormant account of the funds of suitors of the High Court.

(3) The Accountant shall comply with an order of the Chief Justice under this section.

(4) In this section "investments" means, in relation to the dormant account of the funds of suitors, assets other than cash.

Disposal of part of funds of suitors

35.—(1) The financial institution shall pay out of the general cash account to the Exchequer such sums as the Chief Justice, from time to time, directs, not exceeding 97.5 per cent of the aggregate of the amounts in the form of money standing in the dormant account of the funds of suitors of the High Court and the special account for small balances, as may be required for the purposes of *subsection* (*2*).

(2) The sums paid to the Exchequer pursuant to an order under *subsection* (*1*) may be applied from time to time, by the Minister, with the consent of the Minister for Finance, for the purposes of defraying the costs of providing, managing and maintaining court buildings under section 5(*d*) of the Courts Service Act 1998.

Deficiency in funds of suitors

36.—Where, by virtue of the compliance by the financial institution with a direction under *section 35*, the funds of suitors are not sufficient to enable suitors to be fully indemnified, the Minister for Finance shall, for the purpose of enabling them to be so indemnified, advance out of the Central Fund or the growing produce thereof such sum as he or she considers necessary.

Publication of notices by Accountant

37.—(1) The Accountant shall, not later than 3 months after the compliance by the financial institution concerned with a direction under *section 35*—

(*a*) first given after the passing of this Act, and

(*b*) each subsequent such direction where the sums paid to the Exchequer pursuant thereto exceed €100,000,

cause a notice of the payment of the sums to the Exchequer pursuant to the direction to be published in *Iris Oifigiúil*, the Law Society Gazette, two national daily newspapers and by such other means (if any) as he or she considers appropriate.

(2) The accountant shall, upon compliance by a financial institution with a direction under *section 35*, make all reasonable efforts to serve a notice in writing of the payment of the sums to the Exchequer pursuant to such a direction on such persons as have an entitlement to any of the funds for the time being standing to the credit of the dormant account of the funds of suitors of the High Court.

(3) The expenses incurred by the Accountant in complying with this section may where the Chief Justice so consents be paid out of funds standing for the time being in the dormant account of the funds of suitors of the High Court.

Register of funds of suitors

38.—(1) The Accountant shall establish and maintain a register of funds of suitors of the High Court (in this section referred to as the "register").

(2) The register shall contain the following particulars—

(*a*) the title of the proceedings to which the funds to which Order 77 of the Rules of the Superior Courts applies relate,

(*b*) the names of the parties to those proceedings and the addresses at which they ordinarily reside,

(*c*) the ledger account number,

(*d*) the value of the investments realised in accordance with *section 34* on the date of their realisation,

(*e*) the date on which those funds were paid into the dormant account of the funds of suitors of the High Court,

(*f*) if those funds were repaid to the ledger account, the date on which they were so repaid,

(*g*) the account number of the special account for small balances,

(*h*) the moneys paid over to the special account for small balances, and

(i) such other matters as are provided for by rules of court or the President of the High Court directs.

Chapter 2

Miscellaneous Provisions

Definitions

39.—In this Chapter—

"Act of 1976" means the Family Home Protection Act 1976;

"Act of 1981" means the Courts Act 1981;

"Act of 1989" means the Judicial Separation and Family Law Reform Act 1989;

"Act of 1991" means the Courts Act 1991;

"Act of 1995" means the Family Law Act 1995;

"Act of 1996" means the Family Law (Divorce) Act 1996.

Proceedings heard otherwise than in public

40.—(1) In this section "court" includes the Master of the High Court.

(2) For the purposes of this section each of the following shall be a "relevant enactment"—

(*a*) section 2(1B) (inserted by section 20 of the Courts Act 1971) of the Legitimacy Act 1931;

(*b*) section 45 of the Courts (Supplemental Provisions) Act 1961 (in so far as it relates to matrimonial causes or matters, or minor matters);

(*c*) section 25 of the Family Law (Maintenance of Spouses and Children) Act 1976;

(*d*) section 10 of the Act of 1976;

(*e*) section 36 of the Status of Children Act 1987;

(*f*) section 34 of the Act of 1989;

(*g*) section 7 of the Maintenance Act 1994;

(*h*) section 33 of the Act of 1995;

(*i*) section 38 of the Act of 1995;

(*j*) section 38 of the Act of 1996;

(*k*) section 16 of the Domestic Violence Act 1996.

(3) Nothing contained in a relevant enactment shall operate to prohibit—

(*a*) the preparation by a barrister at law or a solicitor or a person falling within any other class of persons specified in regulations made by the Minister and publication of a report of proceedings to which the relevant enactment relates, or

(*b*) the publication of the decision of the court in such proceedings,

in accordance with rules of court, provided that the report or decision does not contain any information which would enable the parties to the proceedings or any child to which the proceedings relate to be identified and, accordingly, unless in the special circumstances of the matter the court, for reasons which shall be specified in the direction, otherwise directs, a person referred to in *paragraph* (*a*) may, for the purposes of preparing such a report, attend the proceedings subject to any directions the court may give in that behalf.

(4) Nothing contained in a relevant enactment shall operate to prohibit a party to proceedings to which the enactment relates from supplying copies of, or extracts from, orders made in the proceedings to such persons and in accordance with such conditions (if any) as may be prescribed by order of the Minister.

(5) Nothing contained in a relevant enactment shall operate to prohibit a party to proceedings to which the enactment relates from being accompanied, in such proceedings, in court by another person subject to the approval of the court and any directions it may give in that behalf.

(6) Nothing contained in an enactment that prohibits proceedings to which the enactment relates from being heard in public shall operate to prohibit the production of a document prepared for the purposes or in contemplation of such proceedings or given in evidence in such proceedings, to—

(*a*) a body or other person when it, or he or she, is performing functions under any enactment consisting of the conducting of a hearing, inquiry or investigation in relation to, or adjudicating on, any matter, or

(*b*) such body or other person as may be prescribed by order made by the Minister, when the body or person concerned is performing functions consisting of the conducting of a hearing, inquiry or investigation in relation to, or adjudicating on, any matter as may be so prescribed.

(7) Nothing contained in an enactment that prohibits proceedings to which the enactment relates from being heard in public shall operate to prohibit the giving of information or evidence given in such proceedings to—

(*a*) a body or other person when it, or he or she, is performing functions under any enactment consisting of the conducting of a hearing, inquiry or investigation in relation to, or adjudicating on, any matter, or

(*b*) such body or other person as may be prescribed by order made by the Minister, when the body or person concerned is performing functions consisting of the conducting of a hearing, inquiry or investigation in relation to, or adjudicating on, any matter as may be so prescribed.

(8) A court hearing proceedings under a relevant enactment shall, on its own motion or on the application of one of the parties to the proceedings, have discretion to order disclosure of documents, information or evidence connected with or arising in the course of the proceedings to third parties if such disclosure is required to protect the legitimate interests of a party or other person affected by the proceedings.

(9) A hearing, inquiry or investigation referred to in *subsection* (*6*) or (*7*) shall, in so far as it relates to a document referred to in *subsection* (*6*) or information or evidence referred to in *subsection* (*7*), be conducted otherwise than in public and no such document, information or evidence shall be published.

(10) This section shall apply to proceedings brought, and decisions of a court made, whether before or after the commencement of this section.

Interest on costs, charges or expenses of certain judgments, orders or decrees

41.—(1) Section 30 of the Act of 2002 is amended by the substitution of the following subsection for subsection (1):

"(1) Subject to section 23 of the Act of 1981, interest on the amount of costs, charges or expenses awarded to a party in proceedings in a court, to which section 27 of the Debtors (Ireland) Act 1840 applies, pursuant to a judgment, order or decree of the court, shall—

(*a*) not be payable until—

(i) if the amount aforesaid is agreed by the parties to the proceedings, the date of such agreement, or

(ii) in default of agreement—

(I) the date on which a certificate of taxation (which expression includes an interim certificate of taxation) in respect of the amount aforesaid is issued by a taxing master of the High Court or by a county registrar exercising the powers of such a taxing master, as may be appropriate, or

(II) if appropriate, in the case of proceedings in the Circuit Court, the date on which a county registrar measures the amount aforesaid in accordance with rules of court, and

(*b*) be payable at the rate for the time being standing specified in section 26 of the Debtors (Ireland) Act 1840, from the appropriate date aforesaid until that amount is paid.".

(2) Subsections (3) and (4) of section 30 of the Act of 2002 are repealed.

(3) The amendments to section 30 of the Act of 2002 effected by this section apply to—

(*a*) actions brought on or after the commencement of this section, and

(*b*) actions pending on the date of such commencement.

Certain officers to act as registrar of Central Criminal Court

42.—The Eighth Schedule to the Courts (Supplemental Provisions) Act 1961 is amended by the insertion, in paragraph 6, of the following subparagraph:

"(1A) Each officer nominated under subparagraph (1) of this paragraph who stands directed to act as registrar to the High Court under that subparagraph shall (in addition to any other duties which may be assigned to him or her by the officer for the time being managing the Central Office) act as registrar to the Central Criminal Court as and when directed to so act by the officer for the time being managing the Central Office.".

Amendment of section 27 of Court Officers Act 1926

43.—Section 27 of the Court Officers Act 1926 is amended by the substitution of the following subsections for subsections (1) and (2):

"(1) In the event of the temporary absence or the temporary incapacity through illness of any Taxing-Master or in the event of the office of any Taxing-Master being vacant the Courts Service may appoint a deputy to execute the office of such Taxing-Master during such absence, incapacity or vacancy.

(1A) In any of the following cases, namely—

(*a*) the temporary absence or the temporary incapacity through illness of the Master of the High Court,

(*b*) the office of the Master of the High Court being vacant, or

(*c*) any other case in which the Courts Service considers it desirable that the following power be exercised,

the Courts Service may appoint one or more than one deputy to execute the office of the Master of the High Court or, as the case may be, to execute such office concurrently with the Master of the High Court.

(2) A deputy appointed under this section shall while his appointment continues have and exercise all the powers and authorities and shall perform and fulfil all the duties and functions of the officer whose deputy he is—

(*a*) in a case falling within subsection (1) or subsection (1A)(*a*) or (*b*) of this section, in place of their being exercised, performed and fulfilled by that officer, and

(*b*) in a case falling within paragraph (*c*) of subsection (1A), concurrently with their being exercised, performed and fulfilled by that officer.".

Amendment of section 38 of Court Officers Act 1926

44.—Section 38 of the Court Officers Act 1926 is amended by the substitution of the following subsections for subsection (3):

"(3) The county registrar of the county, county borough or other area (other than the county or county borough of Dublin) in which the Central Criminal Court is, for the time being, sitting shall perform the following functions, that is to say:

(*a*) the function of acting as registrar to that court, and

(*b*) the function of performing such powers and carrying out of such duties in relation to that court as are assigned to the registrar of the Central Criminal Court by rules of court,

when requested to so do by the officer for the time being managing the Central Office of the High Court.

(4) The functions performable by a county registrar pursuant to a request under subsection (3) shall be performed by a member of the staff of the Circuit Court Office in the county concerned to whom

those functions have been delegated by that county registrar.".

Amendment of Courts (Supplemental Provisions) Act 1961

45.—(1) Section 2 of the Courts (Supplemental Provisions) Act 1961 is amended by the insertion, in subsection (1), of the following definition:

" 'market value' means, in relation to land, the price that would have been obtained in respect of the unencumbranced fee simple were the land to have been sold on the open market, in the year immediately preceding the bringing of the proceedings concerned, in such manner and subject to such conditions as might reasonably be calculated to have resulted in the vendor obtaining the best price for the land.".

(2) The Third Schedule to the Courts (Supplemental Provisions) Act 1961 is amended, in column (3), by the substitution of—

(*a*) "market value" for "rateable valuation" in each place that it occurs, and

(*b*) "€3,000,000" for "£200" (inserted by section 2(1)(*d*) of the Act of 1981) in each place that it occurs.

Amendment of Registration of Title Act 1964

46.—Section 18 of the Registration of Title Act 1964 is amended by—

(*a*) the substitution, in subsection (2) (amended by section 3 of the Act of 1991), of—

(i) "market value" for "rateable valuation", and

(ii) "€3,000,000" for "£200",

and

(*b*) the insertion of the following subsection:

"(4) In this section 'market value' means, in relation to land, the price that would have been obtained in respect of the unencumbranced fee simple were the land to have been sold on the open market, in the year immediately preceding the bringing of the proceedings concerned, in such manner and subject to such conditions as might reasonably be calculated to have resulted in the vendor obtaining the best price for the land.".

Amendment of Succession Act 1965

47.—Section 6 of the Succession Act 1965 is amended by—

(*a*) the substitution, in subsection (3) (inserted by section 4 of the Act of 1981), of—

(i) "market value" for "rateable valuation", and

(ii) "€3,000,000" for "£200",

and

(*b*) the insertion of the following subsection:

"(5) In this section 'market value' means, in relation to land, the price that would have been obtained in respect of the unencumbranced fee simple were the land to have been sold on the open market, in the year immediately preceding the bringing of the proceedings concerned, in such manner and subject to such conditions as might reasonably be calculated to have resulted in the vendor obtaining the best price for the land.".

Amendment of Act of 1976

48.—Section 10 of the Act of 1976 is amended by—

(*a*) the substitution, in subsection (4) (inserted by section 13 of the Act of 1981), of—

(i) "market value" for "rateable valuation", and

(ii) "€3,000,000" for "£200",

and

(*b*) (i) the repeal of paragraphs (*a*) and (*c*) of subsection (5), and

(ii) the deletion, in paragraph (*b*) of subsection (5), of the words "or where such chattels are or immediately before such disposal or removal, were in a family home the rateable valuation of which does not exceed £20",

(*c*) the insertion of the following subsection:

"(8) In this section 'market value' means, in relation to land, the price that would have been obtained in respect of the unencumbranced fee simple were the land to have been sold on the open market, in the year immediately preceding the bringing of the proceedings concerned, in such manner and subject to such conditions as might reasonably be calculated to have resulted in the vendor obtaining the best price for the land.".

Amendment of section 1 of Courts (No. 3) Act 1986

49.—The Courts (No. 3) Act 1986 is amended by the substitution of the following section for section 1:

"1.—(1) Proceedings in the District Court in respect of an offence may be commenced by the issuing, as a matter of administrative procedure, of a document (in this section referred to as a 'summons') to the prosecutor by the appropriate office.

(2) The issue of a summons may, in addition to being effected by any method by which the issue of a summons could be effected immediately before the enactment of *section 49* of the Act of 2004, be effected by transmitting it by electronic means to the person who applied for it or a person acting on his or her behalf.

(3) An application for the issue of a summons may be made to the appropriate office by or on behalf of the Attorney General, the Director of Public Prosecutions, a member of the Garda Síochána or any person authorised by or under an enactment to bring and prosecute proceedings for the offence concerned.

(4) The making of an application referred to in subsection (3) of this section may, in addition to being effected by any method by which the making of an application for a summons could be effected immediately before the enactment of *section 49* of the Act of 2004, be effected by transmitting it to the appropriate office by electronic means.

(5) Where an application for the issue of a summons is made to—

(*a*) an office referred to in paragraph (*a*) of the definition of 'appropriate office' in this section, the summons may, instead of its being issued by that office, be issued by an office referred to in paragraph (*b*) of that definition, or

(*b*) an office referred to in paragraph (*b*) of that definition, the summons may, instead of its being issued by that office, be issued by an office referred to in paragraph (*a*) of that definition.

(6) A summons shall—

(*a*) specify the name of the person who applied for the issue of the summons,

(*b*) specify the application date as respects the summons,

(*c*) state shortly and in ordinary language particulars of the alleged offence, the name of the person alleged to have committed the offence and the address (if known) at which he or she ordinarily resides,

(*d*) notify that person that he or she will be accused of that offence at a sitting of the District Court specified by reference to its date and location and, insofar as is practicable, its time, and

(*e*) specify the name of an appropriate District Court clerk.

(7) For the avoidance of doubt, particulars of the penalty to which a person guilty of the offence concerned would be liable are not required to be stated in a summons.

(8) Where the issue of a summons is effected in accordance with

subsection (2) of this section, references to an original summons in any enactment relating to the service of summonses (whether the references employ the word 'summons' or the expression 'original document') shall be construed as references to a true copy of the summons.

(9) In any proceedings—

(*a*) a document purporting to be a summons shall be deemed to be a summons duly applied for and issued, and

(*b*) the date specified in the summons as being the application date shall be deemed to be such date,

unless the contrary is shown.

(10) In any proceedings in which the issue of a summons was effected in accordance with subsection (2) of this section, a true copy of the summons shall, unless the contrary is shown, be evidence of the summons concerned.

(11) A summons duly issued under this Act shall be deemed for all purposes to be a summons duly issued pursuant to the law in force immediately before the passing of this Act.

(12) Any provision made by or under any enactment passed before the passing of this Act relating to the time for making a complaint in relation to an offence shall apply, with any necessary modifications, in relation to an application under subsection (3) of this section.

(13) The procedures provided for in this section in relation to applications for, and the issue of, summonses are without prejudice to any other procedures in force immediately before the passing of this Act whereby proceedings in respect of an offence can be commenced and, accordingly, any of those other procedures may be adopted, where appropriate, as if this Act had not been passed.

(14) In this section—

'Act of 2004' means the *Civil Liability and Courts Act 2004*;

'application date' means, in relation to a summons, the date on which the application for the issue of the summons was received by the appropriate office;

'appropriate District Court clerk' means, in relation to a summons, a District Court clerk assigned to any district court area in the district court district in which a judge of the District Court has jurisdiction in relation to the offence to which the summons relates;

'appropriate office' means, in relation to a summons—

(*a*) the office of any District Court clerk assigned to any district court area in the district court district in which a judge of the District Court has jurisdiction in relation to the offence to which the summons relates, or

(*b*) any office of the Courts Service designated by the Courts Service for the purpose of receiving applications referred to in subsection (3) of this section;

'prosecutor' includes a person acting on behalf of the prosecutor;

'summons' has the meaning assigned to it by subsection (1);

'true copy' means, in relation to a summons the issue of which was effected in accordance with subsection (2), a document that purports to be a reproduction in writing of the summons certified by the prosecutor as being a true copy thereof.".

Amendment of Act of 1989

50.—Section 31 of the Act of 1989 is amended by—

(*a*) the substitution, in subsection (3), of—

(i) "market value" for "rateable valuation", and

(ii) "€3,000,000" for "£200",

and

(*b*) the insertion of the following subsection:

"(6) In this section 'market value' means, in relation to land, the price that would have been obtained in respect of the unencumbranced fee simple were the land to have been sold on the open market, in the year immediately preceding the bringing of the proceedings concerned, in such manner and subject to such conditions as might reasonably be calculated to have resulted in the vendor obtaining the best price for the land.".

Amendment of Act of 1995

51.—Section 38 of the Act of 1995 is amended by—

(*a*) the substitution, in subsection (3), of—

(i) "market value" for "rateable valuation", and

(ii) "€3,000,000" for "£200",

(*b*) the repeal of subsection (5), and

(*c*) the insertion of the following subsection:

"(9) In this section 'market value' means, in relation to land, the price that would have been obtained in respect of the unencumbranced fee simple were the land to have been sold on the open market, in the year immediately preceding the bringing of the proceedings concerned, in such manner and subject to such conditions as might reasonably be calculated to have resulted in the vendor obtaining the best price for the land.".

Amendment of Act of 1996

52.—Section 38 of the Act of 1996 is amended by—

(*a*) the substitution in subsection (2) of—

(i) "market value" for "rateable valuation", and

(ii) "€3,000,000" for "£200",

(*b*) the repeal of subsection (4), and

(*c*) the insertion of the following subsection:

"(8) In this section 'market value' means, in relation to land, the price that would have been obtained in respect of the unencumbranced fee simple were the land to have been sold on the open market, in the year immediately preceding the bringing of the proceedings concerned, in such manner and subject to such conditions as might reasonably be calculated to have resulted in the vendor obtaining the best price for the land.".

Amendment of Planning and Development Act 2000

53.—(1) Section 90 of the Act of 2000 is amended, in subsection (5), by—

(*a*) the substitution of—

(i) "market value" for "rateable valuation" in each place that it occurs, and

(ii) "€3,000,000" for "£200" in each place that it occurs,

and

(*b*) the insertion of the following paragraph:

"(*d*) In this subsection 'market value' means, in relation to land, the price that would have been obtained in respect of the unencumbranced fee simple were the land to have been sold on the open market, in the year immediately preceding the bringing of the proceedings concerned, in such manner and subject to such conditions as might reasonably be calculated to have resulted in the vendor obtaining the best price for the land.".

(2) Section 160 of the Act of 2000 is amended, in subsection (5), by—

(*a*) the substitution of—

(i) "market value" for "rateable valuation" in each place that it occurs, and

(ii) "€3,000,000" for "£200" in each place that it occurs, and

(*b*) the insertion of the following paragraph:

"(*e*) In this subsection 'market value' means, in relation to land, the price that would have been obtained in respect of the unencumbranced fee simple were the land to have been sold on the open market, in the year immediately preceding the bringing of the proceedings concerned, in such manner and subject to such conditions as might reasonably be calculated to have resulted in the vendor obtaining the best price for the land.".

(3) In this section "Act of 2000" means the Planning and Development Act 2000.

Exclusion of certain witnesses, etc.

54.—(1) The court in a personal injuries action may, upon the application of a party to the action, direct that a person (other than another party to the action or an expert witness) who it is intended will be called to give evidence at the trial of the action shall not attend that trial until he or she is called to give evidence.

(2) Where a court gives a direction under *subsection (1)*, it may give all such other directions as it considers necessary or expedient to secure that a witness to whom the first-mentioned direction applies does not—

(*a*) communicate with other witnesses who it is intended will be called to give evidence at the trial of the action concerned, or

(*b*) receive information such as might influence him or her when giving evidence.

(3) In this section "expert witness" means, in relation to a personal injuries action, a person who it is intended will be called as a witness to give expert evidence at the trial of that action.

Amendment of Act of 2002

55.—Section 46 of the Act of 2002 is amended by—

(*a*) the substitution of the following subsections for subsections (3), (4) and (5):

"(3) Subject to subsection (6), if judgment in the proceedings concerned is not delivered before the expiration of 2 months from the date on which it is reserved, the President of the Court shall, as soon as may be after—

(*a*) the said expiration, and

(*b*) the expiration of each subsequent period of 2 months (if judgment is not delivered first),

list the proceedings or cause them to be listed before the judge who reserved judgment therein and shall give notice in writing to the parties to the proceedings of each date on which the proceedings are listed in accordance with this section.

(3A) If, apart from this subsection, subsection (3) would operate to require the President of the Court to do anything referred to in that subsection during a period when the court is in vacation, then that subsection shall be construed as requiring that President to do that thing as soon as may be after the expiration of that period.

(4) Where proceedings are listed before a judge in accordance with subsection (3), the judge shall specify the date on which he or she proposes to deliver judgment in the proceedings.

(5) The date specified by a judge under subsection (4) shall, in relation to the proceedings concerned, be entered in the register and where the proceedings concerned have been listed more than once in accordance with subsection (1), there shall be entered in the register on each occasion on which they are so listed the date, for the time being, standing so specified.",

(*b*) the deletion of paragraph (*b*) of subsection (9),

(*c*) the substitution of the following subsection for subsection (10):

"(10) In this section references to a judge shall, in the case of a court constituted of more than one judge, be construed as references to the judge who, among the judges of which the court was constituted, ranks first in order of precedence in accordance with section 9 (inserted by section 9 of the Courts (No. 2) Act 1997) of the Courts of Justice Act 1924.",

(*d*) the insertion of the following definition in subsection (11):

" 'President of the Court' means—

(*a*) in relation to the District Court, the President of the District Court,

(*b*) in relation to the Circuit Court, the President of the Circuit Court,

(*c*) in relation to the High Court, the President of the High Court,

(*d*) in relation to the Supreme Court, the Chief Justice;".

Increase in number of judges of High Court, Circuit Court and District Court

56.—The Courts and Court Officers Act 1995 is amended by—

(*a*) the substitution of the following section for section 9 (inserted by section 2 of the Courts and Court Officers (Amendment) Act 2003):

"9.—The number of ordinary judges of the High Court shall not be more than 31.",

(*b*) the substitution of the following section for section 10 (inserted by section 26 of the Act of 2002):

"10.—The number of ordinary judges of the Circuit Court shall not be more than 33.", and

(*c*) the substitution of the following subsection for subsection (1) (inserted by section 27(1) of the Act of 2002) of section 11:

"(1) The number of judges of the District Court in addition to the President of the District Court shall not be more than 54.".

Appendix 2

CIVIL LIABILITY AND COURTS ACT 2004 (COMMENCEMENT) ORDER 2004

S.I. No. 544 of 2004

I, Michael McDowell, Minister for Justice, Equality and Law Reform, in exercise of the powers conferred on me by section 1(2) of the Civil Liability and Courts Act 2004 (No. 31 of 2004), hereby order as follows:

1. This Order may be cited as the Civil Liability and Courts Act 2004 (Commencement) Order 2004.

2. In this Order "Act of 2004" means the Civil Liability and Courts Act 2004 (No. 31 of 2004).

3. (1) The day on which this Order is made is appointed to be the day on which sections 1, 5, 6, 8, 19, 21, 22, 25, 26, 29, 39, 41, 42, 43, 44, 54 and 55 of the Act of 2004 shall come into operation.

(2) The 31st day of March, 2005 is appointed to be the day on which sections 7, 9, 10, 11, 12, 13, 14, 15, 16, 17, 18, 20, 23, 24, 27, 28 and 40 of the Act of 2004 shall come into operation.

GIVEN under my Official Seal,
this 20th day of September, 2004.

Michael McDowell
Minister for Justice, Equality and Law Reform.

EXPLANATORY NOTE

(This is not part of the instrument and does not purport to be a legal interpretation)

This Order appoints the 20th day of September 2004 as the day on which the following sections of the Civil Liability and Courts Act 2004 come into operation: Sections 1, 5, 6, 8, 19, 21, 22, 25, 26, 29, 39, 41, 42, 43, 44, 54 and 55.

This Order also appoints the 31st day of March 2005 as the day on which the following sections of the Civil Liability and Courts Act 2004 come into operation: Sections 7, 9, 10, 11, 12, 13, 14, 15, 16, 17, 18, 20, 23, 24, 27, 28 and 40.

Appendix 3

RULES OF THE SUPERIOR COURTS (PERSONAL INJURIES) 2005

Order 1A: S.I. No. 248 of 2005

We, the Superior Courts Rules Committee, constituted pursuant to the provisions of the Courts of Justice Act, 1936, section 67, and reconstituted pursuant to the provisions of the Courts of Justice Act, 1953, section 15, by virtue of the powers conferred upon us by the Courts of Justice Act, 1924, section 36, and the Courts of Justice Act, 1936, section 68 (as applied by the Courts (Supplemental Provisions) Act, 1961, section 48), and the Courts (Supplemental Provisions) Act, 1961, section 14, and of all other powers enabling us in this behalf, do hereby make the following Rules of Court.

Dated this 4th day of May, 2005.

John L Murray
Joseph Finnegan
Brian McCracken
Richard Johnson
William McKechnie
Edmund Honohan
Patrick Groarke
Patrick O'Connor
Michael Cush
Anthony Hunt
Matthew Feely
Noel Rubotham

I concur in the making of the following Rules of Court.

Dated this 19th day of May, 2005.

MICHAEL McDOWELL
Minister for Justice, Equality and Law Reform

S.I. No. 248 of 2005
Rules of the Superior Courts (Personal Injuries) 2005

1. These Rules shall come into operation on the 2nd day of June 2005.

2. These Rules shall be construed together with the Rules of the Superior Courts 1986 to 2005 and may be cited as the Rules of the Superior Courts (Personal Injuries) 2005.

3. Order 1 of the Rules of the Superior Courts is hereby amended by the substitution for rule 2 thereof, of the following:

   "2. An originating summons for the commencement of plenary proceedings with pleadings and to be heard on oral evidence (in these Rules called a plenary summons) shall, save in admiralty proceedings, and save in personal injuries actions as defined in Order 1A, be in the Form No. 1 in Appendix A, Part I".

4. The Rules of the Superior Courts are hereby amended by the insertion immediately following Order 1 of the following Order as Order 1A:

"Order 1A

PROCEDURE BY PERSONAL INJURIES SUMMONS

I. PRELIMINARY

Definitions

1. In this Order unless the context or subject matter otherwise requires—

"the Act" means the Civil Liability and Courts Act 2004;

"personal injuries action" has the same meaning as in section 2 of the Act and "action" shall be interpreted accordingly;

"personal injury" includes any disease and any impairment of a person's physical or mental condition

"personal injuries summons" means a summons by which a personal injuries action is instituted in accordance with rule 3 of this Order

"plaintiff" includes a deceased person, where a personal injuries action is instituted for the benefit of dependants of a deceased person;

"pleading" has the same meaning as in section 2 of the Act;

"Personal Public Service Number" means the Personal Public Service Number allocated and issued to a person under section 223 (inserted by section 14 of the Social Welfare Act 1998) of the Social Welfare (Consolidation) Act 1993.

Application of this Order

2. (1) The provisions of this Order shall apply to personal injuries actions and to all proceedings in personal injuries actions.

(2) Save where otherwise expressly provided by this Order, in the event that any conflict shall arise between the provision of any rule of this Order and any other provision of these Rules, the provision of the rule of this Order shall, in respect of personal injuries actions, prevail.

(3) Without prejudice to the generality of sub-rule 2, Order 19, rules 1 and 3 and Order 21, rule 6 shall not apply in personal injuries actions.

II. Commencement of Proceedings

Personal injuries summons

3. A personal injuries action shall be instituted by an originating summons, for the commencement of plenary proceedings with pleadings and hearing on oral evidence, which shall be in the Form No. 1 in Appendix CC, to be called a personal injuries summons.

4. Save where otherwise expressly provided by this Order, the provisions of these Rules which apply to a plenary summons shall, with appropriate modifications, apply to a personal injuries summons.

5. (1) Where the action is being instituted for the benefit of dependants of a deceased person, the personal injuries summons shall specify the date of birth and Personal Public Service Number of the deceased person.

(2) Where the action is being instituted for the benefit of dependants of a deceased person, the name, address and date of birth of each such dependant shall be stated in the personal injuries summons.

(3) Where a plaintiff has not been issued with a Personal Public Service Number, this shall be stated in the personal injuries summons.

6. Where a plaintiff alleges that he was unable, at the time at which a personal injuries summons was issued, to include in the personal injuries summons any of the information required by this Order to be specified in the personal injuries summons, he shall include in the personal injuries summons a statement of the reasons why it is claimed that any such information could not be provided at the time of issue of the summons. The plaintiff shall, at the time the personal injuries summons is served or as soon as may be thereafter (whether by amendment or otherwise) provide such of the information required by this Order as was not included in the personal injuries summons.

III. Pleadings

7. (1) No statement of claim shall be required in a personal injuries action.

(2) Save where otherwise expressly provided by this Order, the provisions of these Rules which apply to a statement of claim shall, where appropriate and with appropriate modifications, apply to a personal injuries summons.

8. An appearance to a personal injuries summons shall be in the Form No. 5 in Appendix A, Part II of these Rules. A defence shall be delivered by each defendant in the Form No. 2 in Appendix CC within eight weeks of the service on such defendant of the plaintiff's personal injuries summons. Where any defendant makes a counterclaim, such counterclaim shall be in the Form No. 3 in Appendix CC and shall be appended to the defence.

9. A plaintiff who wishes to join issue with a defendant's defence may deliver a reply, within six weeks of the delivery of the defence. Any reply shall, if it contains any assertion or allegation of fact, be verified upon oath in accordance with rule 10. A plaintiff shall deliver a defence to any counterclaim within eight weeks of the delivery by such defendant to the plaintiff of the defendant's counterclaim. A defence to a counterclaim shall be in the Form No. 2 in Appendix CC, with such modifications as may be necessary, and shall comply with the requirements of the Act applicable to a defence.

IV. Verification of facts alleged

10. (1) An affidavit of verification of a pleading or of further information requiring under section 14(1), 14(2) or 14(3) of the Act to be verified on oath shall be in the Form No. 4 in Appendix CC. If the affidavit is not separate to the pleading or other document concerned, it may be endorsed upon such pleading or other document.

(2) A copy of the affidavit of verification shall be delivered to the party to whom the pleading or other document is to be delivered. Where the affidavit is endorsed upon the pleading or other document, the copy of the affidavit shall be delivered within the time prescribed by these Rules for delivery of such pleading or other document. Otherwise, the affidavit shall be delivered within the time prescribed by section 14 of the Act for lodgment of the affidavit in court.

(3) An affidavit of verification shall be lodged in court as required by section 14(4) of the Act by filing the same in the Central Office.

(4) Where the copy of the affidavit of verification is delivered

subsequent to delivery of the pleading or other document, the time prescribed by these Rules for delivery of any pleading or other document in reply shall run from the date of delivery of such copy.

V. Interlocutory Applications

11. (1) The following applications in a personal injuries action shall be made by motion to the Court on notice to the opposing party or parties, grounded upon an affidavit sworn by or on behalf of the moving party:

(i) An application by a defendant under section 10(3) of the Act for a stay or dismissal of the action by reason of a plaintiff's failure to comply with section 10 of the Act;

(ii) An application by a defendant under section 11(3) of the Act for a stay or dismissal of the action by reason of a plaintiff's failure to provide further information requested under section 11(1) or section 11(2) of the Act;

(iii) An application by a plaintiff under section 12(3) of the Act for a stay of the action or for judgment by reason of a defendant's failure to comply with section 12 of the Act;

(iv) An application for an order for the delivery by the opposing party of further and better particulars of any pleading delivered by such party;

(v) An application by a party wishing to have evidence in the action given by affidavit, under section 19 of the Act.

An order sought in an application referred to in paragraphs (i), (ii), (iii) or (iv) of this sub-rule shall not be made unless:

(a) the moving party shall have first written to the relevant opposing party requesting that such party agree to the moving party's request;

(b) a period of twenty eight days for compliance with the moving party's request has been allowed; and

(c) the party requested has failed, refused or neglected to comply with such request.

(2) No application for judgment or for other relief in default of pleading shall be granted in a personal injuries action unless the moving party has satisfied the Court that he has verified his previous pleadings in that action on oath.

VI. Mediation

12. (1) A request by a party for a direction of the Court under section 15 of the Act that a mediation conference be held shall be made by motion to the Court on notice to the opposing party or parties, grounded upon an affidavit sworn by or on behalf of the moving party.

(2) Where the Court directs that a mediation conference be held, it may adjourn the proceedings for such time as it considers appropriate to enable the mediation conference to be held.

(3) Where the Court directs that a mediation conference be held, it may extend the time for compliance by the parties or any of them with any provision of these Rules or any order of the court in the proceedings.

(4) The report under section 16 of the Act of the person appointed under section 15(4) of the Act to be the chairperson of a mediation conference shall be by way of affidavit which shall verify:

(a) his or her appointment as mediator;
(b) whether the mediation conference was or was not held;
(c) if not held, the reasons why the mediation conference did not take place;
(d) if held,
  (i) the time and place at which the mediation conference was held;
  (ii) the parties in attendance;
  (iii) whether or not a settlement has been reached in the action and
  (iv) the terms of any settlement signed by the parties.

VII. Formal Offers

13. Copies of the plaintiff's notice of an offer of terms of settlement required by section 17(1) of the Act and of the defendant's notice required by section 17(2) of the Act shall be lodged in court by being filed (together with an affidavit as to the service of the same on the opposing party) in the Central Office as soon as may be after the expiry of the prescribed period referred to in section 17(3) of the Act. Such notice shall be in the Form No. 5 in Appendix CC.

VIII. Pre-trial hearing

14. (1) A person presiding over a pre-trial hearing directed by the Court under section 18 of the Act may at such hearing give such directions and make such orders as may be necessary for the purposes

of determining what matters relating to the action are in dispute.

(2) Any direction given or order made at a pre-trial hearing by a person, other than a Judge, presiding over such hearing, may be appealed to the Court by a party affected."

5. Order 4 of the Rules of the Superior Courts is hereby amended by the substitution for rule 2 thereof, of the following:

"2. Save in the case of a personal injuries summons as defined in Order 1A, the indorsement of claim on a plenary summons shall be entitled "General Indorsement of Claim" and there shall be an indorsement of the relief claimed and the grounds thereof expressed in general terms in such one of the forms in Appendix B, Part II as shall be applicable to the case, or, if none be found applicable, then such other similarly concise form as the nature of the case may require. The indorsement of claim on a personal injuries summons shall be as provided by Order 1A."

6. Order 13 of the Rules of the Superior Courts is hereby amended by insertion of the following, immediately following rule 6:

"6A. In case of default of appearance by any defendant to a personal injuries summons as defined in Order 1A, the plaintiff (without delivering a statement of claim) may apply to the Court by motion for judgment in the action in default of appearance upon filing in the Central Office an affidavit or affidavits of service of the personal injuries summons and an affidavit verifying the contents of the said personal injuries summons."

7. Order 13A of the Rules of the Superior Courts is hereby amended by the substitution for rule 3 thereof, of the following:

"3. In the case of default of appearance by any defendant to an originating summons or other originating document, the plaintiff shall:

(1) in the case of a plenary summons, (other than a personal injuries summons as defined in Order 1A), deliver a statement of claim by filing the same in the Central Office; or,

(2) in the case of a special summons, file a grounding affidavit in the Central Office; or,

(3) in the case of a personal injuries summons, a summary summons or other originating document, file an affidavit in the Central Office verifying the contents of such personal injuries summons, summary summons or other originating document;

and in any such case, shall file an affidavit or affidavits of service of the originating document concerned, and thereupon may apply to court for a judgment in default of appearance".

8. Order 19 of the Rules of the Superior Courts is hereby amended by the substitution for sub-rule 1 of rule 5 thereof, of the following:

   "(1) In every personal injuries action (within the meaning of the Civil Liability and Courts Act 2004) pleadings shall conform to the requirements of section 13 of the Civil Liability and Courts Act 2004. In all other cases alleging a wrong within the meaning of the Civil Liability Acts 1961 and 1964, particulars of such wrong, any personal injuries suffered and any items of special damage shall be set out in the statement of claim, defence or counterclaim (as the case may be) and particulars of any contributory negligence shall be set out in the defence."

9. Order 58 of the Rules of the Superior Courts is hereby amended by the substitution for sub-rule 4 of rule 3 thereof, of the following:

   "(3) Subject to any relevant provision of statute, the Supreme Court shall have power to enlarge the time appointed by these Rules or fixed by any other order enlarging time for the service of a notice of appeal to the Supreme Court upon such terms (if any) as it may direct, and any such enlargement may be ordered although the application for same is not made until after the expiration of the time appointed or allowed."

10. Order 121 of the Rules of the Superior Courts is hereby amended by the insertion immediately following its rule 8, of the following:

    "9. The delivery or service of any notice for the purposes of section 8 or section 17 of the Civil Liability and Courts Act 2004 shall be in the manner prescribed in section 4 of that Act".

11. Order 122 of the Rules of the Superior Courts is hereby amended by the substitution for rule 7 thereof, of the following:

    "7. Subject to any relevant provision of statute, the Court shall have power to enlarge or abridge the time appointed by these Rules, or fixed by any order enlarging time, for doing any act or taking any proceeding, upon such terms (if any) as the Court may direct, and any such enlargement may be ordered although the application for same is not made until after the expiration of the time appointed or allowed."

12. The forms in Schedule 1 following shall be inserted as Appendix CC to the Rules of the Superior Courts. The form in Schedule 2 following shall be inserted as Form No. 5 in Appendix A, Part II to the Rules of the Superior Courts.

O.1A, r.3 **SCHEDULE 2**

Appendix CC
PERSONAL INJURIES ACTIONS (CIVIL LIABILITY AND COURTS ACT 2004)
No. 1
PERSONAL INJURIES SUMMONS

THE HIGH COURT

20…… No. ……

Between

A.B.

Plaintiff

and

C.D.

Defendant

To the defendant ________________________________ (occupation)

who is ordinarily resident at ________________________________

in the County of ________________________________

This personal injuries summons requires you to enter an appearance in person or by solicitor in the Central Office, Four Courts, Dublin in the above action within eight days after the summons has been served on you (exclusive of the day of such service).

And TAKE NOTICE that if you do not enter an appearance the plaintiff may proceed in this action, and judgment may be given in your absence.

BY ORDER,
Chief Justice of Ireland,

the day of two thousand ………………………

N.B.: This summons is to be served within twelve calendar months from the date hereof, unless the time for service has been extended by the Court.

The defendant may appear to this summons by entering an appearance either personally or by solicitor at the Central Office, Four Courts, Dublin.

INDORSEMENT OF CLAIM

The plaintiff's claim is for the reliefs set out herein for personal injuries suffered by the plaintiff [or state capacity in which the plaintiff sues] as follows:

[The indorsement of claim on a personal injuries summons shall—

(a) set out, in numbered paragraphs, full and detailed particulars of—
   (i) the nature of the claim and of each allegation, assertion or plea comprising that claim;
   (ii) the injuries to the plaintiff alleged to have been occasioned by the wrong of the defendant;
   (iii) the acts of the defendant constituting the said wrong and the circumstances relating to the commission of the said wrong;
   (iv) each instance of negligence by the defendant, and

(b) contain a schedule of full particulars of all items of special damage in respect of which the plaintiff is making a claim.

The following is a suggested format in which the indorsement might be presented:

1. Description of the parties;
2. The nature of the claim;
3. The acts of the defendant alleged to constitute a wrong, each instance of negligence by the defendant, all other relevant circumstances in relation to the commission of the said wrong and any other assertion or plea concerning same;
4. The injuries to the plaintiff alleged to have been occasioned by the wrong of the defendant;
5. The reliefs sought;
6. (Where appropriate) the particulars required by Order 4, rule 3A.

SCHEDULE

Particulars of Items of Special Damage

(Full particulars should be set out. Add additional sheets if necessary)

(Particulars of a general allegation should be set out in the indorsement under the paragraph containing such allegation and headed "Particulars of

…etc." Where same are lengthy, they may alternatively be scheduled to the indorsement or set out in additional sheets appended to the Personal

Injuries Summons at time of issue and service.)]

(Signed) ____________________

This summons was issued by the plaintiff.

OR

This summons was issued by , solicitor for the plaintiff, whose registered place of business is ____________________ .

The plaintiff's personal details are as follows:

1. The address at which the Plaintiff ordinarily resides is:
   (state address accurately). The plaintiff's address for service, if different from the plaintiff's address mentioned above, should also be stated here:

   ____

   ____

2. Plaintiff's occupation:
3. Plaintiff's date of birth: Day: Month Year
4. Plaintiff's Personal Public Service Number:
   (If the Plaintiff has not been issued with a Personal Public Service Number, this must be stated)

INDORSEMENT OF SERVICE

This summons was served by me at _________________________ on the defendant ____________________ on ______ day the ________________ day of ___________, 20 ____.

Indorsed the day of 20 ____.

(Signed) (Address)

O.1A, r.8

No. 2
PERSONAL INJURIES DEFENCE

THE HIGH COURT

20…… No. ……

Between

A.B.

Plaintiff

and

C.D.

Defendant

Delivered on the day of two thousand ………………………by AB of (registered place of business) solicitor for the defendant.

TAKE NOTICE that the defence of the defendant to the claim of the plaintiff made by personal injuries summons dated the day of two thousand ………………………is as follows:

[A defence to a personal injuries action shall:

(a) specify—
  (i) the allegations specified, or matters pleaded, in the personal injuries summons of which the defendant does not require proof,
  (ii) the allegations specified, or matters pleaded in the personal injuries summons of which he or she requires proof,
  (iii) the grounds upon which the defendant claims that he or she is not liable for any injuries suffered by the plaintiff, and
  (iv) where the defendant alleges that some or all of the personal injuries suffered by the plaintiff were occasioned in whole or in part by the plaintiff's own acts, the grounds upon which he or she so alleges, and

(b) contain full and detailed particulars of each denial or traverse, and of each allegation, assertion or plea, comprising the defendant's defence and, where appropriate, a counter-schedule setting out the defence to items of special damage claimed by the plaintiff.

COUNTER-SCHEDULE

DEFENCE TO ITEMS OF SPECIAL DAMAGE CLAIMED BY THE PLAINTIFF

(add additional sheets if necessary)

(Particulars of a general denial, traverse, allegation, assertion or plea should be set out in the Defence under the paragraph containing same and headed "Particulars of …etc." Where same are lengthy, they may alternatively be scheduled to the Defence or set out in additional sheets appended to the Defence at time of service.)]

(Signed)______________________

O.1A, r.8 No. 3

PERSONAL INJURIES COUNTERCLAIM

INDORSEMENT OF COUNTERCLAIM

The defendant's counterclaim is for the reliefs set out herein for personal injuries suffered by the defendant as follows:

[A personal injuries counterclaim shall:

(a) set out, in numbered paragraphs, full and detailed particulars of—
   (i) the nature of the counterclaim and of each allegation, assertion or plea comprising that counterclaim;
   (ii) the injuries to the defendant alleged to have been occasioned by the wrong of the plaintiff;
   (iii) the acts of the plaintiff constituting the said wrong and the circumstances relating to the commission of the said wrong;
   (iv) each instance of negligence by the plaintiff, and

(b) contain a schedule of full particulars of all items of special damage in respect of which the defendant is making a claim.

The following is a suggested format in which the indorsement might be presented:

1. Description of the parties;

2. The nature of the counterclaim;

3. The acts of the plaintiff alleged to constitute a wrong, each instance of

negligence by the plaintiff, all other relevant circumstances in relation to the commission of the said wrong and any other assertion or plea concerning same;

4. The injuries to the defendant alleged to have been occasioned by the wrong of the plaintiff;
5. The reliefs sought;
6. (Where appropriate) the particulars required by Order 4, rule 3A.

SCHEDULE

Particulars of Items of Special Damage

(Full particulars should be set out.

Add additional sheets if necessary)

(Particulars of a general allegation should be set out in the indorsement under the paragraph containing such allegation and headed "Particulars of …etc." Where same are lengthy, they may alternatively be scheduled to the indorsement or set out in additional sheets appended to the counterclaim at time of service.)]

This defendant's personal details are as follows:

1. Address of defendant's ordinary residence:
   (state address accurately). The defendant's address for service, if different from the address mentioned above, should be stated here:
2. Defendant's occupation:
3. Defendant's date of birth: Day: Month Year
4. Defendant's Personal Public Service Number:
   (If the Defendant has not been issued with a Personal Public Service Number, this must be stated)

(Signed)______________________

O.1A, r.10

No. 4
AFFIDAVIT OF VERIFICATION

THE HIGH COURT

20...... No. ......

Between

A.B.

Plaintiff

and

C.D.

Defendant

I, AB, ...of .... , the (plaintiff, defendant or state other capacity or authority) in the above-entitled proceedings, aged eighteen years and upwards MAKE OATH and say as follows:

1. I beg to refer to the contents of the (personal injuries summons, defence, reply, further information etc. – as the case may be) delivered herein on behalf of the (plaintiff/ defendant) on the .....day of ....20.... *[upon which this affidavit is endorsed] *[and upon a true copy of which marked "A" I have signed my name prior to the swearing hereof].

2. The assertions, allegations and information contained in the said (personal injuries summons, etc.) which are within my own knowledge are true. I honestly believe that the assertions, allegations and information contained in the said (personal injuries summons, etc.) which are not within my own knowledge are true.

3. I am aware that it is an offence to make a statement in this affidavit that is false or misleading in any material respect and that I know to be false or misleading.

SWORN etc.

*Delete if inapplicable.

O.1A, r.13 No. 5

NOTICE OF OFFER OF TERMS OF SETTLEMENT

THE HIGH COURT

20…… No. ……

Between

A.B.

Plaintiff

and

C.D.

Defendant

TAKE NOTICE that for the purposes of section 17 of the Civil Liability and Courts Act 2004 the *plaintiff/defendant is willing to settle the above-entitled action upon the following terms:

TERMS OTHER THAN THOSE AS TO COSTS:

TERMS AS TO COSTS:

[or]

TAKE NOTICE that for the purposes of section 17 of the Civil Liability and Courts Act 2004 the defendant is not prepared to pay any sum of money to the plaintiff in settlement of above-entitled action.

Signed:_______________

Date:

*Delete whichever inapplicable

O.1A, r. 8

SCHEDULE 2
Appendix A, Part II
No. 5

MEMORANDUM OF APPEARANCE TO PERSONAL INJURIES SUMMONS

Between

AB

Plaintiff

and

CD

Defendant

Enter an Appearance for CD, the defendant in this personal injuries action.

Dated ______________________

Signed ____________________ EF

Solicitor for the defendant

The registered place of business of EF is ______________________.

*[or CD, the defendant in person

The address at which CD ordinarily resides is ____________________ .

The address for service of CD is ________________________________]

To: The Registrar of the Central Office.

Take Notice that I have this day entered an appearance at the Central Office, Four Courts, Inns Quay, Dublin 7** [, for the above defendant to the personal injuries summons in this action].

Dated ____________________________

Signed ____________________________

To: ______________________________

*Insert if applicable

**Delete if appearance is by defendant in person.

Appendix 4

CC02 – PERSONAL INJURIES ACTIONS; PROCEDURE FOR CONDUCT OF PROCEEDINGS

Civil Liability and Courts Act 2004
Personal Injuries Actions

1. Part 2 of the Civil Liability and Courts Act 2004 ("the Act"), which applies to personal injuries actions as defined in section 2 of the Act, inter alia, makes changes in the procedure for conduct of such proceedings and makes provision for the content and verification by affidavit of personal injuries summonses and pleadings, and for the consequences of failure to comply with the requirements of the Act. With the exception of certain provisions referred to in section 6 of the Act, a provision of Part 2 applies only to such proceedings brought after commencement of the provision concerned.

2. The Civil Liability and Courts Act 2004 (Commencement) Order 2004 (S.I. 544 of 2004) provided, inter alia, for the commencement in effect of various provisions of Part 2 of the Act as of the 31st March 2005.

3. Pending the coming into operation of rules of court regulating in detail the procedure and prescribing the forms to be used in such proceedings, and subject to paragraph 6 of this practice direction, the forms referred to in this practice direction and appended hereto are to be used in such proceedings instituted from the 31st March 2005.

4. A personal injuries summons used to commence proceedings in the Circuit Court in respect of a personal injuries action shall comply with the requirements of Part 2 of the Act including, in particular, sections 10, 13(1)(a) and 14 of the Act, and shall be in Form 1.

5. A defence in a personal injuries action shall comply with the requirements of the Act including, in particular sections 12(1), 13(1)(b) and 14 of the Act, and shall be in Form 2. Where any counterclaim is made, it shall comply with the requirements of the Act including, in particular, sections 12(2) and 14 of the Act, and shall be appended to the defence. A defence to a counterclaim shall, with such modifications as may be necessary,

comply with the requirements of the Act applicable to a defence.

6. An affidavit of verification of a pleading or of further information requiring under section 14 of the Act to be verified by affidavit shall be in Form 3. The affidavit of verification may be endorsed upon such pleading or other document. An affidavit in such form must be filed in the Circuit Court Office in the ordinary way and in any event within the period specified in section 14(4) of the Act. The form of affidavit of verification in Form 3 shall be used in proceedings brought before the 31st March 2005 in the circumstances referred to in section 14(8)(b) of the Act.

7. A notice containing a party's formal offer within the meaning of section 17 of the Act shall be in Form 4.

8. An application for any interlocutory order referred to Part 2 of the Act may be made by motion on notice in the ordinary way.

9. Subject to the requirements of section 4 of the Act concerning service of notices of claim under section 8 of the Act and of formal offers under section 17 of the Act, the existing arrangements and requirements as to the issue, service or delivery of pleadings and other documents continue to apply in personal injuries actions.

10. This practice direction shall cease to have effect on the coming into effect of the rules of court referred to above.

Dated this 31st day of March 2005

Esmond Smyth
President of the Circuit Court

Form 1

AN CHÚIRT CHUARDA
THE CIRCUIT COURT

CIRCUIT COUNTY OF

PERSONAL INJURIES SUMMONS

BETWEEN

.... Plaintiff

AND

.... Defendant

You are hereby required within ten days after the service of this Personal Injuries Summons upon you, to enter, or cause to be entered, with the County Registrar at his office at ....
an Appearance to answer the claim of ....
(*state plaintiff's name and occupation*) of .... (*state the address at which the plaintiff ordinarily resides*)............................
the plaintiff herein.

And take notice that, unless you do enter an Appearance you will be held to have admitted the said claim, and the plaintiff may proceed therein and judgment may be given against you in your absence without further notice.

And further take notice that, if you intend to defend the proceeding on any grounds, you must not only enter an Appearance, but also within six weeks after Appearance deliver a statement in writing showing the nature and grounds of your Defence.

The Appearance may be entered by posting same to the said Office and by giving copies thereof to the Plaintiff or his Solicitor by post and the defence may be delivered by posting same to the Plaintiff or his Solicitor.

INDORSEMENT OF CLAIM

[*The indorsement of claim on a personal injuries summons shall be entitled "Indorsement of Claim" and shall:*

(a) set out, in numbered paragraphs, full and detailed particulars of—
(i) the nature of the claim and of each allegation, assertion or plea comprising that claim;

(ii) *the injuries to the plaintiff alleged to have been occasioned by the wrong of the defendant;*

(iii) *the acts of the defendant constituting the said wrong and the circumstances relating to the commission of the said wrong;*

(iv) *each instance of negligence by the defendant,*

(b) *contain a schedule of full particulars of all items of special damage in respect of which the plaintiff is making a claim, and*

(c) *give details of the basis upon which jurisdiction is claimed*

The following is a suggested format in which the indorsement might be presented:

1. DESCRIPTION OF PARTIES

2. WRONG ALLEGED AGAINST THE DEFENDANT (OR AGAINST EACH DEFENDANT)

3. PARTICULARS OF THE ACTS OF THE DEFENDANT (OR OF EACH DEFENDANT) CONSTITUTING THE WRONG AND OF THE CIRCUMSTANCES RELATING TO THE COMMISSION OF THE WRONG
(Full particulars should be set out)

4. PARTICULARS OF EACH INSTANCE OF NEGLIGENCE BY THE DEFENDANT (OR BY EACH DEFENDANT)
(Full particulars should be set out)

5. PARTICULARS OF THE INJURIES TO THE PLAINTIFF OCCASIONED BY THE WRONG OF THE DEFENDANT (OR OF EACH DEFENDANT)

6. RELIEFS CLAIMED

SCHEDULE

PARTICULARS OF ITEMS OF SPECIAL DAMAGE
(Full particulars should be set out. Add additional sheets if necessary)]
[If applicable, insert the particulars required by Order 5, rule 5A]

The personal details of the plaintiff are as follows:

1. The address at which the Plaintiff ordinarily resides is:

   (State address accurately. The plaintiff's address for service, if different from the plaintiff's address mentioned above, should also be stated here.)

2. Plaintiff's occupation:

3. Plaintiff's date of birth: Day: Month: Year.

4. Plaintiff's Personal Public Service Number:

   (If the Plaintiff has not been issued with a Personal Public Service Number, this must be stated)

Dated the day of 2005.

Signed: ________________________

Plaintiff/Solicitors for the Plaintiff

To: __________________________________

The Defendant/Solicitors for the Defendant

Form 2

AN CHÚIRT CHUARDA
THE CIRCUIT COURT

CIRCUIT COUNTY OF

PERSONAL INJURIES DEFENCE

BETWEEN

.... Plaintiff

AND

.... Defendant

Defence of the Defendant..

of..

delivered the day of two thousand by..................

....Defendant/Solicitor for the Defendant

[*Here insert details of the Defence.*

A Defence to a personal injuries action shall:

(a) specify—

(i) the allegations specified, or matters pleaded, in the personal injuries summons of which the defendant does not require proof,

(ii) the allegations specified, or matters pleaded in the personal injuries summons of which he or she requires proof,

(iii) the grounds upon which the defendant claims that he or she is not liable for any injuries suffered by the plaintiff, and

(iv) where the defendant alleges that some or all of the personal injuries suffered by the plaintiff were occasioned in whole or in part by the plaintiff's own acts, the grounds upon which he or she so alleges, and

(b) contain full and detailed particulars of each denial or traverse, and of each allegation, assertion or plea, comprising the defendant's Defence and, where appropriate, a counter-schedule setting out the defence to items of special damage claimed by the plaintiff.

The following is a suggested format in which the defence might be presented:

1. *THE DEFENDANT DOES NOT REQUIRE PROOF OF THE FOLLOWING ALLEGATIONS SPECIFIED OR MATTERS PLEADED IN THE PERSONAL INJURIES SUMMONS:*

2. *THE DEFENDANT REQUIRES PROOF OF THE FOLLOWING ALLEGATIONS SPECIFIED OR MATTERS PLEADED IN THE PERSONAL INJURIES SUMMONS:*

3. *THE GROUNDS UPON WHICH THE DEFENDANT CLAIMS THAT (S)HE IS NOT LIABLE FOR ANY INJURIES SUFFERED BY THE PLAINTIFF ARE AS FOLLOWS:*

*4. *THE GROUNDS UPON WHICH THE DEFENDANT CLAIMS THAT SOME OR ALL OF THE INJURIES SUFFERED BY THE PLAINTIFF WERE OCCASIONED IN WHOLE OR IN PART BY THE PLAINTIFF'S OWN ACTS ARE AS FOLLOWS:*

5. *DEFENCE TO RELIEFS CLAIMED BY THE PLAINTIFF.*

COUNTER-SCHEDULE

DEFENCE TO ITEMS OF SPECIAL DAMAGE CLAIMED BY THE PLAINTIFF
(add additional sheets if necessary)]

Signed: ____________________________

Defendant/Solicitors for the Defendant

To: ______________________________________

Plaintiff/Solicitors for the Plaintiff

And
The County Registrar

*delete if inapplicable

Form 3

AFFIDAVIT OF VERIFICATION

[Title as in the action]

[The title need not be repeated where the affidavit is endorsed upon the pleading or other document]

I, *AB*, ………………..of …………………. , the (*plaintiff, defendant or state other capacity or authority*) in the above-entitled proceedings, aged eighteen years and upwards MAKE OATH and say as follows:

1. I beg to refer to the contents of the (*personal injuries summons, defence, reply, further information etc. – as the case may be*) delivered herein on behalf of the (plaintiff/ defendant) on the …..day of …………..20…. *[upon which this affidavit is endorsed] *[and upon a true copy of which marked "A" I have signed my name prior to the swearing hereof].
2. The assertions, allegations and information contained in the said (*personal injuries summons, etc.*) which are within my own knowledge are true. I honestly believe that the assertions, allegations and information contained in the said (*personal injuries summons, etc.*) which are not within my own knowledge are true.
3. I am aware that it is an offence to make a statement in this affidavit that is false or misleading in any material respect and that I know to be false or misleading.

SWORN etc.

*Delete if inapplicable.

Form 4

AN CHÚIRT CHUARDA
THE CIRCUIT COURT

CIRCUIT COUNTY OF

NOTICE OF OFFER OF TERMS OF SETTLEMENT

BETWEEN

.... Plaintiff

AND

.... Defendant

TAKE NOTICE that for the purposes of section 17 of the Civil Liability and Courts Act 2004 the *plaintiff/defendant is willing to settle the above-entitled action upon the following terms:

TERMS OTHER THAN THOSE AS TO COSTS:

TERMS AS TO COSTS:

[*or*]

TAKE NOTICE that for the purposes of section 17 of the Civil Liability and Courts Act 2004 the defendant is not prepared to pay any sum of money to the plaintiff in settlement of above-entitled action.

Dated:

Signed:

To: The *Defendant/Plaintiff

*Delete whichever inapplicable

Appendix 5

DISTRICT COURT (PERSONAL INJURIES) RULES 2005

Order 39A: S.I. No. 257 of 2005

The District Court Rules Committee, in exercise of the powers conferred on them by section 91 of the Courts of Justice Act, 1924, section 72 of the Courts of Justice Act, 1936, section 17 of the Interpretation Act, 1937 [as applied by section 48 of the Courts (Supplemental Provisions) Act, 1961] and section 34 of the Courts (Supplemental Provisions) Act, 1961, do hereby, with the concurrence of the Minister for Justice, Equality and Law Reform, make the following rules of court:

1. These rules may be cited as the District Court (Personal Injuries) Rules 2005.
2. These rules shall come into operation on the 3rd day of June 2005 and shall be read together with all other District Court rules for the time being in force.
3. The District Court Rules 1997 (S.I. No.93 of 1997) are hereby amended:

....

(vii) by the insertion immediately following Order 39 of the following Order as Order 39A:

"Order 39A

PERSONAL INJURIES PROCEEDINGS

1. In this Order unless the context or subject matter otherwise requires—
"the Act" means the Civil Liability and Courts Act 2004;
"personal injuries proceedings" means an action for the recovery of damages,
in respect of a wrong, for—
(a) personal injuries,
(b) both such injuries and damage to property (but only if both

have been caused by the same wrong), or

(c) under section 48 of the Civil Liability Act 1961,

but shall not include an action where the damages claimed include damages for false imprisonment or trespass to the person; and "proceedings" shall be interpreted accordingly;

"personal injury" includes any disease and any impairment of a person's physical or mental condition;

"personal injuries summons" means a summons by which personal injuries proceedings are instituted in accordance with rule 3 of this Order;

"plaintiff" includes a deceased person, where personal injury proceedings are instituted for the benefit of dependants of a deceased person;

"pleading" has the same meaning as in section 2 of the Act;

"Personal Public Service Number" means the Personal Public Service Number allocated and issued to a person under section 223 (inserted by section 14 of the Social Welfare Act 1998) of the Social Welfare (Consolidation) Act 1993;

2. (1) The provisions of this Order shall apply to personal injuries proceedings.

(2) Save where otherwise expressly provided by this Order, in the event that any conflict shall arise between the provision of any rule of this Order and any other provision of these Rules, the provision of the rule of this Order shall, in respect of personal injuries proceedings, prevail. For the avoidance of doubt and without prejudice to the generality of the foregoing, Order 39, rule 3 and sub-rules (1) and (4) of rule 4 shall not apply in personal injuries proceedings.

3. (1). Personal injuries proceedings shall be instituted by the issue for service upon each defendant named therein of a personal injuries summons in the Form No. 39A.1, Schedule C.

(2) Save where otherwise expressly provided by this Order, the provisions of these Rules which apply to a civil summons shall, with appropriate modifications, apply to a personal injuries summons.

4. A personal injuries summons shall specify:

(i) the plaintiff's name, the address at which he or she ordinarily resides and his or her occupation,

(ii) the plaintiff's Personal Public Service Number (and where a plaintiff has not been issued with a Personal Public Service Number, this shall be stated in the personal injuries summons),

(iii) the defendant's name, the address at which he or she ordinarily resides (if known to the plaintiff) and his or her occupation (if known to the plaintiff).

5. A personal injuries summons shall—

(a) set out full and detailed particulars of—

(i) the nature of the claim and of each allegation, assertion or plea comprising that claim;

(ii) the injuries to the plaintiff alleged to have been occasioned by the wrong of the defendant;

(iii) the acts of the defendant constituting the said wrong and the circumstances relating to the commission of the said wrong;

(iv) each instance of negligence by the defendant, and

(b) contain a schedule of full particulars of all items of special damage in respect of which the plaintiff is making a claim.

6. Each defendant who intends to defend the proceedings shall deliver to the plaintiff (or his solicitor) and to the Clerk a defence in the Form 39A.2, Schedule C within twenty eight days after the service upon him of the personal injuries summons. Where any defendant makes a counterclaim, such counterclaim shall be in the Form 39A.3, Schedule C and shall be appended to the defence.

7. (1) An affidavit of verification of a pleading or of further information requiring under section 14(1) or (2) of the Act to be verified on oath shall be in the Form 39A.4, Schedule C. The affidavit may be endorsed upon the pleading or other document concerned, or may exhibit such pleading or other document.

(2) A copy of the affidavit of verification shall be delivered to the party to whom the pleading or other document is to be delivered. Where the affidavit is endorsed upon the pleading or other document, it shall be delivered within the time prescribed by these Rules for delivery of such pleading or other document. Otherwise, the affidavit shall be delivered within the time prescribed by section 14 of the Act for lodgment of the affidavit in court.

(3) Where the affidavit of verification is delivered subsequent to delivery of the pleading or other document, the time prescribed by these Rules for delivery of any pleading or other document in reply shall run from the date of delivery of the affidavit of verification.

(4) An affidavit of verification shall be lodged in Court as required by section 14(4) of the Act by lodging the original affidavit duly stamped with the Clerk.

8. (1) The following applications in personal injuries proceedings shall, subject to the following rules of this Order, be made by application to the Court by application on notice to the opposing party or parties

in the Form 39A.5, Schedule C, grounded upon an affidavit sworn by or on behalf of the moving party:

(i) An application under section 9(2) of the Act (in the absence of agreement between or among the parties) for the extension of the period provided for in this Order or otherwise in these Rules, within which any document may be served or thing may be done;

(ii) An application by a defendant under section 10(3) of the Act for a stay or dismissal of proceedings by reason of a plaintiff's failure to provide the information necessary to comply with section 10 of the Act;

(iii) An application by a defendant under section 11(3) of the Act for a stay or dismissal of proceedings by reason of a plaintiff's failure to provide further information requested under section 11(1) or section 11(2) of the Act;

(iv) An application by a plaintiff under section 12(3) of the Act for a stay of proceedings or for judgment by reason of a defendant's failure to provide the information necessary to comply with section 12 of the Act;

(v) An application by a party for a direction of the Court under section 15 of the Act that a mediation conference be held;

(vi) An application to the Court to order the delivery by the opposing party of further and better particulars of any pleading delivered by such party;

(vii) An application by a party wishing to have evidence in the action given by affidavit, under section 19 of the Act;

(viii) An application by a party wishing to have an approved person appointed to carry out any investigation and to give any evidence in the action in relation to any matter, under section 20 of the Act.

No application described in this sub-rule shall be issued unless:

(a) the moving party shall have first written to the relevant opposing party requesting that such party agree to any extension proposed or (as the case may be) provide the information identified in, or agree to, the moving party's request;

(b) a period of fourteen days for compliance with the moving party's request has been allowed; and

(c) the party requested has failed, refused or neglected to comply with such request.

(2) Any order made on such application shall be in the Form 39A.6, Schedule C.

(3) No application for judgment in default of defence shall be granted in personal injuries proceedings unless the moving party has satisfied the Court that he has verified his personal injuries summons in those proceedings on oath in accordance with this Order.

9. (1) Where the Court directs that a mediation conference be held, it may adjourn the proceedings for such time as it considers appropriate to enable the mediation conference to be held.

(2) Where the Court directs that a mediation conference be held, it may extend the time for compliance by the parties or any of them with any provision of these Rules or any order of the Court in the proceedings.

(3) The report under section 16 of the Act of the person appointed under section 15(4) of the Act to be the chairperson of a mediation conference shall be by way of affidavit which shall verify:

- (a) his or her appointment as mediator;
- (b) whether the mediation conference was or was not held;
- (c) if not held, the reasons why the mediation conference did not take place;
- (d) if held,
  - (i) the time and place at which the mediation conference was held;
  - (ii) the parties in attendance;
  - (iii) whether or not a settlement has been reached in the proceeding and
  - (iv) the terms of any settlement signed by the parties.

10. Copies of the plaintiff's notice of an offer of terms of settlement required by section 17(1) of the Act and of the defendant's notice required by section 17(2) of the Act shall be lodged in Court by being delivered (together with an affidavit as to the service of the same on the opposing party) to the Clerk as soon as may be after the expiry of the prescribed period referred to in section 17(3) of the Act. Such notice shall be in the Form 39A.7, Schedule C. Such notice shall not be given or produced to the Judge prior to the determination of the proceedings.

11. A pre-trial hearing as provided for in section 18 of the Act shall be held in personal injuries proceedings where the Court, on the application by motion on notice to the opposing party or parties by the party wishing to apply for a pre-trial hearing, considers that a pre-trial hearing is appropriate. A Judge presiding over a pre-trial hearing may

at such hearing give such directions and make such orders as may be necessary for the purposes of determining what matters relating to the proceedings are in dispute."

4. The Forms numbered 39A.1 to 39A.7 inclusive in Schedule 1 hereof shall be added to the Forms in Schedule C of the District Court Rules 1997 (S.I. No. 93 of 1997).

O.39A, r.3 **No. 39A.1**

Schedule C

AN CHUIRT DUICHE THE DISTRICT COURT

District Court Area of District No.

PERSONAL INJURIES SUMMONS

CIVIL LIABILITY AND COURTS ACT 2004, SECTION 10

Between ....

who is ordinarily resident at ....

in the County of ....

Personal Public Service Number (PPSN) (if none, please state "none") ....

.... (state plaintiff's occupation) .... Plaintiff

and ....

who is ordinarily resident at ....

in the County of ....

.... (state defendant's occupation) .... Defendant

INDORSEMENT OF CLAIM

[A personal injuries summons shall contain an indorsement entitled "Indorsement of Claim" which shall:

(a) set out, in numbered paragraphs, full and detailed particulars of—
   (i) the nature of the claim and of each allegation, assertion or plea comprising that claim;
   (ii) the injuries to the plaintiff alleged to have been occasioned by the wrong of the defendant;
   (iii) the acts of the defendant constituting the said wrong and the circumstances relating to the commission of the said wrong;
   (iv) each instance of negligence by the defendant,
(b) contain a schedule of full particulars of all items of special damage in respect of which the plaintiff is making a claim, and
(c) give details of the basis upon which jurisdiction is claimed.

The following is a suggested format in which the indorsement might be presented:

1. DESCRIPTION OF PARTIES
2. WRONG ALLEGED AGAINST THE DEFENDANT (OR AGAINST EACH DEFENDANT)
3. PARTICULARS OF THE ACTS OF THE DEFENDANT (OR OF EACH DEFENDANT) CONSTITUTING THE WRONG AND OF THE CIRCUMSTANCES RELATING TO THE COMMISSION OF THE WRONG
   (Full particulars should be set out)
4. PARTICULARS OF EACH INSTANCE OF NEGLIGENCE BY THE DEFENDANT (OR BY EACH DEFENDANT)
   (Full particulars should be set out)
5. PARTICULARS OF THE INJURIES TO THE PLAINTIFF OCCASIONED BY THE WRONG OF THE DEFENDANT (OR OF EACH DEFENDANT)
6. RELIEFS CLAIMED

SCHEDULE

PARTICULARS OF ITEMS OF SPECIAL DAMAGE

(Full particulars should be set out. Add additional sheets if necessary)

[If applicable, insert the particulars required by Order 39, rule 4(1A)]

YOU ARE HEREBY required personally to appear at the sitting of the District Court for the hearing of civil proceedings to be held at .... on the .... day of ....20 ...... at ...... a.m./p.m. to answer the said claim.

IF YOU DISPUTE THE PLAINTIFF'S CLAIM and intend to defend the proceedings you (or your solicitor) should deliver a Defence to the plaintiff's claim within twenty eight days of the date of receipt of this personal injuries summons.

Dated this .... day of .... 20 .

Signed ....
Plaintiff/Solicitor for the Plaintiff

The plaintiff's address for service, if different from the plaintiff's address mentioned above, should be stated here:

To ....

of ....
the above-named defendant.

O.39A, r.6 **No. 39A.2**

Schedule C

AN CHUIRT DUICHE THE DISTRICT COURT

District Court Area of District No.

PERSONAL INJURIES DEFENCE

CIVIL LIABILITY AND COURTS ACT 2004, SECTION 12

Between ....

who is ordinarily resident at ....

in the County of ....

Personal Public Service Number (PPSN) (if none, please state "none") ....

.... (state plaintiff's occupation) .... Plaintiff

and ....

who is ordinarily resident at ....

in the County of ....

.... (state defendant's occupation) .... Defendant

Defence of the Defendant...

of ....

delivered the day of two thousand by ....

.... Defendant/Solicitor for the Defendant

[Here insert details of the Defence.

A Defence to a personal injuries action shall:

(a) specify—
- (i) the allegations specified, or matters pleaded, in the personal injuries summons of which the defendant does not require proof,
- (ii) the allegations specified, or matters pleaded in the personal injuries summons of which he or she requires proof,
- (iii) the grounds upon which the defendant claims that he or she is not liable for any injuries suffered by the plaintiff, and
- (iv) where the defendant alleges that some or all of the personal injuries

suffered by the plaintiff were occasioned in whole or in part by the plaintiff's own acts, the grounds upon which he or she so alleges, and

(b) contain full and detailed particulars of each denial or traverse, and of each allegation, assertion or plea, comprising the defendant's Defence and, where appropriate, a counter-schedule setting out the defence to items of special damage claimed by the plaintiff.

The following is a suggested format in which the defence might be presented:

1. THE DEFENDANT DOES NOT REQUIRE PROOF OF THE FOLLOWING ALLEGATIONS SPECIFIED OR MATTERS PLEADED IN THE PERSONAL INJURIES SUMMONS:

2. THE DEFENDANT REQUIRES PROOF OF THE FOLLOWING ALLEGATIONS SPECIFIED OR MATTERS PLEADED IN THE PERSONAL INJURIES SUMMONS:

3. THE GROUNDS UPON WHICH THE DEFENDANT CLAIMS THAT (S)HE IS NOT LIABLE FOR ANY INJURIES SUFFERED BY THE PLAINTIFF ARE AS FOLLOWS:

*4. THE GROUNDS UPON WHICH THE DEFENDANT CLAIMS THAT SOME OR ALL OF THE INJURIES SUFFERED BY THE PLAINTIFF WERE OCCASIONED IN WHOLE OR IN PART BY THE PLAINTIFF'S OWN ACTS ARE AS FOLLOWS:

5. DEFENCE TO RELIEFS CLAIMED BY THE PLAINTIFF

COUNTER-SCHEDULE

DEFENCE TO ITEMS OF SPECIAL DAMAGE CLAIMED BY THE PLAINTIFF
(add additional sheets if necessary)]

Signed ______________________________
Defendant/Solicitor for the Defendant

To _________________________________
Plaintiff/Solicitor for the Plaintiff

And to the Clerk of the District Court

at

*delete if inapplicable

O.39A, r.6 **No. 39A.3**

Schedule C

AN CHUIRT DUICHE THE DISTRICT COURT

District Court Area of District No.

PERSONAL INJURIES COUNTERCLAIM

CIVIL LIABILITY AND COURTS ACT 2004, SECTION 12

INDORSEMENT OF COUNTERCLAIM

[A personal injuries counterclaim shall contain an indorsement entitled "Indorsement of Counterclaim" which shall:

(a) set out, in numbered paragraphs, full and detailed particulars of-
  (i) the nature of the claim and of each allegation, assertion or plea comprising that claim;
  (ii) the injuries to the defendant alleged to have been occasioned by the wrong of the plaintiff;
  (iii) the acts of the plaintiff constituting the said wrong and the circumstances relating to the commission of the said wrong;
  (iv) each instance of negligence by the plaintiff,
(b) contain a schedule of full particulars of all items of special damage in respect of which the defendant is making a claim, and
(c) give details of the basis upon which jurisdiction is claimed.

The following is a suggested format in which the indorsement might be presented:

1. DESCRIPTION OF PARTIES

2. WRONG ALLEGED AGAINST THE PLAINTIFF (OR AGAINST EACH PLAINTIFF)

3. PARTICULARS OF THE ACTS OF THE PLAINTIFF (OR OF EACH PLAINTIFF) CONSTITUTING THE WRONG AND OF THE CIRCUMSTANCES RELATING TO THE COMMISSION OF THE WRONG
(Full particulars should be set out)

4. PARTICULARS OF EACH INSTANCE OF NEGLIGENCE BY THE

PLAINTIFF (OR BY EACH PLAINTIFF)
(Full particulars should be set out)

5. PARTICULARS OF THE INJURIES TO THE DEFENDANT OCCASIONED BY THE WRONG OF THE PLAINTIFF (OR OF EACH PLAINTIFF)

6. RELIEFS CLAIMED BY THE DEFENDANT

SCHEDULE

PARTICULARS OF ITEMS OF SPECIAL DAMAGE

(Full particulars should be set out. Add additional sheets if necessary)

[If applicable, insert the particulars required by Order 39, rule 4(1A)]

This defendant's personal details are as follows:

1. Address of defendant's ordinary residence:
(state address accurately)

2. Defendant's occupation:

3. Defendant's Personal Public Service Number:
(If the defendant has not been issued with a Personal Public Service Number, this must be stated)

4. The defendant's address for service, if different from the address mentioned above, should be stated here:

Dated this .... day of .... 20 .

Signed ____________________________
Defendant/Solicitor for the Defendant

O.39A, r.7 **No. 39A.4**

Schedule C

AN CHUIRT DUICHE THE DISTRICT COURT

District Court Area of District No.

VERIFYING AFFIDAVIT

CIVIL LIABILITY AND COURTS ACT 2004, SECTION 14

Between ....

who is ordinarily resident at ....

in the County of ....

Personal Public Service Number (PPSN) (if none, please state "none") ....

.... (state plaintiff's occupation) .... Plaintiff

and

....

who is ordinarily resident at ....

in the County of ....

.... (state defendant's occupation) .... Defendant

[The title need not be repeated where the affidavit is endorsed upon the pleading or other document]

I, AB, ………………..of …………………, the (plaintiff, defendant or state other capacity or authority) in the above-entitled proceedings, aged eighteen years and upwards MAKE OATH and say as follows:

1. I beg to refer to the contents of the (personal injuries summons, defence, reply, further information etc. - as the case may be) delivered herein on behalf of the (plaintiff/ defendant) on the …..day of ………….20…. *[upon which this affidavit is endorsed] *[and upon a true copy of which marked "A" I have signed my name prior to the swearing hereof].

2. The assertions, allegations and information contained in the said (personal injuries summons, etc.) which are within my own knowledge are true. I honestly believe that the assertions, allegations and

information contained in the said (personal injuries summons, etc.) which are not within my own knowledge are true.

3. I am aware that it is an offence to make a statement in this affidavit that is false or misleading in any material respect and that I know to be false or misleading.

SWORN before me at.............................

in the County of ....this ...... day of .... 200..., and I know the deponent

....

Deponent
Commissioner for Oaths/Practising Solicitor

*Delete if inapplicable.

O.39A, r.8 **No. 39A.5**

Schedule C

AN CHUIRT DUICHE THE DISTRICT COURT

District Court Area of District No.

NOTICE OF APPLICATION

CIVIL LIABILITY AND COURTS ACT 2004

Between ....

who is ordinarily resident at ....

in the County of ....

Personal Public Service Number (PPSN) (if none, please state "none") ....

.... (state plaintiff's occupation) .... Plaintiff

and

....

who is ordinarily resident at ....

in the County of ....

.... (state defendant's occupation) .... Defendant

TAKE NOTICE that the above-named *plaintiff/*defendant will apply to the District Court sitting at ....on the ....day of..........20..... at............a.m./p.m., for the following relief pursuant to the Civil Liability and Courts Act 2004 (hereinafter the "Act") or otherwise in personal injuries proceedings:

* An order under section 9(2) of the Act for the extension of the period for the service of (state matter in which extension of time is sought);

* An order under section 10(3) of the Act for a stay or dismissal of the proceedings by reason of the plaintiff's failure to provide the information necessary to comply with section 10 of the Act;

* An order under section 11(3) of the Act for a stay or dismissal of proceedings by reason of the plaintiff's failure to provide further information requested under section 11(1) or section 11(2) of the Act;

* An order under section 12(3) of the Act for a stay of proceedings or for

judgment by reason of a defendant's failure to provide the information necessary to comply with section 12 of the Act;

* A direction of the Court under section 15 of the Act that a mediation conference be held;

* An order for the delivery of further and better particulars by the *plaintiff/ *defendant;

* An order allowing evidence in the action to be given by affidavit, under section 19 of the Act;

* An order appointing an approved person to carry out any investigation and to give evidence in the action, under section 20 of the Act.

Which application shall be grounded upon the affidavit of ....sworn on ....

Dated this .... day of .... 20 .

Signed

Solicitor for the *plaintiff/*defendant

To: District Court Clerk at ....

And:.................... Solicitor for the *plaintiff/*defendant

of ....

in the County of ....

O.39A, r.8 **No. 39A.6**

Schedule C

AN CHUIRT DUICHE THE DISTRICT COURT

District Court Area of District No.

ORDER

CIVIL LIABILITY AND COURTS ACT 2004

Between ....

who is ordinarily resident at ....

in the County of ....

Personal Public Service Number (PPSN) (if none, please state "none") ....

.... (state plaintiff's occupation) .... Plaintiff

and

....

who is ordinarily resident at ....

in the County of ....

.... (state defendant's occupation) .... Defendant

WHEREAS on the hearing of an application by motion dated ....
.... 20..............of the above-named *Plaintiff/*Defendant

The Court being satisfied that the respondent was duly served with notice of the application herein

AND ON HEARING what was alleged by the applicant *and the respondent IT IS HEREBY ORDERED:

* under section 9(2) of the Act that the period for (state relevant matter) be extended by

* under section 10(3) of the Act that *the plaintiff's action shall not proceed any further until the plaintiff (state condition) *the plaintiff's action be dismissed

* under section 11(3) of the Act that *the plaintiff's action shall not proceed

any further until the plaintiff (state condition) *the plaintiff's action be dismissed

* under section 12(3) of the Act that *the action shall not proceed any further until the defendant (state condition) *judgment be entered for the plaintiff in the amount of € ....
* under section 15 of the Act that a mediation conference be held in respect of the proceedings under the chairmanship of [name] .... of (address) who is hereby appointed chairman of the mediation conference and who is hereby directed to report to the Court on the outcome of said conference in the form and manner prescribed by Order 39A of the District Court Rules not later than .... 20...... and that the within proceedings be adjourned to .... 20...... to facilitate such mediation.
* that the *plaintiff/*defendant do deliver the further and better particulars of the *personal injuries summons/*defence/*counterclaim/*defence to counterclaim herein sought by letter dated .... 20 ...... within the period of .... of the date of this order.
* under section 19 of the Act that the evidence at the hearing of the within action of .... may be given by affidavit.
* under section 20 of the Act that .... of.........................., being for the time being an approved person within the meaning of said section be and is hereby appointed to carry out an investigation into the following matter arising in the within proceedings, namely

to be completed not later than ....20.... and if necessary to give evidence at the hearing of the within action in the action of the outcome of such investigation

Dated this .... day of .... 20 .

Signed

Judge of the District Court

O.39A, r.10 **No. 39A.7**

Schedule C

AN CHUIRT DUICHE THE DISTRICT COURT

District Court Area of District No.

NOTICE AS TO TERMS

CIVIL LIABILITY AND COURTS ACT 2004

Between ....

who is ordinarily resident at ....

in the County of ....

Personal Public Service Number (PPSN) (if none, please state "none") ....

.... (state plaintiff's occupation) .... Plaintiff

and

....

who is ordinarily resident at ....

in the County of ....

.... (state defendant's occupation) .... Defendant

TAKE NOTICE that for the purposes of section 17 of the Civil Liability and Courts Act 2004 the *plaintiff/defendant is willing to settle the above-entitled action upon the following terms:

TERMS OTHER THAN THOSE AS TO COSTS:

TERMS AS TO COSTS:

[or]

TAKE NOTICE that for the purposes of section 17 of the Civil Liability and Courts Act 2004 the defendant is not prepared to pay any sum of money to the plaintiff in settlement of above-entitled action.

Signed: ....

Date: ....

To: ....

Solicitor for the *plaintiff/*defendant

And to: District Court Clerk at

*delete whichever inapplicable.

Given this 11th day of April 2005

Peter Smithwick Chairman
Uinsin Mac Gruairc
John P Brophy
Mary C Devins
Thomas E O'Donnell
Hugh O'Neill
Noel Rubotham
Elizabeth Hughes Secretary

I concur in the making of the foregoing rules

Dated this 20th day of May 2005

Michael McDowell
Minister for Justice, Equality and Law Reform

Appendix 6

CIVIL LIABILITY AND COURTS ACT 2004 (BODIES PRESCRIBED UNDER SECTION 15) ORDER 2005

S.I. No. 168 of 2005

I, Michael McDowell, Minister for Justice, Equality and Law Reform, in exercise of the powers conferred on me by section 15 of the Civil Liability and Courts Act 2004 (No. 31 of 2004), hereby order as follows:

1. This Order may be cited as the Civil Liability and Courts Act 2004 (Bodies Prescribed under Section 15) Order 2005.

2. Each of the bodies specified in the Schedule to this Order is prescribed for the purposes of section 1 5(4)(b)(ii)(II) of the Civil Liability and Courts Act 2004 (No. 31 of 2004).

SCHEDULE

Friary Law
Mediation Forum—Ireland
Mediators Institute Ireland
The Bar Council
The Chartered Institute of Arbitrators Irish Branch
The Law Society of Ireland

GIVEN under my Official Seal,
this 31st day of March 2005.
Michael McDowell
Minister for Justice, Equality and Law Reform.

EXPLANATORY NOTE

(This note is not part of the Instrument and does not purport to be a legal interpretation.)

This Order relates to the nomination of chairpersons of mediation conferences in personal injuries actions, in the event that the parties do not agree on the chairperson. In such cases, the chairperson shall be appointed by the Court and shall be either a practising barrister or practising solicitor of not less than 5 years standing or a person nominated by one of the bodies prescribed in this Order. This Order prescribes six bodies which can nominate chairpersons.

Appendix 7

CIVIL LIABILITY AND COURTS ACT 2004 (SECTION 17) ORDER 2005

S.I. No. 169 of 2005

I, Michael McDowell, Minister for Justice, Equality and Law Reform, in exercise of the powers conferred on me by section 17 of the Civil Liability and Courts Act 2004 (No. 31 of 2004), hereby order as follows:

1. This Order may be cited as the Civil Liability and Courts Act 2004 (Section 17) Order 2005.

2. In this Order "Act of 2004" means the Civil Liability and Courts Act 2004 (No. 31 of 2004).

3. For the purposes of section 17 of the Act of 2004, the prescribed date is the date upon which the personal injuries summons is served on the defendant.

4. (1) For the purposes of section 17 of the Act of 2004, the prescribed period shall, in the case of proceedings in the Circuit Court or the High Court, be the period commencing on the prescribed date and ending on the expiration of 14 days after the service of the notice of trial in those proceedings.

(2) For the purposes of section 17 of the Act of 2004, the prescribed period shall, in the case of proceedings in the District Court, be the period commencing on the prescribed date and ending on the expiration of 4 days after the delivery of the defence in those proceedings.

GIVEN under my Official Seal,
this 31st day of March 2005
Michael McDowell
Minister for Justice, Equality and Law Reform.

EXPLANATORY NOTE

(This note is not part of the Instrument and does not purport to be a legal interpretation.)

This Order prescribes the date after which formal offers shall be made in personal injuries actions and the period after which they shall be lodged in court.

Index